Motor Development and Movement Experiences for Young Children (3-7)

Motor Development and Movement Experiences for Young Children (3-7)

DAVID L. GALLAHUE, Ed.D.

Indiana University
Bloomington, Indiana

John Wiley & Sons, Inc. New York, London, Sydney, Toronto

Library of Congress Cataloging in Publication Data:

Gallahue, David L

   Motor development and movement experiences for young children.

   Includes bibliographies and index.
   1. Motor learning. 2. Movement, Psychology of. I. Title. [DNLM: 1. Child
development. 2. Motor skills. 3. Movement—In infancy and childhood. WE103 G162m]

BF723.M6G34   155.4'23   75-37676
ISBN 0-471-29042-4

Printed in the United States of America

10 9 8 7 6 5 4

To Ellie, David Lee, and Jennifer,
"The Sunshine of My Life"

Preface

The motor development and movement education of preschool and primary grade children has become a topic of considerable interest in recent years. Educators from the areas of early childhood education, elementary education, special education, growth and development, and physical education have become increasingly aware of the many important contributions that movement can make to the cognitive and affective development of children as well as to their psychomotor behavior.

Motor Development and Movement Experiences for Young Children is dedicated to the task of helping teachers and parents deal more knowledgeably and effectively with children through the medium of movement. The book has been written in such a manner that current theory, research, and practical application are merged into a workable whole.

The first five chapters provide the reader with a basis of knowledge concerning the psychomotor development of young children. Chapter 1 contains an overview of the role of movement in child development. Chapter 2 deals with the growth and development of young children. Chapters 3, 4, and 5 are concerned with the contribution of movement of the psychomotor, cognitive, and affective development of children, respectively. Special attention is paid to perceptual-motor development and self-concept development in these chapters.

Chapters 6 through 11 focus on activity ideas for young children. Too often, books of this nature merely present undefined lists and descriptions of activities with little or no indication of their intent. The movement experiences contained in each of these chapters are categorized according to their general and specific objectives, thus enabling the reader to select activities based on children's needs. It should also be noted that the movement experiences are not graded according to the approximate age or grade level of their appropriateness. It has been my experience that grade level estimates are misleading and often serve to underestimate the ability level of children. The activities within the text have, however, been sequenced in a simple to complex manner.

Chapter 6 deals with a variety of individualized movements experiences for enhancing fundamental movement abilities. Chapter 7 provides the reader with a limited number of traditional games found useful in enhancing fundamental locomotor and manipulative skills. Chapters 8, 9, and 10 deal with movement experiences designed to enhance rhythmic perceptual-motor and visual, tactile, and auditory abilities. Chapter 11 presents game activities designed to enhance a variety of academic concepts.

The last two chapters of the book are concerned with the role of play in the lives of children, the many different forms that early childhood education takes, and the role of movement in this education. It is the intent of these chapters to acquaint the reader more fully with the nature of children's play and the role of movement in preschool education.

A great deal of library research and program experimentation has gone into the preparation of this book. The state of our knowledge concerning the motor development and movement experiences of preschool and primary grade children is in the embryonic stages. A great deal of theory and conjecture exists concerning how children develop motorically and the types of experiences that best foster this development. Unfortunately, however, comparatively little exists in terms of hard experimental data. It is the intent of this text to synthesize the current pertinent information on motor development that does exist and to present a series of classroom-tested movement experiences that help achieve a variety of psychomotor, cognitive, and affective objectives.

The reader should note that there has been an attempt to blend the newer movement education concepts of teaching movement with the more traditional forms of physical education. The approach taken is not one of which school of thought is better or best, but rather what movement experiences can we as parents and teachers of young children utilize to help them develop to their fullest potential.

I would like to express my heartfelt thanks to the boys and girls of the "Challengers" Motor Development Programs as well as the undergraduate and graduate students from a variety of disciplines who have assisted so ably with the Challengers and in the program experimentation necessary for the development of this text. My special appreciation is extended to Bruce McClenaghan for his tireless assistance with the Challengers.

Photography credits go to Lawrence Manning and James McKittrick. I also thank Phi Delta Kappa Education Fraternity for their permission to use numerous photographs, and Betty Garrett for typing the manuscript.

No author can complete a task of this nature without the complete cooperation and support of his family. For this, I especially wish to thank my wife Ellie, and children, David Lee and Jennifer, for their supreme patience and moral support, and to Him who makes all things possible.

David L. Gallahue

Bloomington, Indiana
October 1975

Contents

Chapter 1   Movement with Meaning   **1**

Chapter 2   Growth, Development, and the Young Child   **21**

Chapter 3   Psychomotor Development of Young Children   **49**

Chapter 4   Psychomotor Development and the Cognitive Behavior of Young Children   **81**

Chapter 5   Psychomotor Development and the Affective Behavior of Young Children   **107**

Chapter 6   Individualized Movement Experiences for Enhancing Fundamental Movement Abilities   **127**

Chapter 7   Active Games for Enhancing Fundamental Movement Abilities   **177**

Chapter 8   Movement Experiences for Enhancing Fundamental Rhythmic Abilities   **215**

Chapter 9   Movement Experiences for Enhancing Perceptual-Motor Abilities   **259**

Chapter 10   Movement Experiences for Enhancing Visual, Tactile, and Auditory Abilities   **289**

Chapter 11   Movement Experiences for Enhancing Academic Abilities   **315**

xii

Chapter 12 Children's Play Toys, and Play Spaces   **353**

Chapter 13 Education of Young Children   **379**

Author Index   **401**

Subject Index   **405**

Motor Development and Movement Experiences for Young Children (3-7)

Chapter 1

Movement with Meaning

CONTENTS

Introduction
Psychomotor Development
    Movement Abilities
        Phases of Motor Development
    Physical Abilities
        Physical Fitness
        Motor Fitness
Cognitive Development
    Perceptual-Motor Concepts
    Academic Concept Readiness
Affective Development
    Self Concept
    Peer Relations and Play
Conclusion
Suggested Readings

The Child is the Father of the Man
William Wadsworth

INTRODUCTION

Parents and teachers of young children are becoming increasingly aware of the importance of providing their children with meaningful movement experiences. There is a growing realization among early childhood educators, special educators, and physical educators that the so-called play experiences engaged in by preschool and primary-grade children play an important role in *learning to move* and *learning through movement.* For young children movement is at the very center of their life. It permeates all facets of their development, whether in the psychomotor, cognitive, or affective domains of human behavior. In this chapter we will take a cursory look at the contribution that movement can make to each of these domains. Subsequent chapters will more closely examine the role of movement in psychomotor, cognitive and affective development. The unity of man makes it impossible to separate these three areas of human behavior. Therefore the astute reader will be aware of the complex interaction between these domains, and will take care not to separate them in his or her thinking or dealing with children.

PSYCHOMOTOR DEVELOPMENT

The primary contribution of movement programs for young children is in the development of psychomotor competencies. Psychomotor development is at the very heart of the movement education program and should be viewed as an avenue by which both cognitive and affective competencies can also be enhanced. Psychomotor development refers to *learning to move* with control and efficiency through space. It is often referred to simply as motor development (the terms will be used interchangeably) and is subdivided here into two aspects, namely *movement abilities* and *physical abilities.*

With preschool and primary-grade children the term "movement abilities" refers to the development and refinement of a wide variety of fundamental movements. These movement abilities are developed and refined to a point that children are capable of operating with considerable ease and efficiency within their environment. As they mature, the fundamental movement abilities that were developed when they were younger are applied to a wide variety of games and sports that, hopefully, are engaged in as a part of their daily life experiences. The fundamental movement abilities of striking an object in an underhand, sidearm, or overarm pattern, for example, are elaborated upon and found in numerous sport and recreational pursuits such as golf, tennis, and baseball.

The joy of efficient movement

The term "physical abilities" refers to the young child's ever-increasing ability to function and operate within the environment with regard to his or her level of physical fitness and motor ability. Children's physical abilities are influenced by a variety of health- and performance-related factors that in turn influence their movement abilities.

Movement Abilities

Movement behavior may be categorized into three broad and sometimes overlapping categories. These categories represent the primary focus of the motor development specialist when working with children in a movement education program. The first and most basic of these movement categories is referred to as stability. *Stability* abilities are those developing patterns of movement that permit young children to gain and maintain a point of origin for the explorations that they make through space. Stability abilities are sometimes referred to as nonlocomotor movements because they involve such stationary activities as bending, stretching, twisting, and turning. They also include activities in which a *premium* is placed on maintaining equilibrium such as with inverted supports (tip-up, tripod, or headstand) and rolling movements (forward, backward, or sideward rolls).

At the time when stability abilities are developing, fundamental locomotor abilities are also being enhanced. *Locomotion* involves projection of the body into external space by altering its location in either a vertical or horizontal plane. Such activities as running, jumping, skipping, and galloping are commonly thought of as locomotor in nature. It is through locomotion that children are able to effectively explore the world about them.

The third aspect of developing movement abilities in young children involves the development of fundamental manipulative abilities. *Gross motor manipulation* involves imparting force to objects such as in throwing, striking, pushing and pulling toys, and receiving force from objects as with catching, trapping, and stacking toys. It is through the manipulation of objects that children are able to come into actual physical contact with objects in their world.

Phases of Motor Development.*

The movement education of preschool and primary-grade children involves the development of fundamental, locomotor, manipulative, and stability movement abilities. Upon closer examination of movement behavior throughout the life cycle, we find that these three categories permeate human movement from infancy through adulthood. That is, locomotor, manipulative, and stability movement activities are experienced at all levels in the total life experience which may be classified motorically into developmental stages. These developmental stages correspond roughly with the phases of development outlined in the following paragraphs (see Figure 1.1).

The *reflexive movements* of the fetus and newborn are considered to represent the first phase of motor development. Reflexive behaviors are subcortically controlled. They preceed and operate concurrently with the

---

*For a detailed discussion of the movement abilities of young children and the phases of motor development, see *A Conceptual Approach to Moving and Learning,* by Gallahue, Werner, and Luedke, Wiley, 1975.

APPROXIMATE AGE (IN YEARS)	PHASE OF MOTOR DEVELOPMENT	CORRESPONDING DEVELOPMENTAL STAGE
-5 to 1	Reflexive behavior	Utero infancy
0–2	Rudimentary movement abilities	Infancy
2–7	Fundamental movement abilities	Early childhood
7–10	General movement abilities	Middle childhood
11–13	Specific movement abilities	Later childhood
14+	Specialized movement abilities	Adolescence and adulthood

Figure 1.1 The phases of motor development and the developmental stage sequence.

development of *rudimentary movement abilities.* Rudimentary movements begin developing in the infant from shortly after birth to approximately 2 years of age. They involve locomotor activities such as creeping, crawling, and walking. They include manipulative experiences such as reaching, grasping, and releasing objects and also involve the stability movements of gaining control of the head, neck, and trunk along with learning how to sit and stand unaided.

The third phase of motor development is referred to as the *fundamental movement abilities* phase. This phase was discussed briefly in the preceding paragraphs and is the primary concern of this book. Developing fundamental movement abilities involves attaining acceptable levels of performance in a variety of basic movement skills beginning around the second year of life and continuing through the preschool years and primary grades to about age 7 years. This age range encompasses the period of time commonly referred to as early childhood.

Boys and girls in the intermediate grades (third, fourth, and fifth grades) are generally considered to be in middle childhood. This stage of development gives rise to a fourth phase of motor development, namely the *general movement abilities* phase. General movement abilities closely resemble the fundamental movement abilities of the preceding phase because they involve many of the same movements. The difference, however, lies in the fact that these fundamental movements are now elaborated upon, more highly developed, and approached as sport skills that are applied to a wide variety of lead-up activities for individual, dual, and team sports. The rudimentary movement of striking, for example, is now approached as the general sport skills of striking a softball, golf ball, or tennis ball and applied to lead-up

Developing rudimentary stability abilities.

games such as fungo, low-hole golf, and tennis volley rather than the *official* sport.

A fifth phase of development is the *specific movement abilities* phase, which corresponds with the developmental stage of later childhood and preadolescence (sixth, seventh, and eighth grades). This phase of motor development is similar to the previous one except that the child is developmentally more mature and more capable of coping with the physical and psychological demands brought about through greater emphasis on form, skill, and accuracy in the performance of more advanced lead-up games and the official sport itself.

The final phase of motor development is the *specialized movement abili-*

ties phase beginning around high school and continuing through adulthood. The specialized skill phase involves application of the knowledges gained in the preceding phases to a selected few lifetime activities that are engaged in on either a recreational or competitive level on a regular basis. One of the primary goals of education is to develop individuals to a point that they become happy, healthy, contributing members of society. We must not lose sight of this lofty but worthy goal and proceed to view the hierarchical development of movement abilities as stepping stones to the specialized movement skill level. We must cease to view young children as miniature adults who can be programed to perform at this phase in such potentially high-pressure, physiologically and psychologically questionable activities as Little League Baseball and Pee Wee Football. We must truly begin to view children as *children* and structure meaningful movement experiences appropriate for their particular developmental level. Only when we recognize that the progressive development of movement abilities in a developmentally appropriate sequence is imperative to the balanced motor development of children will we truly be contributing to the total development of each individual. Specialized skill development can and should play a role in our lives, but it is unfair to children to require that they specialize in one or two skill areas at the expense of developing their abilities and appreciations for many other areas.

The reader is cautioned to view the age ranges for each phase of motor development in general terms only. Children will often be seen to function at different phases depending on their experiential background and hereditary makeup. For example, it is entirely possible for a 10-year-old to function at the specialized movement skill phase in stability activities involving gymnastic-type movements but only at the rudimentary or fundamental movement phase in a variety of manipulative or locomotor activities involving such activities as throwing, catching, or running. Although we should continue to encourage this precocious behavior in gymnastics, we should also be very concerned that the child catches up to his or her age mates in the other areas and develops at least an acceptable level of proficiency in them. We must, therefore, refer to the phases of motor development as convenient guidelines of where the *majority* of children are functioning at a given point in time. Rigid adherence to the age classifications is unwise and in direct conflict with the principle of individual differences.

Physical Abilities

The physical development aspects of the psychomotor domain may be classified as either *physical fitness* or *motor fitness* (see Figure 1.2).

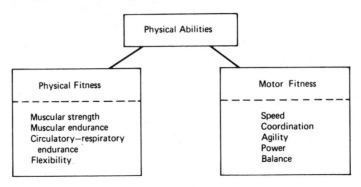

Figure 1.2 The physical fitness and motor fitness components of physical ability.

These terms, however, are elusive and difficult to define to the mutual satisfaction of experts in the field.

Physical fitness.

Fitness is a relative term that may refer to such things as spiritual, emotional, and social fitness as well as physical fitness. As a result, the concept of "total fitness" has developed over the years and is probably best exemplified by Mathews's statement that "a child who is fit enjoys robust health, a fine looking physique, a satisfactory level of social and emotional adjustment and a proficiency in the basic skills of movement."[1] Agreement on a suitable definition of physical fitness is difficult and is generally done so in broad terms because the level of fitness required of one individual may not be the same as that required of another. Hence physical fitness is generally considered to be the ability to perform one's daily tasks without undue fatigue. It also is a state in which ample reserves of energy should be available for recreational pursuits and to meet energy needs. Muscular strength, muscular endurance, circulatory–respiratory endurance, and muscular flexibility are generally considered to be the components of physical fitness and are discussed in detail in Chapter 3.

Motor Fitness.

The concept of motor ability or "motor fitness," as it is often termed, is also an elusive one that has been studied extensively over the past several years

---

[1] Mathews, Donald K. *Measurement in Physical Education,* Philadelphia: Saunders, 1973, p.5.

and is classified by some experts as being a part of physical fitness. Hockey's statement probably best summarizes the debate:

> Many factors associated with the development of skill have erroneously been referred to as physical fitness components. It should be kept in mind that only factors that relate to the development of health and increase the functional capacity of the body should be classified as physical fitness components. Those that are necessary for skillful performance of an activity should be classified as motor ability components.[2]

Motor ability (motor fitness) is generally thought of as one's performance abilities as influenced by the factors of speed, agility, balance, coordination, and power.

The generality and specificity of one's motor abilities has been debated and researched for years with the bulk of recent research evidence in favor of its specificity.[3,4] For years many physical educators somehow let themselves believe that motor abilities were general in nature; as a result, the term "*general* motor ability" came into vogue. It was assumed that because an individual excelled in a certain sport, corresponding ability would be automatically carried over to other activities. Although this often does occur, it is probably due to the individual's personal motivation, numerous activity experiences, and several specific sport aptitudes rather than transfer or carryover of skills from one activity to another. In an effort to avoid confusion between the terms "motor ability" and "general motor ability" we will instead refer to the factors of speed, agility, balance, coordination, and power as elements of "motor fitness."

COGNITIVE DEVELOPMENT

Another important outcome of a well-rounded movement education program for young children is the enhancement of fundamental cognitive concepts. Throughout the history of man, philosophers, psychologists, and educators have indicated that a relationship exists between the functioning of the body and the mind. From the Greek philosophers of Socrates and Plato to the educational theorists of the twentieth century there has been a great deal of philosophical support. The fact is, however, that little had been done

[2]Hockey, Robert V. *Physical Fitness,* St. Louis: C. V. Mosby, 1973, p. 6.

[3] Henry, Franklin M. "Influence of Motor and Sensory Sets on Recreation Latency and Speed of Discrete Movements," *The Research Quarterly,* October 1960.

[4] Henry, Franklin M., and Donald Rogers, "Increased Response Latency for Complicated Movements and a 'Memory Drum' Theory of Neuromotor Reaction," *The Research Quarterly,* October 1960.

of an experimental or practical nature prior to the 1960s to put this philosophical construct into operation. A look at psychology, education, and child growth and development textbooks prior to this time makes this point abundantly clear. Topics were generally segregated or categorized under distinctly separate chapter headings with little consideration given to the interrelations between motor and cognitive functioning. Not until the growth of popularity of the works of Jean Piaget has there been a true shift in favor of recognizing the importance of movement in the development of both psychomotor and cognitive aspects of the child's behavior. Piaget, a developmental psychologist, emphasizes the tremendous importance of movement as an information-gathering device for children to learn about themselves and their world. Physical educators,[5,6] and special educators[7-9] have since been quick to capitalize on this point and have developed a series of motor-training programs designed to enhance children's cognitive abilities.

The movement experiences of preschool and primary-grade children can be effectively used as a medium for *learning through movement.* Educators are now recognizing that important perceptual–motor skills and fundamental academic concepts can be effectively dealt with in a movement education program. This is not meant to imply that movement is the primary or sole mode by which cognitive abilities can or should be developed. It is, however, meant to say that movement can, through good teaching, be effectively used as a tool for enhancing children's cognitive awareness of themselves and the world around them. The proper use of the "teachable moment" along with the emphasis placed on the development of cognitive concepts of *why, what, how,* and *when* in relation to one's movement can play an important role in helping children get ready for learning by supplementing and reinforcing information that is dealt with in the traditional setting of the nursery school or classroom.

There are two primary aspects of cognitive development that may be dealt with effectively through the movement education portion of the child's day. The first of these aspects is the various perceptual–motor concepts involving the development of body awareness, spatial awareness, directional awareness, and establishment of an effective time–space orientation. The second aspect of cognitive development involves the development and reinforcement of increased understandings and appreciations of fundamental academic concepts involving science, mathematics, the language arts, and social studies through the medium of movement. The bulk of available evidence

[5] Cratty, Bryant J. *Intelligence in Action,* Englewood Cliffs, N. J.: Prentice–Hall, 1973.

[6] Humphrey, James *Child Learning,* Dubuque, Iowa: W. C. Brown, 1974.

[7] Getman, G. and E. Kane *The Physiology of Readiness,* Minneapolis: P.A.S.S. Inc., 1964.

[8] Kephart, Newell C. *The Slow Learner in the Classroom,* Columbus, Ohio: Charles E. Merrill, 1971.

[9] Frostig, Marianne *Move, Grow, Learn,* Chicago: Follett, 1969.

indicates that both types of cognitive concepts, whether perceptual–motor or academic in nature, may be enhanced through active involvement in carefully selected and directed movement activities. It should be noted, however, that there is little support for the notion that increased movement abilities will have a correspondingly positive affect on the native intelligence of children. The use of movement as a method of enhancing cognitive development is *not* a panacea. Only through the combined and coordinated efforts of parents, classroom teachers, and the physical education teacher will truly positive inroads be made into the child's development of cognitive abilities.

Developing concepts of "in," "on," "through" with inner tubes.

Perceptual–Motor Concepts

The process of interacting with our environment is a combination of perceptual and motor processes, which are not independent of one another, as is often assumed. The dash that appears in the term "perceptual–motor" signifies the *interdependence* of one on the other. This becomes apparent when we recognize that efficient and effective movement is dependent on accurate perceptions of ourselves and our world and that the development of one's perceptual abilities is dependent, in part, on movement.

The development of perceptual–motor abilities is a process of both maturation and experience, and as a result all children develop at their own individual rate. Not all children are at the same ability level upon entering school, and although nothing can be done about the maturational component of this process, parents and teachers can have an important influence on the experience component.

The development of perceptual–motor abilities involves the establishment and refinement of kinesthetic sensitivity to one's world through movement. This kinesthetic sensitivity involves the development and refinement of an adequate *space* structure and *temporal* (time) structure. All movement occurs in space and involves an element of time, and the development of these structures is basic to efficient functioning in a variety of other areas. In order to enhance children's knowledge of their spatial world we should involve them in movement activities designed to contribute to their body awareness, directional awareness, and spatial awareness. The temporal world of children may be correspondingly enhanced through activities that involve synchrony, rhythm and the sequencing of movements. Selected visual, auditory, and tactile abilities may also be reinforced through movement in a variety of carefully selected activities (see Figure 1.3). Chapters 9 and 10 deal with enhancing a variety of perceptual–motor abilities through movement.

Academic Concept Readiness

Movement activities for young children can enhance the understanding of fundamental academic concepts when they are integrated with material dealt with during the academic portion of the day. Textbooks by Humphrey,[10] Cratty,[11] and others have presented in operational terms how specific types of activity might be effectively used to enhance the acqui-

---

[10] Humphrey, James. *Child Learning,* Dubuque, Iowa: W. C. Brown, 1974. *Op. cit.*

[11] Cratty, Bryant J. *Active Learning: Games to Enhance Academic Abilities,* Englewood Cliffs, N. J.: Prentice–Hall, 1971.

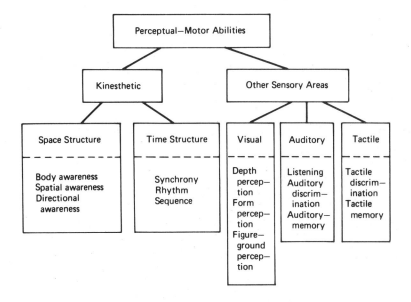

Figure 1.3 The sensory components of perceptual–motor development.

sition of language-arts competencies, basic mathematical operations, and social studies and science concepts. There are a variety of indirect and direct reasons why this occurs. Among them is the fact that active participation is fun. It is often a more natural approach that more closely approximates the needs and interests of children. Active participation in a game in which academic concepts are being dealt with makes it difficult for children's attention to be diverted by extraneous stimuli. Also, a large proportion of today's children place a high negative value on academic understandings but have a high positive regard for physical abilities. Using active games as a learning medium tends to pair pleasurable and highly regarded activity with that which may not be as highly valued, and thus tends to give more pleasure to the practice of the academic skill. Lastly, active learning through movement activities enables children to deal in concrete terms with their world rather than in the abstract.[13]

Children generally regard movement as fun and do not equate it with the

[13] Cratty, Bryant J. *Intelligence in Action,* Englewood Cliffs, N. J. Prentice–Hall, 1973.

routine "work" of the classroom. It should be noted, however, that *not all* children benefit best in the enrichment of their academic abilities through active participation in movement activities. On the contrary, there is an overwhelming amount of evidence that indicates that the traditionally silent and relatively immobile form of thought is quite effective for many individuals. The point to be made here is that *some* children benefit greatly from a program that integrates movement activities with academic concept development and that *most* young children will probably realize at least some improvement. Chapter 11 presents a variety of appropriate activities designed to enhance selected academic abilities.

AFFECTIVE DEVELOPMENT

A third important but often overlooked outcome of a good movement education program for young children is enhancement of the affective domain. Affective development involves dealing with children's increasing ability to act, interact, and react effectively with other people as well as with themselves. It is often referred to as "social–emotional development," and its successful attainment is of crucial importance to preschool and primary grade children. For without sufficient social and emotional competencies, children will encounter continual difficulty in relating effectively to their peers, adults, and even themselves.

> "A good or poor parent, an affluent or culturally deprived environment, and the quality and quantity of stimulation given children will largely determine whether they view their world as one that they can control or as one that controls them."[12]

The movement experiences engaged in by young children play an important role in children's perception of themselves as individuals as well as how they are able to relate to their peers and utilize their free time. Astute parents and teachers will recognize the vital importance of balanced social–emotional growth. They will study the developmental characteristics of children and gather the necessary understandings of their behavior in at least the following two areas: (1) self-concept and (2) peer relations and play. This knowledge will enable them to encourage and structure meaningful movement experiences that will strengthen children's social–emotional growth and be in accordance with their developmental needs, interests, and capabilities.

Self-concept

Preschoolers and primary-grade children are active, energetic, and emerg-

---

[12] Gallahue, David L., Werner Peter H. and Luedke George C. *A Conceptual Approach to Moving & Learning,* New York: Wiley, 1975.

ing beings. They are engrossed in play and utilize play experiences as a means of finding out more about themselves and their bodies. The important beginnings of self-concept or "self-esteem," as it is often termed, is formed in the preschool years. Young children generally view themselves on one end of two extremes in all that they do. Their egocentric nature does not permit them to view themselves objectively in light of their particular strengths and weaknesses. They are unable to fully grasp the concept that one's abilities to do things lie somewhere *between* these self-limiting poles. The "right–wrong," "good–bad" world that children live in plays a key role in how they view themselves. Since their world is one of play and vigorous activity, the successes and failures that they experience play an important role in the establishment of a stable self-concept. If children experience repeated failure in their play world and are unable to perform the fundamental movement tasks of early childhood, they are likely to encounter difficulties in establishing a stable positive concept of themselves.

Based on this knowledge it becomes important for parents and teachers of young children to structure meaningful movement experiences that are within children's developmental capabilities. Ones that reduce the failure potential, thereby enhancing the success potential. It is not enough to say that "failure is a fact of life" or that "if one does not know failure he cannot appreciate success." We must be ever mindful a preschooler is developmentally unable to utilize such logic due to his egocentric nature. The possibility and risk of failure must be *gradually* introduced to children in a manner that is educationally appropriate. We must endeavor to instil the noble concept that each person is a unique individual with a variety of limitations as well as capabilities. Positive feelings toward oneself will help form the basis for developing this concept.

Movement experiences that permit exploration and problem solving on the part of children are very worthwhile. They permit children to solve movement problems or challenges within the limits of their own abilities and do not require the emulation of a predetermined criterion of performance. In this way each child is permitted to achieve a measure of success bounded only by the limits of his or her capabilities.

Movement experiences that have an adventure or "pseudo-danger" element to them are of value in enhancing children's self-concept. Activities such as those that permit children to climb trees or a jungle gym, balance several feet off the ground on a rope ladder or balance beam, or crawl through a homemade tunnel all incorporate an element of adventure in which children must overcome their natural fears and uncertainties to accomplish a "dangerous" task. The feelings of exhileration and self-satisfaction with accomplishing such a task helps to promote an "I can" attitude

Time to relax and enjoy.

within children and enhance their self-esteem. Chapter 5 will take a detailed look at the role of movement in self-concept development.

Peer Relations and Play

While children are engaged in learning about themselves and their world they are also involved in learning how to interact with their peers. Children gradually move through various stages in the establishment of successful relations with members of their peer group. The first is the egocentric stage, in which they literally view themselves as the center of the universe during the first 2 years of life. The egocentric child is content to play alone with very limited contact with other children. The second stage is that of parallel play. Three- and 4-year old children exhibit behavior characteristic of this stage, in which they are content to play alongside other children but do not enter into group activities for extended periods of time. At about age 5 years, children enter the the group-play stage. This stage is characterized by the ability to play in small groups for increasing periods of time followed by the ability to play in large groups and in team-type efforts by age 7 or 8 years.

Movement serves as a primary vehicle by which children progress through each of the play stages. The wise parent and teacher will recognize that wholesome peer relations are a developing phenomena. They will be careful to view children's difficulty with sharing, playing together, and concern for others' feelings as factors that must be dealt with understandingly in light of each child's developmental level. Through wise guidance, movement can be used as an effective tool in helping children develop each of these abilities.

The world of preschool and primary-grade children is a play world. Play serves as a primary vehicle by which they learn about themselves and the world about them. If asked "what did you do today," young children characteristically respond by saying "play." Care must be taken not to view such a response as a frivolous remark or unnecessary part of their daily life. Play must be viewed in the perspective that it is the work of children. That is, through play, whether individual or group, active or quiet, children develop fundamental understandings of the world in which they live.

The development of fundamental movement abilities contributes to children's use of leisure time. The ability to perform a wide variety of locomotor, manipulative, and stability-type movements in an acceptable manner enables children to pursue a variety of play-type activities. Children who do not move well are hindered in their pursuit of leisure-time activities that involve the use and development of their movement abilities. As a result, a negative cycle that witnesses poor movement abilities being formed due to lack of opportunity or encouragement is established. The constructive use of leisure time can be enhanced through the possession of efficient movement abilities. Although gross motor activities are only one way of engaging in leisure they are important ones for most children and adults. Chapter 12 deals with the play of children, their toys, and appropriate playing spaces.

CONCLUSION

The movement activities engaged in by young children play a very important role in the development of their psychomotor, cognitive, and affective abilities. Young children are involved in the important and exciting task of *learning to move* effectively and efficiently through their world. They are developing a wide variety of fundamental movement abilities, enhancing their physical abilities, and learning to move with joy and control. Children also *learn through movement.* Movement serves as a vehicle by which they explore all that is around them. It aids in developing and reinforcing a variety of perceptual–motor and academic concepts. It also serves as a medium for encouraging affective development in which effective and efficient movement contributes to enhancing a positive self-concept, wholesome peer relations, and the worthy use of leisure time through constructive play. Figure 1.4 provides an overview of the interrelated nature of the psychomotor, cognitive, and affective domains as applied to movement.

An increasing number of educators and parents are beginning to realize that reciting the alphabet, being able to count to 100, and writing one's name are not the important learning tasks for young children. Readiness for learning is more than parroting facts and figures, it is a state of developmentally integrated maturity rather than the ability to memorize isolated facts. Children who have developed the following abilities are well on their way to success in school:

1. To love themselves and value their existence as human beings.
2. To possess the fundamental motor and perceptual abilities necessary for cognitive and motor learning.
3. To be able to interpret the meanings of other people's behavior as well as their own.
4. To understand the difference between thoughts and actions and to recognize that feelings are harmless to others.
5. To be able to communicate feelings and emotions as well as thoughts and ideas with words.
6. To wonder and inquire.

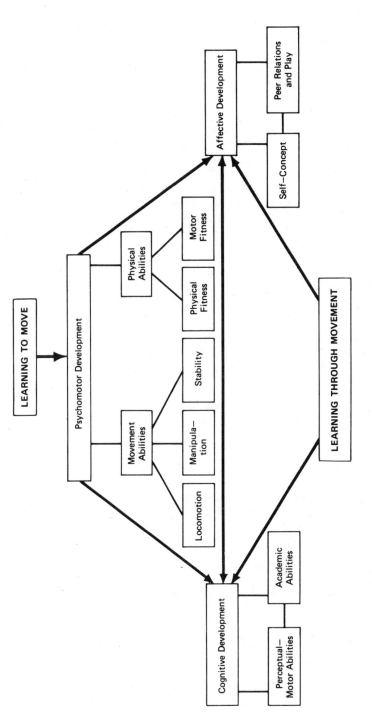

Figure 1.4 The interrelated nature of motor development affects cognitive and affective behavior as well as psychomotor development.

7. To be able to risk failure as a necessary part of learning.
8. To understand that complicated questions do not have simple answers in a complex and inconsistent world.
9. To have a mind of their own and to be able to make decisions.
10. To trust their environment and the people in it and to know when to ask for help.

Surely movement plays a key role in the development of these crucial concepts. It is time that we take a fresh and serious look at movement in light of its contributions to the *total* child rather than playing lip service to its potential value. We must begin to view movement in light of its educational potential for enhancing psychomotor, cognitive, and affective development. The following chapters are dedicated to this end.

SUGGESTED READINGS

Annarino, Anthony A. *Fundamental Movement and Sport Skill Development,* Columbus, Ohio: Charles E. Merrill, 1973.

Dauer, Victor. *Essential Movement Experiences for Preschool and Primary Grade Children,* Minneapolis: Burgess, 1972.

Gallahue, David L., Peter H. Werner, and George C. Luedke, *A Conceptual Approach to Moving and Learning,* New York: Wiley, 1975.

Harrow, Anita J. *A Taxonomy of the Psychomotor Domain,* New York: David McKay Company, 1972.

Latchaw, Majorie, and Glen Egstrom, *Human Movement,* Englewood Cliffs, N. J.: Prentice–Hall, 1969.

MacKenzie, Marlin M. *Toward A New Curriculum in Physical Education,* New York: McGraw–Hill, 1969.

Metheny, Eleanor. *Movement and Meaning,* New York: McGraw–Hill, 1968.

Miller, Arthur G., John T. F. Cheffers, and Virginia Whitcomb, *Physical Education: Teaching Human Movement in the Elementary Schools,*Englewood Cliffs, N. J.: Prentice–Hall, 1974.

North, Marion. *Body Movement for Children,* Boston: Plays, Inc., 1971.

Schurr, Evelyn. *Movement Experiences for Children: A Humanistic Approach to Elementary School Physical Education,* Englewood Cliffs, N. J.: Prentice–Hall, 1975.

Seidel, Beverly et al. *Sports Skills: A Conceptual Approach to Meaningful Movement,* Dubuque, Iowa: W. C. Brown, 1975.

Sweeney, Robert T. (ed.). *Selected Readings in Movement Education,* Reading, Massachusetts: Addison–Wesley, 1970.

Vannier, Maryhelen, Mildred Foster, and David L. Gallahue, *Teaching Physical Education in Elementary Schools,* Philadelphia: W. B. Saunders, 1973.

Chapter 2

Growth, Development, and the Young Child

CONTENTS

Introduction
Human Development Defined
Models of Child Development
Conceptual Viewpoints of Child Development
  Erik Erikson
  Jean Piaget
Characteristics of Young Children
  Preschool Age Children (2 to 5)
    Psychomotor Characteristics
    Cognitive Characteristics
    Affective Characteristics
    Implications for the Motor Development
      Program
  Primary Grade Children (5 to 7)
    Psychomotor Characteristics
    Cognitive Characteristics
    Affective Characteristics
    Implications for the Motor Development
      Program
Conclusion
Suggested Readings

The Secret in Education Lies in Respecting the Pupil
Ralph Waldo Emerson

INTRODUCTION

Prior to embarking on the construction of a movement education program for preschool and primary-grade children, it is crucial that we clearly understand various concepts of growth and development as well as the needs, interests, and developmental characteristics of young children. Only in this way can we devise and implement developmentally appropriate movement experiences for them.

The basis of any sound educational program lies in a thorough understanding of the characteristic needs of the individuals being dealt with. All too often this principle of program development is neglected or minimized. We become engrossed in our subject matter and end up teaching *content* rather than *children.* There is a vast difference implied between the teaching of content and the teaching of children. The teacher of content molds or modifies the learner to fit the subject matter, whereas the teacher of children utilizes the subject matter as a tool to be modified and geared to the needs, interests, and abilities of the learner.

This chapter deals with the process of child development and the characteristics of children in an effort to develop more knowledgeable teachers of *children.* It should be noted, however, that the best way to gain an understanding or "feel" for the needs, interests, and abilities of children is through active involvement with them and the careful observation of their behavior.

HUMAN DEVELOPMENT DEFINED

The terms "growth" and "development" are often used interchangeably, but there is a difference in emphasis implied by each. *Growth* in its purest sense refers to an increase in the size of the body or its parts as the child progresses toward maturity. In other words, growth is an increase in the structure of the body brought about by the multiplication of cells. The term "growth," however, is often referred to in the totality of physical change and as a result it becomes more inclusive and takes on the same meaning as development.

Development in its purest sense refers to changes in the individual's level of functioning. It is the emerging and broadening of the child's ability to function on a higher level, whether in the psychomotor, cognitive, or affective domains of human behavior. The study of human development is concerned with *what* occurs and *how* it occurs in the organism on its journey from conception through maturity and on to eventual death. It is a continuous process which encompasses all of the interrelated dimensions of man's existence, and care must be taken not to consider each of these dimensions as autonomous.

The interwoven elements of maturation and experience play a key role in the developmental process. *Maturation* is an aspect of development used to specifically designate qualitative changes that enable one to progress to higher levels of functioning. Maturation is primarily innate; that is, it is genetically determined and resistant to external or environmental influences. Maturation is characterized by a fixed order of progression in which the pace may vary but the sequence of appearance of characteristics generally does not. For example, the progression and approximate ages at which the infant learns to sit, stand, and walk are highly influenced by maturation. The *sequence* of appearance of these abilities is fixed and resistent to change with only the *rate* of appearance being altered by the environmental influences of experience.

Experience refers to factors within the environment that may alter or modify the appearance of various developmental characteristics through the process of learning. The experiences that children are exposed to may have an affect on the rate of onset of certain patterns of behavior.

The developmental aspects of both maturation and experience are complexly interwoven. Determining the separate contribution of each of these processes is impossible. In fact, a heated debate over the relative merits of the two has raged throughout the literature for over a century. The trend now, however, is to recognize the unique importance of each and their dependence on one another. As a result, the term *adaptation* has come into vogue and is often used to refer to the complex interplay between the individual and the environment. Figure 2.1 illustrates how the factors of growth and maturation and adaptation are all directly related to the developing child and indirectly related to one another.

MODELS OF CHILD DEVELOPMENT

During the past half century several developmental theorists have closely studied the phenomena of child development. Such notables are Sigmund Freud, Erik Erikson, Arnold Gesell, Robert Havighurst, and Jean Piaget, who have each made valuable contributions to the knowledge of children. Each has constructed models of the developing child that depict the many phases and stages that are passed through on the journey to maturity. Each of the models have several similarities but reflect their originator's philosophical leanings and particular interests in the study of children. A cursory look at the models of growth and development proposed by the above theorists

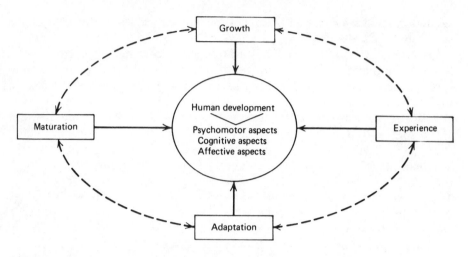

Figure 2.1 Related components of human development.

should adequately illustrate this point and provide a basis for more knowledgeable study of child development as well as show the important role that movement plays in each model.

Freud's psychoanalytic theory of human behavior may be viewed as a model of child development even though his work centered around personality. His famous psychosexual stages of development reflect various zones of the body with which the child seeks gratification of the id (i.e., the unconscious source of motives, desires, passions, and pleasure seeking) at certain general age periods. The ego mediates between the pleasure-seeking behavior of the id and the super ego (i.e., common sense, reasons, and conscience).[1] The oral, anal, phallic, latency, and genital stages of personality development represent the terms applied to the pleasure-seeking zones of the body that come into play at different age periods. Each stage relies heavily on physical sensations and motor activity.

Erikson, a student of Freud, focused his attention on the influence of society on development rather than sex. He described eight stages of man and put them on a continuum, emphasizing factors in the environment as facilitators of change rather than heredity.[2] Erikson's view of human development acknowledges factors within the individual's experiential back-

---

[1] Freud, Sigmund. *The Ego and the Id,* New York: Norton, 1962.
[2] Erikson, Erik. *Childhood and Society,* New York: Norton, 1963.

ground as having more to do with one's development than generally given credit for. His view of the importance of motor development in childhood is more implied than explicit, but he clearly points out the importance of success-oriented movement experiences as a means of reconciling the developmental crises that each child passes through.

The freedom of efficient movement.

A brief look at Gesell's theory of growth and development also reveals a great deal of emphasis on the physical and motor components of human behavior.[3] Gesell took great pains to document and describe general age

[3] Gesell, Arnold. *The Embryology of Behavior,* New York: Harper, 1945.

periods for the acquisition of a wide variety of rudimentary movement skills and viewed these skills as important indicators of social and emotional growth. Gesell also described various ages when the child is in "nodal" periods or when he is "out of focus" with his environment. A nodal stage refers to the child exhibiting a high degree of mastery over situations in the immediate environment, being balanced in behavior, and generally pleasant to be with. Being out of focus refers to just the opposite, namely exhibiting a low degree of mastery over situations in the immediate environment, being unbalanced or troubled in behavior, and generally unpleasant to be with.[4]

A fourth developmental model, that of Robert Havighurst, views development as an interplay between biological, social, and cultural forces in which the child is continually enhancing his abilities to function effectively in society.[5] Havighurst has viewed development as a series of tasks that must be achieved within a certain framework of time to ensure proper functioning of the individual. These crucial tasks arrise from three main sources: (1) physical maturation, (2) cultural pressure, and (3) a combination of (1) and (2) that forms the individual's unique personality or self. Havighurst's model stresses that there are teachable moments when the body is ripe and when society requires successful completion of a task. As with the aforementioned models, the tasks described by Havighurst rely heavily on movement, play, and physical activity for their development.

The last and currently most popular developmental theory among parents and educators is that of Jean Piaget, who places primary emphasis on the acquisition of cognitive thought processes and has gained insight to the development of cognitive structures through careful observation of infants and children.[6] The genius in Piaget's work lies in his uncanny ability to pick out subtle clues in children's behavior that give us indications of their cognitive functioning. Piaget views these subtle indicators as milestones in the hierarchy of cognitive development. A great deal of emphasis is placed on movement as a primary agent in the acquisition of increased cognitive functioning, particularly during infancy and the preschool years. Piaget terms the developmental periods as sensorimotor (birth to 2 years), preoperational (2–7 years), concrete operations (7–12 years), and formal operations (12 years and over). Piaget does not directly concern himself with the individual

---

[4] Gesell, Arnold, et al. *The First Five Years of Life: A Guide to the Study of the Preschool Child,* New York: Harper, 1940.

[5] Havighurst, Robert. *Developmental Tasks and Education,* New York: Longmans, Green and Company, 1952.

[6] Piaget, Jean. *The Psychology of the Child,* New York: Basic Books, 1969.

beyond age 15 years because he has established his intellectual capabilities by this time.

The point to be made from the above paragraphs is that even though each theorist looks at the phenomena of child development from a somewhat different point of view, close inspection reveals that they are remarkably congruent on many aspects. Each places a degree of emphasis on movement, motor development, and play as important facilitators of enhanced functioning. They each differ, however, in the particular aspect of development emphasized. It must be remembered that man is a multidimensional being and that no one developmental model adequately covers all dimensions. There is plenty of room for different areas of emphasis, but care must be taken not to suscribe to one to the exclusion of all others. Such a move would be unwise and without scientific support. As parents and educators, we must constantly be aware of the interrelatedness of our children's behavior and dispel the notion that the psychomotor, cognitive, and affective domains of human behavior are independent of one another. Figure 2.2 illustrates the

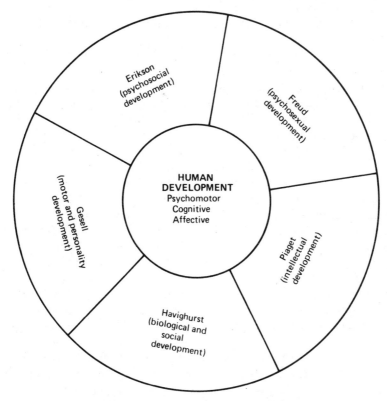

Figure 2.2 The interrelationship of theoretical models of child development.

interrelatedness of each of the developmental models discussed and the particular interest area of each theorist.

We can learn a great deal from the developmental models discussed above, but we must be selective in our application of this knowledge. That is, we must *attempt* to recognize all points of view and select what most adequately describes each *individual child.*

CONCEPTUAL VIEWPOINTS OF CHILD DEVELOPMENT

Close inspection of the five models of child development discussed in the preceding section as well as study of others reveals a distinct tendency for each to group around one of three similar but independent conceptual frameworks. These frameworks or viewpoints are classified here as either *age–stage, developmental task,* or *developmental milestone* concepts of child development.

The age–stage concept refers to periods of time that are characterized by certain types of behavior. These general descriptions of specific behaviors occur at various ages and last for arbitrary lengths of time. Each stage (i.e., typical behavior) generally covers a period of 1 year or more. Most who expound an age–stage scheme have divided childhood, or even the entire life cycle, into 10 stages or less. The age–stage concept is probably the most popular among parents and educators and is often reflected in our thinking and speech when we say, "she is just going through a stage," or "I will be happy when he is out of that stage." Freud, Erikson, and Gesell each view child development through the age–stage concept.

The second conceptual viewpoint of child development is referred to as the developmental task concept. A developmental task is an important accomplishment that the individual must achieve by a *certain* time if he is going to function effectively and meet the demands placed upon him by society. Developmental task proponents view the accomplishment of particular tasks within a certain span of time as prerequisite to smooth progression to higher levels of functioning. This concept of development differs from the age–stage view in that it is *predictive* of later success or failure based on the individual's performance at an earlier stage and does not merely attempt to *describe* typical behavior at a particular age. Havighurst's view of child development is an excellent example of use of the developmental task concept.

The developmental milestone concept represents the third and final conceptual framework from which children's behavioral patterns are viewed. Developmental milestones are similar to developmental tasks except for their emphasis. Rather than representing accomplishments that take place if the individual is to adapt to the environment, this concept refers to the strategic indicators of how far development has progressed. The accomplishment of a developmental milestone may or may not in itself be crucial to adjustment in the world as with a developmental task. Milestones are merely convenient guidelines by which the rate and extent of development can be gauged. As with age–stage concepts, they are descriptive rather than predictive but unlike them, they more readily view development as a continual unfolding and intertwining of developmental processes rather than a neat transition from one stage to another.

Realization of the fact that the many models of child development tend to group under three broad concepts enables us to view the phenomena of child development in more objective terms. Each concept has merit and probably operates to a certain degree throughout the developmental process. The crucial young years are ones which do, in fact, require the achievement of certain important *tasks* such as learning to walk, talk, and take solid foods by a certain age in order for normal functioning to be established. These years also house a variety of *stages* that all children pass through at more or less the same age and a variety of *milestones* that are achieved as subtle indicators of how far development has progressed.

The following pages contain summaries of two theories representing different conceptual points of view. The age–stage theory of Erik Erikson and the developmental milestone theory of Jean Piaget are considered. These two theories have been selected because of their thoroughness, popularity, and implications for movement.

Erik Erikson

The psychoanalytic theory of Erik Erikson[7] represents adherence to the age–stage concept of human development. It is an experience-based theory widely acclaimed by educators and psychologists. The following is an overview of Erikson's theory presented in outline form for ease of understanding and clarity. Note the numerous implications for movement throughout the theory but particularlly during the first four stages.

1. **Acquiring a sense of basic trust versus mistrust** (infancy):

   a. For the neonate, trust requires a feeling of physical comfort and a minimum of fear or uncertainty.

---

[7] Erikson, Erik. "Eight Ages of Man," *Childhood and Society,* New York: Norton, 1963, pp. 247–274.

b. A sense of basic trust helps the individual to accept new experiences willingly.

c. Bodily experiences provide the basis for a psychological state of trust.

d. The infant learns to trust "mother," himself and the environment through mother's perception of his needs and demands. A mutual trust and willingness to face situations together between mother and child is established.

2. **Acquiring a sense of autonomy versus doubt and shame** (toddler):

a. Continued dependency creates a sense of doubt in capacity.

b. The child is bombarded by conflicting pulls of asserting himself and denying himself the right and capacity to make this assertion.

c. The child needs guidance and support lest he find himself at a loss and become forced to turn against himself with shame and doubt.

d. The child explores and accomplishes new feats.

e. Proper development of the ego, which spells healthy growth, permits awareness of self as an autonomous unit.

f. The child experiences frustration as a reality of life (a natural part of life, not a total threat).

g. Play allows children to develop autonomy within their own boundaries.

h. Autonomy is developed by realizing that the environment and oneself can be controlled. The child develops concepts of frontward, backward, upward, downward, and so on.

i. The child violates mutual trust to establish autonomy in distinct areas.

3. **Acquiring a sense of initiative versus guilt** (play age):

a. Avid curiosity, feelings of guilt, and anxiety develop. The conscience is established.

b. Specific tasks are mastered. Assumes responsibility for himself and his world. Realizes life has a purpose.

c. The child initiates behavior, the implications of which go beyond himself. This includes feelings of discomfort and guilt by the frustration of autonomy of others. He experiences guilt with a desire to curtail all initiative that conflicts with the pull toward a continuance of his searching initiative.

d. The child discovers that in his greater mobility, his is not unlike the adults of his environment. The use of language has improved permitting him to expand his fields of activity and imagination.

e. The child will incorporate into his conscience what the parent really is as a person and not merely what he tries to teach the child.

f. Awareness of sex differences develops, and the child finds pleasurable accomplishment in manipulating meaningful toys.

g. Most guilt and failure quickly become compensated for by a sense of accomplishment. The future absolves the past.

4. **Acquiring a sense of industry versus inferiority** (school age):

a. This stage is marked by development of the skills necessary for life in general and preparation for marriage and family life.

b. The child needs to find a place among his peers rather than adults.

c. The child works on mastering social skills to become a competent self, striving for a sense of accomplishment for having done well, he wards off failure at any price.

d. All activities reflect competition.

e. Boys and girls play separately. Play loses importance at the end of this phase.

f. Beginning with puberty, involvement in play merges into semiplayful and eventually real involvement in work.

g. The child recognizes that he must eventually break with his accustomed family life.

h. Dependence on the parent as the child's major influence shifts to dependence on social institutions.

5. **Acquiring a sense of identity versus role confusion** (puberty–adolescence):

a. During this stage there is rapid body growth and sexual maturity. Identity to masculinity or feminity develops. Feelings of acceptance or rejection by peers are important. Conflict arises when one's peers say one thing and society says another.

b. Identity is essential for making adult decisions (vocation and marriage partner).

c. Youth will select as significant adults people who have come to mean the most.

d. The individual slowly moves into society as an interdependent member.

e. A sense of identity assures the individual a definite place within his own corner of society.

6. **Acquiring a sense of intimacy versus isolation** (young adult–late teens, early twenties):

    a. The individual accepts himself and goes on to accept others by fusing his personality with others.

    b. Childhood and youth are at an end. The individual seriously settles to the task of full participation in the community, and begins to enjoy life with adult liberties and responsibilities.

    c. The individual shows readiness in ability and willingness to share mutual trust, regulate cycles of work, procreation, and recreation.

7. **Acquiring a sense of generativity versus self-absorption** (adulthood):

    a. The individual shows interest in the next generation rather than being caught up with his own problems (i.e., wants to advance the coming generation).

    b. Generativity refers to the course one establishes and pursues with one's mate in society in order to assure for the next generation the hope, virtues, and wisdom he has accumulated. It also includes parental responsibility for society's efforts and interests in child care, education, the arts and sciences, and traditions.

8. **Acquiring a sense of integrity versus despair** (mature adult, and old age):

    a. The individual accomplishes the fullest sense of trust as the assured reliance on another's integrity.

    b. A different love of one's parents is established. Integrity provides a successful solution to an opposing sense of despair.

    c. Fulfillment of this stage involves a sense of wisdom and a philosophy of life which often extends beyond the life cycle of the individual and which is directly related to the future of new developmental cycles.

Jean Piaget

    The developmental milestone theory of Jean Piaget[8] is currently among the most popular of the developmental theories postulated by experts in the field. The following is a summary of Piaget's theory presented in outline form. Note the numerous implications for movement throughout the phases of development, but particularly during the sensory–motor phase.

[8] Maier, Henry. *Three Theories of Child Development*, New York: Harper, 1969.

1. **Sensory–motor phase** (0–2 years): The major developmental tasks are coordination of the infant's actions or motor activities and perceptions into a tenuous whole.

   a. *Use of reflexes* (0–1 month): There is a continuation of prenatal reflexes. They are spontaneous repetitions caused by internal and external stimulations. Rhythm is established through practice, and habits are formed that later emerge as voluntary movements.
   b. *Primary circular reactions* (1–3 months):
      i. Reflexive movement is gradually replaced by voluntary movements.
      ii. Neurological maturity must be reached first before sensations can be understood.
      iii. What previously had been automatic behavior is repeated voluntarily.
      iv. More than one sensory modality can be used at a time.
      v. Accidentally acquired responses become new sensory–motor habits.
      vi Primary circular reactions refer to the assimilation of a previous experience and the recognition of the stimulus that triggers the reaction.
      vii. New or past experiences have no meaning unless they become part of the primary circular reaction pattern.
   c. *Secondary circular reactions* (3–9 months):
      i. The infant tries to make events last and tries to make events occur.
      ii. The focus of the infant is on retention, not repetition.
      iii. The infant tries to create a state of permanency.
      v. Primary circular reactions are repeated and prolonged by secondary reactions.
      vi. Two or more sensory–motor experiences as related to one experimental sequence or schema.
      vii. Vision is the prime coordinator but other sensory modalities are also used.
      viii. Imitation, play, and emotion begin to appear at this stage.
   d. *Application of the secondary schemata to new situations* (8–12 months):
      i. This is characterized by the child's ability to distinguish means from ends (i.e., producing the same result more than one way).
      ii. The child uses previous behavioral achievements primarily as the basis for adding new ones to his expanding repertoire.

       iii. There is increased experimentation; ends and means are differentiated by experimenting.
       iv. Adaptation is an end result of experimentation.
       v. The infant can experience action by observation.
  e. *Tertiary circular reactions* (12–18 months):
       i. There is discovery of new means through active experimentation.
       ii. The beginnings of curiosity and novelty-seeking behavior are developing.
       iii. Reasoning comes into play and is developed.
       iv. Failure to remember is failure to understand.
       v. The infant develops spatial relationships upon discovering objects as objects.
       vi. Imitation develops.
       vii. Play is very important because it repeats the action phase.
  f. *Invention of new means through mental combinations* (2 years):
       i. There is a shift from sensory–motor experiences to an increased reflection about these experiences. This is the stepping stone to the next phase, which is an advanced level of intellectual behavior.
       ii. Objects become permanent. He discerns himself as one object among many and he perceives and uses objects for their own innate qualities.
       iii. The child begins to relate the object to new actions without actually perceiving all of the actions.
       iv. Sensory–motor patterns are slowly replaced by semimental functionings.
       v. Imitation copies the action itself or the symbol of the action.
       vi. Parallel play comes into existence.
       vii. Identification, as a mental process, becomes evident at the end of 2 years. It depends on the level of intellectual development of the child.
       viii. This period is characterized by the creation of means and not merely the discovery of means (insight).

2. **Preoperational phase** (2–4 years):
  a. This is a period of transition from self-satisfying behavior and rudimentary socialized behavior.
       i. Continuous investigation of his world develops.
       ii. The child knows the world only as he see it.
       iii. The child is egoncentric rather than autistic, as in the sensory-motor phase.

Happiness is . . . .

   iv. Assimilation is the paramount role of the child.
   v. Play occupies most of his awake hours. Emphasis on how and why becomes a primary tool for adaptation.
  vi. Imaginary play is important.
 vii. Language repeats and replaces sensory–motor history.
viii. Events are judged by outward appearance regardless of their objective logic.
  ix. Either the qualitative or quantative aspects of an event are experienced, not both at once. The child cannot merge concepts of objects, space, and causality into temporal interrelationships with a concept of time.

3. **Intuitive thought phase** (4–7 years):

  a. There is widening social interest in the world about him.
  b. There is reduced egocentricity and increased social participation.
  c. The first real beginning of cognition occurs here.
  d. Speech replaces movement to express thinking.
  e. The child can think of only one idea at a time.

f. The child tries to adjust new experiences to previous patterns of thinking.
g. The child becomes aware of relationships.
h. Conservation of quantity, such as permanency and continuity, must be mastered before a concept of numbers can be developed.
i. Play enacts the rules and values of elders.
j. Parallel play continues.

4. **Concrete operations phase** (7–11 years):

a. The child becomes aware of alternative solutions.
b. The child acquires reversibility which is the capacity of relating an event or thought to a total system of interrelated parts in order to conceive the event or thought from beginning to end or end to beginning.
c. Operational thought develops mental capacity. It is the capacity to order and relate experience to an organized whole.
d. The concrete operational thought level presupposes that mental experimentation still depends on perception.
e. The child examines parts to gain knowledge of the whole.
f. The child establishes systems of classifications of organizing parts into a hierarchial system.
g. Perceptions are more accurate.
h. The child applies interpretation of perceptions of the environment knowingly.
i. Play is used for understanding physical and social world.
j. Play loses its assimilative characteristics and becomes a balanced subordinate process of cognitive thought.
k. Curiosity finds expression in intellectual experimentation rather than active play.
l. The child becomes interested in rules and regulations.

5. **Formal operations phase** (11–15 years):

a. Childhood ends and youth begins.
b. The individual enters into the world of ideas.
c. There is a systematic approach to problems.
d. There is logical deduction by implication.
e. The individual thinks beyond the present (vertically).
f. The individual can dream and does not need reality.
g. Deduction by hypothesis and judgment by implication enable reasoning beyond cause and effect.

CHARACTERISTICS OF YOUNG CHILDREN

Preschool-age Children (2–5 years)

During the past decade there has been a tremendous surge of interest and study of the preschool stage of life. This heightened interest has been brought about by two important factors. The first of these is the growing realization that the young years are crucial for optimal lifelong physical, mental, emotional, and social development. The second factor is our rapidly changing North American culture. Many mothers now work full– or part-time in order to supplement the family income. As a result, thousands of children are being cared for in private homes, day-care centers, or nursery schools for at least a portion of the day. There is a great deal of concern for providing quality experiences for the child during these hours of nonfamily care.

Prior to the 1960s very little importance was attached to the preschool years as facilitators of later development. This period of time was generally looked upon as the "frivilous" play era of children's lives. Play was generally viewed as being of little or no real value by all but a few. Most specialists in child growth and development played "lip service" to the values of play but rarely went beyond that. It is now realized, primarily through the work of Piaget, that the play of children is of crucial importance to their gaining many of the important knowledges that are necessary for success in our world.

Play is what young children do when they are not eating, sleeping, or complying with the wishes of adults. It occupies most of their waking hours, and it may literally be viewed as the child's equivalent of the work of adults. Children's play serves as the primary mode by which they learn about their bodies and its movement capabilities. It also serves as an important facilitator of cognitive and affective growth in the young child as well as an important means of developing both fine and gross motor skills.

Preschool children are actively involved in enhancing their cognitive abilities in a variety of ways. These early years are a period of important cognitive development that have been termed the *preoperational thought phase* by Piaget. For it is during this time that children develop cognitive functions that will eventually result in logical thinking and concept formation. Young children are not capable of thinking from any point of view other than their own. They are extremely egocentric and view almost everything in terms of themselves. For preschoolers, their perceptions dominate their thinking and what is experienced at a given moment in time has a great influence on them. During this preconceptual phase of cognitive development, seeing is literally believing. The preschoolers' thinking and logic sees no need to justify conclusions. Even if they did, they would be unable to reconstruct their thoughts and show others how they arrived at their conclusions. Play serves as a vital means by which higher cognitive structures are gradually developed. It provides a multitude of settings and variables for promoting cognitive growth.

The young child needs love, guidance, and assurance.

Affective development is also dramatic during the preschool years. During this period children are involved in the two crucial social–emotional tasks of developing a sense of *autonomy* and *initiative.* Autonomy is expressed through a growing sense of independence, which may be seen in the child's delight in the use of the word "no" to almost any direct question. The answer will often be "no" to a question such as "do you want to play outside?" even though he clearly would like to. This may be viewed as an expression of a new-found sense of independence and ability to manipulate some factors in the environment rather than always an expression of sheer disobedience. A way in which to avoid this natural autonomous reaction to a question is to alter it to form a positive statement such as "let's go play outdoors." In this way, the child is not confronted with a direct "yes" or "no" choice. Care must be taken, however, to remember that children must be given abundant situations in which an expression of their autonomy is reasonable and proper.

Young children's expanding sense of initiative is seen through their curious, exploring, and very active behavior. The child now engages in new experiences such as climbing, jumping, running, and throwing objects for their own sake and the sheer joy of sensing and knowing what he is capable of doing. Failure to develop a sense of initiative as well as a sense of autonomy leads to feelings of shame, worthlessness, and a sense of guilt. Establishing a stable self-concept is crucial to proper affective development in preschoolers because it has an effect on both cognitive and psychomotor functions.

Through the medium of play, preschoolers are developing a wide variety of fundamental locomotor, manipulative, and stability abilities. If they have a stable and positive self-concept, the gradual gain in greater control over their musculature is a smooth one. The timid, cautious, and measured movements of the 2- and 3-year-old gradually give way to the confident, eager, and often wreckless abandon of the 4- and 5-year-old. Preschoolers' vivid imaginations make it possible for them to jump from great heights, climb high mountains, leap over "raging rivers," and run "faster" than an assorted variety of wild beasts.

Children of preschool age are rapidly expanding their horizons. They are asserting their individuality, developing their abilities, and testing their limits as well as the limits of their family and those around them. In short, young children are pushing out into the world in many complex and wondrous ways. Care must be taken, however, to understand their developmental characteristics and their limitations as well as their potentials. Only in this way can we effectively structure movement experiences for them that truly reflect their needs and interests and are within their level of ability.

PSYCHOMOTOR CHARACTERISTICS:

1. Both boys and girls range from about 33 to 47 inches in height and 25 to 53 pounds in weight:[9]

---

[9] Watson, Ernest and George Lowrey, *Growth and Development of Children*, Chicago: Year Book Medical Publishers, 1967.

2. Perceptual–motor abilities are rapidly developing, but confusion often exists in body awareness, directional awareness, temporal awareness, and spatial awareness.
3. Good bladder and bowel control is generally established by the end of this period but accidents sometimes still occur.
4. Children during this period are rapidly developing fundamental movement abilities in a variety of motor skills. Bilateral movements such as skipping, however, often present more difficulty than unilateral movements.
5. Children are active, energetic, and often prefer to run from place to place rather than walk, but they still need short frequent rest periods.
6. Motor abilities are developed to the point that the children are beginning to learn how to dress themselves, although they may need help straightening and fastening articles of clothing.
7. The body functions and processes become well regulated. A state of physiological homeostasis (stability) becomes well established.
8. The body build of both boys and girls is remarkably similar. A back view of boys and girls reveals no readibly observable structural differences.
9. Fine motor control is not established, although gross motor control is developing rapidly.
10. The eyes are not generally ready for extended periods of close work due to farsightedness, which is characteristic of both preschool and primary-grade children. Also binocular vision is often not completely established.

COGNITIVE CHARACTERISTICS:

1. There is a constantly increasing ability to express thoughts and ideas verbally.
2. A fantastic imagination enables imitation of both actions and symbols with little concern for accuracy or the proper sequencing of events.
3. There is continuous investigation and discovery of new symbols that have a primarily personal reference.
4. The "how" and "why" of the child's actions are learned through almost constant play.
5. There is a preoperational thought phase of development, resulting in a period of transition from self-satisfying behavior to fundamental socialized behavior.

AFFECTIVE CHARACTERISTICS:

1. During this phase children are egocentric in nature and assume that everyone thinks the way they do. As a result they often seem to be

quarrelsome, exhibit difficulty in sharing, and getting along with others.
2. They are often fearful of new situations, shy, self-conscious, and unwilling to leave the security of that which is familiar.
3. They are learning to distinguish right from wrong and beginning to develop a conscience.
4. Two- and 4-year-olds are often seen to be out-of-bounds in their behavior, while 3- and 5-year-olds are often viewed as stable and conforming in their behavior.
5. Their self-concepts are rapidly developing. Wise guidance, success-oriented experiences, and positive reinforcement are especially important during these years.

IMPLICATIONS FOR THE MOTOR-DEVELOPMENT PROGRAM:

1. Plenty of opportunity for gross motor play must be offered in both undirected and directed settings.
2. The movement experiences of the preschooler should involve primarily movement exploration and problem-solving activities in order to maximize the child's creativity and desire to explore.
3. The movement education program should include plenty of positive reinforcement in order to encourage the establishment of a positive self-concept and reduce the fear of failure.
4. Stress should be placed on developing a variety of fundamental locomotor, manipulative, and stability abilities progressing from the simple to the complex as the children become "ready" for them.
5. Interests and abilities of boys and girls are similar, with no need for separate programs at this stage.
6. Plenty of activities designed specifically to enhance perceptual–motor functioning are necessary.
7. Care should be taken to provide ample opportunities for short rest periods during vigorous performances.
8. Advantage should be taken of the child's great imagination through the use of a variety of drama and imagry activities.
9. Because of their often awkward and inefficient movements, be sure to gear movement experiences to maturity level.
10. Provide a wide variety of activities that require object handling and eye–hand coordination in order to aid in the development of binocular vision.
11. Begin to incorporate bilateral activities such as skipping, alternate galloping and hopping after bilateral movements have been fairly well established.
12. Encourage the children to take an active part in the movement educa-

tion program by "showing" and "telling" others what they can do in order to help overcome tendencies to be shy and self-conscious.

13. Provide convenient access to toilet facilities and encourage the children to accept this responsibility on their own.

14. Provide for individual differences and allow for each child to progress at their own individual rate.

15. Encourage plenty of climbing activities and activities in which the upper trunk muscles are utilized as well as the legs and lower trunk.

16. Establish standards for acceptable behavior and abide by them. Provide wise guidance in the establishment of a sense of doing what is right and proper rather than what is wrong and unacceptable.

17 The motor development program should be prescriptive and based on *each* individual's maturational and readiness level.

18. A multisensory approach should be utilized by the instructor that is, one in which a wide variety of experiences are incorporated using several sensory modalities.

PRIMARY-GRADE CHILDREN (5–7 YEARS)

The primary-grade years are generally considered to range from about ages 5 to about 7 years. They are an extension of the preschool years, which extend from about age 3 to 5 years and are generally considered to be a part of the total time period often referred to as early childhood. Separation of the preschool and primary years here is done in order to dramatize the fact that the primary grades represent the first exposure of most children to formal schooling. The primary years should be viewed as an extension of the preschool years with many overlapping developmental aspects.

Children in the primary grades are generally happy, stable, eager, and able to assume responsibilities. They are able to cope with new situations and are anxious to learn more about themselves and their expanding world. Primary-grade children take the first big step into their expanding world when they enter kindergarten. For many, kindergarten represents the first separation from the home for a regularly scheduled block of time during the day. It is the first step out of the secure play environment of the home and into the world of adults. Entering kindergarten marks the first time that most children are placed in a group situation in which they are not the center of attention. It is a time when sharing, concern for others, and respect for the rights and responsibilities of others is established. In short, kindergarten is a readiness time in whih children begin to make the gradual transition from an egocentric, home-centered play world to the group-oriented world of adult concepts and logic. It is not, however, until the first grade that the first *formal* demands for cognitive understandings are made. The major milestone of the first grader is learning how to read at a fundamental level. The 6-year-old is generally developmentally ready for the important task of "breaking the code" and begins to learn to read. He is also involved in developing the first real understandings of time and money and numerous other cognitive concepts. By the second grade children should be well on their way to being able to meet and surmount the everbroadening array of cognitive, affective, and psychomotor tasks that are put before them.

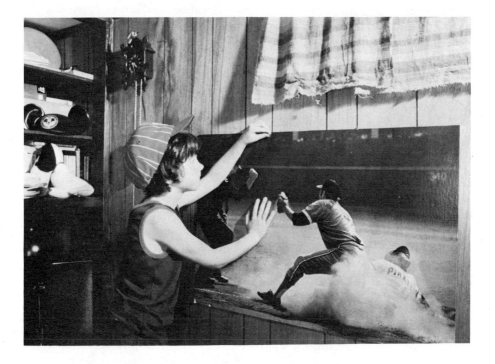

Interests in sports begin developing toward the end of the primary-grade years.

PSYCHOMOTOR CHARACTERISTICS:

1. Both boys and girls range from about 42 to 50 inches in height and 37 to 60 pounds in weight.[10]

[10]Ernest and George Lowrey, *Growth and Development of Children,* Chicago: Year Book Publishers, 1967.

2. Growth is beginning to slow down, especially toward the end of this period. There is, however, a slower but steady pace of increments unlike the more rapid gains in height and weight during the pre-school years.

3. The body begins to lengthen out with only a 2–3-inch annual gain in height and a 3–6-pound yearly gain in weight.

4. The cephalocaudal (head to toe) and proximaldistal (center to periphery) principles of development are now quite evident, in which the large muscles of the body are considerably better developed than the small muscles.

5. Girls are generally about a year advanced beyond boys in physiological development, and separate interests begin to develop toward the end of this period.

6. Hand preference is firmly established with about 90 percent preferring the right hand and only about 10 percent preferring the left.[11]

7. Reaction time is still quite slow, causing difficulty with eye–hand and eye–foot coordination.

8. Both boys and girls are full of energy but often possess a low endurance level and tire easily.

9. The visual perceptual machanisms are not yet fully established. Such perceptual qualities as figure–ground perception, speed of vision, perceptual constancy, and spatial relationships are generally well established by the end of this period.

10. Children are often farsighted during this period and are not ready for extended periods of close work.

11. Fundamental movement abilities are generally well defined by the end of this period. Locomotor abilities are developed to the extent that children are able to gallop, skip, jump, and climb in a mature pattern.

12. Stability abilities are. Both static and dynamic balancing abilities are improved.

13. Basic skills necessary for successful play are fairly well developed.

14. Activities involving the eyes and limbs mature slowly. Such activities as catching, kicking, striking, and throwing need practice.

15. The end of this period marks a transition from refining fundamental movement abilities to the establishment of general movement skills in lead-up games and athletic skills.

COGNITIVE CHARACTERISTICS:

1. Attention span is generally short; however, boys and girls of this age will often spend hours on activities that are of great interest to them.
2. They are eager to learn and to please adults but need assistance and guidance in decision-making.
3. They show good imagination and display extremely creative minds; however, self-consciousness seems to become a factor again toward the end of this period.
4. They are interested in songs, fairy tales, television, movies, rhythmic games, and gymnastic-type activities.
5. They are capable of abstract thinking and deal best with concrete examples and situations.

AFFECTIVE CHARACTERISTICS:

1. Interests of boys and girls are quite similar until the end of this period, at which time they begin to diverge.
2. The child is self-centered and plays poorly in large groups for extended periods of time, although small group situations are handled well.
3. The child is often aggressive, boastful, self-critical, over-reactive, and accepts defeat and winning poorly.
4. There is an inconsistent level of maturity; the child is often less mature at home than school due to parental influence.
5. The child is responsive to authority, "fair" punishment, and discipline.

IMPLICATIONS FOR THE MOTOR DEVELOPMENT PROGRAM:

1. There should be opportunities to refine fundamental movement abilities in the areas of locomotion, manipulation, and stability to a point where they are fluid and efficient.
2. The assurance of being accepted and valued as a human being is important in order to know they have a stable and secure place in their school environment as well as the home.
3. Abundant opportunities for encouragement and positive reinforcement from adults are necessary in order to promote continued development of a positive self-concept.
4. Opportunities and encouragement to explore and experiment through

movement with their bodies and objects in their environment enhance perceptual–motor efficiency.

5. There should be exposure to experiences in which progressively greater amounts of responsibility are introduced to help promote self-reliance.

6. Help in adjusting to the rougher ways of the school playground and neighborhood without being rough or crude themselves is an important social skill to be learned.

7. Opportunities for gradual introduction to group and team activities should be provided at the proper time.

8. Story plays, imaginary, and mimetic activities may be effectively incorporated into the program because of the child's vivid imagination.

9. Activities that incorporate the use of music and creative rhythmics are especially enjoyable at this level and are valuable in enhancing fundamental movement abilities, creativity, and a basic understanding of the components of music and rhythm.

10. Children at this level learn best through active participation. Integration of academic concepts with movement activities provides an effective avenue for reinforcing academic concepts in science, mathematics, social studies, and the language arts.

11. Activities that involve climbing and hanging are beneficial to development of the upper torso and should be included in the program.

12. Discuss play situations involving such topics as taking turns, fair play, cheating, and sportsmanship as a means of establishing a more complete sense of right or wrong.

13. Interests in sports are beginning to develop toward the end of this period. Introduce basic athletic skills and simple lead-up games.

14. *Begin* to stress accuracy, form, and skill in the performance of movement skills toward the end of this period (the general movement-skill stage of development begins around age 7 or 8 years).

15. Encourage children to "think" before engaging in an activity. Help them recognize potential hazards as a meens of reducing their often reckless behavior.

CONCLUSION

Young children are growing, developing, and emerging beings. In the short span of time during 2–7 years of age, a vast multitude of change occurs in their psychomotor, cognitive, and affective development.

Friends.

Several developmental specialists have closely studied the phenomena of human behavior and have constructed a variety of theoretical models of the developmental process. Each of these theories reflect the originator's particular area of interest in certain aspects of development. As a result none paint a *complete* or total picture of the developmental process. One must closely study a variety of models in order to gain a better understanding of child development. Such a study will reveal that most of the models fall into one of three catagories as either age–stage, developmental milestone, or developmental task theories.

Study of the many models of growth and development, along with careful observation and daily contact with young children, enables one to compile a set of developmental characteristics in the psychomotor, affective, and cognitive domains that typify the mythical "average" child. By no means should any of these characteristics be considered to be universally true because one may easily call to mind a number of children who do not exhibit one or more of these characteristics at any given age. Careful study of the developmental characteristics typical of children at varying ages merely enables us to formulate a motor-development program that meets the needs, interests, and developmental capabilities of the *greatest* number of children. It does not guarantee that each child will exactly fit into a predescribed mold. This fact is an important point recognized by most preschool and primary-grade teachers who make room for individual differences through individualized instruction.

Without a clear understanding of children we become teachers of *content* rather than teachers of *children.* If we are to maximize our effectiveness as teachers of children we must know, understand, and accept children for what they are and not "adultize" them and force them into being what we expect them to be.

SUGGESTED READINGS

Caplan, Frank (gen. ed.). *The First Twelve Months of Life,* New York: Grosset and Dunlap, 1973.

Keogh, Jack. F. *Motor Performancy of Elementary School Children,* Monograph, University of California, Los Angeles, Department of Physical Education, 1965.

Lugo, James O., and Gerald L. Hershey, *Human Development, A Multidisciplinary Approach to the Psychology of Individual Growth,* New York: MacMillan, 1974.

Maier, Henry W., *Three Theories of Child Development,* New York: Harper, 1969.

McCandless, Boyd R. *Children—Behavior and Development,* New York: Holt, Rinehart, and Winston, 1967.

Mussen, Paul. H., J. J. Congar, and J. Kagan, *Child Development and Personality,* New York: Harper, 1969.

Rarick, Lawrence, *Physical Activity: Human Growth and Development,* New York: Academic P, 1973.

Smart, Millie S. and Russell C. Smart, *Preschool Children: Development and Relationships,* New York: MacMillan, 1973.

Smart, Millie S. and Russell C. Smart, *School Age Children: Development and Relationships,* New York: MacMillan, 1973.

Sundberg, Ingelman, Axel, *A Child is Born: The Drama of Life Before Birth,* New York: Dell, 1974.

Chapter 3

Psychomotor Development of Young Children

CONTENTS

Introduction
Principles of Motor Development
  Developmental Direction
  Rate of Growth
  Differentiation and Integration
  Readiness for Learning
  Individual Differences
  Phylogenetic and Ontogenetic Behavior
  Maturation and Experience
Rudimentary Movement Abilities in Infancy
  Reflexive Movements Stability and Locomotion
Fundamental Movement Abilities in Early Childhood
Physical Abilities of Children
  Physical Fitness
  Motor Fitness
Conclusion
Suggested Readings

To Move Well is to be Free
The Author

INTRODUCTION

The psychomotor development of young children is one aspect of the total developmental process discussed in the two proceeding chapters. It seems altogether fitting, however, that a book dealing with the role of movement in the education of young children devote at least one complete chapter exclusively to their motor behavior in an effort to more clearly delineate this important aspect of human development.

In recent years there has been growing interest in the motor development of preschool and primary-grade children. No longer are educators content with the vague notion that children somehow magically increase their abilities to function motorically as they advance in age. Physicians, physiologists, physical educators, and educators in general are becoming increasingly aware of the need for accurate information concerning the course of motor development in children and its influence on the developing child.

Several questions must be answered before sound motor development programs can be formulated for preschool and primary-grade children:

1. What principles of motor development affect the motor learning of children?
2. What are the influences of maturation and experience on motor development?
3. When is the optimum time to introduce various skills?
4. What is the role of physical fitness and motor fitness in motor development?

Clarification of these questions is needed in order to develop a more comprehensive understanding of children and their needs. If we fail to answer these questions, we run the risk of repeating many of the same mistakes made by curriculum developers who in the past often took existing high-school curricula and "watered them down" to fit the needs of junior-high and elementary-school children. It would be erroneous to assume that preschool and primary-grade children are identical to their counterparts in the intermediate and upper elementary grades. It would be a tragic mistake to "water down" existing elementary-school curricula in an attempt to meet the needs of younger children, and yet we run the risk of doing just that unless we become more fully acquainted with the many factors of their motor development.

PRINCIPLES OF MOTOR DEVELOPMENT

Developmental Direction

The principle of developmental direction refers to the orderly, predictable sequence of physical development that proceeds from the head to the feet (*cephalocaudal*) and from the center of the body to its periphery (*proximodistal*).

The cephalocaudal aspect of development refers specifically to the gradual progression of increased control over the musculature moving from the head toward the feet. It may be witnessed in the prenatal stages of fetal development as well as later postnatal development. In the developing fetus, for example, the head forms first, and the arms form prior to the legs. Likewise infants exhibit sequential control over the musculature of the head, neck, and trunk, prior to gaining control over the legs. Preschool children are often thought to be clumsy and exhibit poor control over the lower extremities. This is due to incomplete cephalocaudal development.

The second aspect of the developmental direction principle is known as proximodistal development. It refers specifically to the child's progression in control of the musculature from the center of the body to its most distant parts. The young child, for example, is able to control the muscles of the trunk and shoulder girdle prior to gaining much control over the muscles of the wrist, hand, and fingers. This principle of development is utilized by teachers of primary-grade children in the teaching of the less refined elements of manuscript writing prior to the introduction of the more complex and refined movements of cursive writing.

Rate of Growth

The rate of growth for children follows a characteristic pattern universal for all children and resistant to external change. Even the interruption of the normal pace of growth is compensated for by a still unexplained self-regulatory process that comes into operation to help catch the child up to his age mates as much as possible. For example, a severe illness may retard a child's gain in height and weight, but upon recovery from the illness he will have a tendancy to catch up with the other children his age rather than lagging behind in height and weight. The same is seen with the infant born premature (generally under 5 pounds). Despite his low birth weight he still will catch up to the characteristic growth rate of his age mates in a few short years. The self-regulatory process of growth will compensate for *minor* deviations in the growth pattern but it is unable to make up *major* deviations such as in a premature infant weighing under 4 pounds at birth. In this case the infant may suffer permanent deficits in height, weight, and cognitive abilities and be unable to recoup his initial losses.

Differentiation and Integration

The coordinated and progressive intricate interweaving of neural mechanisms of opposing muscle systems into an increasingly mature relationship is characteristic of the developing child's motor behavior. There are two different but related processes associated with this increase of functional complexity known as *differentiation* and *integration*. Differentiation is associated with the gradual progression from the gross globular (overall) movement patterns of infants to the more refined and functional movements of children as they mature. Integration, on the other hand, refers to bringing various opposing muscle and sensory systems into coordinated interaction with one another. For example, the young child gradually progresses from ill-defined corralling movements when attempting to grasp an object to more mature and visually guided reaching and grasping behavior. This differentiation of the movements of the arm, hand, and fingers, followed by integrating the use of the eyes with the movements of the hand to perform rudimentary eye–hand coordination task, is crucial to normal development.

Readiness for Learning

Thorndike, the "grandfather" of learning theory, first proposed the principle of readiness primarily in reference to emotional responses to actions or expected actions. Today's concept of readiness is much broader and is used to refer to readiness for learning. Oxendine has defined readiness to learn as "a condition of the individual that makes a particular task an appropriate one for him to master."[1] There are several factors which in combination promote readiness. The factors are physical and mental maturation, motivation, prerequisite learning, and the child's particular feelings about the situation at hand.

In recent years a great deal of attention has been focused on the concept of developing reading readiness with regard to the appropriate types of experience for preschool and primary grade children to be involved in. Entire educational programs have been built around the principle that chil-

---

[1] Oxendine, J. *Psychology of Motor Learning,* New York: Appleton–Century–Crofts, 1968.

"Readiness" is a key factor in efficient learning.

dren must achieve a certain level of maturation before they are ready to pursue intellectual tasks such as reading and writing. Readiness training is a part of many preschool and primary-grade educational programs. An integral part of these readiness programs in recent years has been the utilization of movement as a means of enhancing basic perceptual–motor qualities such as directional and temporal awareness, as well as body and spatial awareness. The remedial and readiness programs of such noteables as Frostig, Kephart, Getman, and others have been used with varying degrees of success as a means of getting children ready for learning. Each of these programs utilize movement as an integral part of their program. Although it has not been conclusively documented that the inclusion of these perceptual–motor-type experiences have a *direct* effect on the attainment of specific skills necessary for success in school, it is safe to assume that they have at least an indirect influence through enhancement of the child's self-concept and the development of a more positive "I can" attitude.

Individual Differences

The principle of individual difference is of crucial importance. It simply implies that each child is a unique individual with his own timetable for development. This timetable is peculiar to each individual's particular combination of heredity and environmental influences, and although the *sequence* of appearance of developmental characteristics is predictable, the *rate* of appearance may be quite variable.

The "average" age for the acquisition of all sorts of developmental tasks, ranging from learning how to walk (the major developmental task of infancy), to gaining bowel and bladder control (the first restrictions of a civilized society on the child) have been bantered about in the professional literature and the daily conversation of parents and teachers. It must be remembered that these "average ages" are just that and nothing more. They are merely approximations and are meant to serve only as convenient indicators of developmentally appropriate behaviors. It is common to see deviations from the mean of as much as 6 months to 1 year in the appearance of numerous psychomotor abilities. The principle of individual differences is closely linked to the principle of readiness and explains why some children are ready to learn new skills when others are not.

Phylogenetic and Ontogenetic Behavior

Many of the rudimentary abilities of the infant and the fundamental movement abilities of the young child are considered to be phylogenetic in nature. That is, they have a tendency to appear somewhat automatically and in a predictable sequence within the maturing child. Phylogenetic skills are resistant to external environmental influences. Such abilities as the rudimentary manipulative tasks of reaching, grasping, and releasing objects or the stabilizing tasks of gaining control of the gross musculature of the body are examples of phylogenetic skills along with fundamental locomotor abilities such as walking, jumping, and running. Ontogenetic behaviors, on the other hand, are those that depend primarily on learning and environmental opportunities. Such skills as swimming, bicycling, and ice skating are all considered to be ontogenetic. because they do not appear automatically within individuals but require a period of practice and experience and are culturally influenced.

Swimming is an ontogenetic skill.

Maturation and Experience

A great deal of study has been done over the years in an effort to determine the relative merits of both maturation and experience on the learning of a variety of skills. In fact, there has been considerable controversy among hereditarians and environmentalists over this issue for over 100 years. Textbooks are full of the nature versus nurture debates, but little has been settled in the attempt to categorize the effects of each on human behavior. The current trend has been to respect the individual importance of each and to recognize the fact that the influences of both maturation and experience are complexly intertwined.

Students of motor development have recognized the futility of debating the separate merits of maturation and experience and have instead concentrated their research and study on three major questions. The first of these questions deals with the ages at which various skills can be learned most effectively. The researches of Bayley[2], Shirley[3], and Wellman[4] in the 1930s were the first serious attempts to describe at what age a host of rudimentary and fundamental motor abilities appear. Each of these researchers reported a somewhat different timetable for the appearance of numerous phylogenetic skills. They did, however, show amazing consistency in the order of appearance of these abilities. This factor illustrates the combined effect of both intrinsic, or maturationally determined, influences on behavior and extrinsic, or environmentally influenced behaviors. Unfortunately, until recently, little has been done since the early work of the 1930s to more clearly ascertain at what ages both phylogenetic and ontogenetic skills can be learned most effectively. The principle of readiness has been viewed as a cornerstone of our educational system, but unfortunately little more than lip service has been played to its importance, particularly with regard to developing movement abilities. We know that children can develop many movement abilities early in life but we still do not know the best time to introduce specific skills. Only recently has this important question come under serious study. The excellent work being done at the Universities of Wisconsin, Illinois, Purdue, Michigan State, and Indiana represents a first step in answering many of the important questions concerning the age at which fundamental movement patterns can be effectively developed and refined in young children.

The second question being studied by environmentalists and hereditarians deals with the effects of special training on the learning of motor skills. A number of co-twin control studies have been conducted as a means of ascertaining the influence of special practice on early learning. The use of twins enables the researcher to ensure identical hereditary backgrounds and characteristics of the subjects. One twin is given advanced opportunities for practice, while the other is restricted from practicing the same skills over a prescribed length of time. The famous studies of Gesell and Thompson[5],

[2] Bayley, N. "The Development of Motor Abilities During the First Three Years," *Monograph of the Society For Research on Child Development 1*(1), 1–26.

[3] Shirley, M. M. *The First Two Years,* Volume 1, *Postural and Locomotor Development,* Minneapolis: Minnesota U. P., 1931.

[4] Wellman, B. L. "Motor Achievements of Preschool Children," *Childhood Education 13,* 311–316, 1937.

[5] Gesell, A. and H. Thompson, "Learning and Growth in Identical Infant Twins," *Genetic Psychology Monographs, 6,* 1–124, 1929.

McGraw[6], and Hilgard[7] have all demonstrated the inability of early training to hasten maturation to an appreciable degree. However it is important to note that follow-up studies of the co-twin control experiments of both Gesell and McGraw showed that the trained subjects exhibited greater confidence and assurance in the activities in which they had received special training. In other words, special training may not have an influence on the *quantity* or rate of onset of movement skills learned, but it may have an effect on the *quality* of performance of specific skills. Again we see the complex interrelationship between maturation and experience.

The third question being studied is the effect of limited or restricted opportunities for practice on the acquisition of motor skills. Studies of this nature have generally centered on experimentally induced environmental deprivation in animals. Only a few studies have been reported in which children have actually been observed in environments where unusual restrictions of movement or experience have existed. The general consensus of these experiments is that severe restrictions and lack of experience limit one's normal maturation. We need only to look as far as the school playground and observe the girls jumping rope expertly and the boys throwing and catching balls with great skill. When asked to reverse the activities, however, each tends to revert to more primitive patterns of movement. Factors within our culture, unfortunately, often predetermine the types of movement experience that boys and girls engage in.

One of the greatest needs of children is the opportunity to practice skills at a time when they are developmentally ready to benefit the most from them. Special practice prior to being ready maturationally is of dubious benefit. The key is to be able to accurately judge the time at which each individual is "ripe" for learning and then to provide a series of educationally sound and effective movement experiences. All indications are that young children are generally capable of more than we have suspected. It is our job as parents and as educators to accurately determine just what they are capable of and to provide ample opportunities for them to engage in a multitude of movement experiences.

[6] McGraw, M. B. *Growth: A Study of Johnny and Jimmy,* New York: Appleton–Century–Crofts, 1935.

[7] Hilgard, J. R. "Learning and Maturation in Preschool Children," *Journal of Genetic Psychology 41,* 36–56, 1932.

RUDIMENTARY MOVEMENT ABILITIES IN INFANCY*

The most striking progress in the development of movement patterns and physical growth occur during infancy and early childhood. The infant, within a relatively short period, emerges from a completely dependent newborn into a thinking, acting, reacting, and highly mobile individual. In essence, he becomes a young child who has assumed upright posture and is capable of several variations of bipedal locomotion. Numerous investigations and treatises have attempted to qualitatively review and describe the sequential development of fundamental locomotor patterns in children from birth to approximately age 5 years.

Reflexive Movements

According to many kinesiologists and anatomists, the most striking manifestation of movement in the human species is assuredly the development of purposeful locomotion. It must be remembered, however, that during the early weeks and months of life the neonate is in a continuous process of establishing a postural orientation to his spatial world. The reflexive basis for the development of this orientation has not been clearly established.

Many authorities feel that these early reflex movements, along with the generalized motion of many body parts, are important foundations upon which the infant proceeds to higher levels of neuromuscular functioning. Fiorentino[8] contends that primitive reflexes are essential to normal development and that response to these mechanisms prepares the child for progressive development, such as rolling over, sitting, crawling, and standing. Cooper and Glassow[9] suggest that fundamental locomotor movements have a definite reflex action base. Cratty,[10] on the other hand, suggests that there seems to be no direct connection, at least in temporal terms, between these inherent reflexes and the infant's later efforts to assume voluntary quadrupedal and bipedal locomotion. The prominence of these reflexes is such that subcortical control of movements is at a maximum toward the end of

*Special thanks are extended to Dr. David Barlow, University of Delaware, for his contributions to this section.

[8] Fiorentino, Mary. *Reflex Testing Methods for Evaluation of C.N.S. Development,* Springfield, Illinois: Charles C. Thomas, 1963.

[9] Cooper, John and Ruth Glassow, *Kinesiology,* St. Louis: C. V. Mosby, 1972.

[10] Cratty, Bryant J. and M. Marten *Perceptual Motor Efficiency in Children,* Philadelphia: Lea and Febiger, 1969.

the first month and then progressively declines. This is attributed to the onset of cortical inhibition.

During the first days after birth, a number of complex reflex patterns can be elicited in the infant that parallel to a noticeable degree later voluntary efforts of locomotion. These patterns are characteristically referred to as the swimming, crawling, climbing, and walking reflexes. Neurological research on decerebrated animals has shown that these primitive movements are controlled by the spinal cord up to the level of the fourth ventricle.[11] Results of these studies have also been demonstrated in human infants.

Stability and Locomotion.

The infant learns very early how to control his body against the constant influence of the forces of gravity. In the attempts to achieve upright posture and locomotion the infant must first be able to control his body in any of a variety of new postural alignments in a static position prior to undertaking the shifting postural changes that accompany dynamic movements. Obviously the mastery of upright posture and locomotion requires the functional development of equilibrium, which is influenced by cortical control of the vestibular apparatus and neuromuscular mechanisms.

This development of structure and function is rather interesting in that there seems to be a relationship between postural development and an increase in the size of the cerebellum. We know that the cerebellum is primarily concerned with the overall coordination of muscular movement. The cerebellum grows slowly during the first few months but rapidly in the last half of the first year and early part of the second year. This period of rapid growth occurs when a child is starting to acquire erect posture and develop locomotor activities.

The child's rate of growth and development influences the equilibrium of the various body positions. At birth the head is out of proportion in relation to the rest of the body by being approximately one fourth of the total length, as compared with one eighth of the total height of an adult. This condition of extreme disproportionment provides severe mechanical problems initially since stability is directly proportional to weight but indirectly proportional to the distance of the center of gravity of the body above the base of its support. Stability is also directly related to the area of the base on which the body rests. The infant then is unstable when he attempts to sit or stand

---

[11] Fiorentino, Mary. *Ibid.*

because a high center of gravity and a small base of support causes him to be top heavy. This factor, along with the immaturity of the nervous and muscular systems, makes it doubly difficult for the infant to maintain equilibrium when his balance is disturbed.

Skeletal segments serve as mechanical levers in the human which, by muscular action, produce rotary and linear movement. Over 207 pairs of skeletal muscle cover most of the boney skeletal structure, making possible a great variety of motions. Looking at the human skeletal system, the vertebral column at birth is highly flexible and curved forward anteriorly shaped like a "C." Many child-growth and developmental theorists state that purposeful locomotor movements are essential to and ultimately cause the vertebral column to assume its mature curvature, thereby aiding upright posture and gait. Anatomists, on the other hand, suggest that a biological condition of readiness and growth is necessary for the development of the spinal curvatures necessary for efficient weight-bearing functions. It appears that both hypotheses have logical merit and that simultaneous occurrence of these two factors is a distinct possibility.

The upper and lower extremeties of the infant are relatively shorter than in the adult. The hands are also shorter and stubbier, illustrating the proximodistal principle of development. The legs of the infant are short and flexed with the planter surfaces of the feet opposed. The foot is normally flexible, relaxed, and more mobile than that of an older child. The arches of the feet are much less rigid or nonexistent in infancy than at later periods. The fat pad in the bottom of the foot gives the appearance of flat-footedness. Even after a child has started to walk, the ligaments are relaxed and the large muscles, not yet accustomed to maintaining balance, are unable to carry out their new task perfectly. The feet are therefore held wide apart in order to widen the base of support. There is also a tendency to toe out, thus throwing the weight on the inner side of the sole of the foot. Soon after walking is established the bones in the arch take on their adult characteristics even while much of the bone is in cartilaginous form.

Although there is a great variation among children in the age of accomplishment of mature methods of upright locomotion in general, it is not until approximately 3 years after the first step is taken that the art of walking may be considered to be normalized in the child. Many authorities on primate activity believe that man's unique and basic striding ability may be the *most* significant factor that sets him apart from his prehistoric ancestors. Walking in man has often been described as an activity during which the body, step by step, teeters on the edge of catastrophe. Only through the rhythmic forward movement of first one leg and then the other does he keep from falling flat on his face.[12]

---

[12] Gardner, E., D. V. Gray, and R. O'Rahilly, *Anatomy,* Philadelphia; W. B. Saunders, 1969.

FUNDAMENTAL MOVEMENT ABILITIES IN EARLY CHILDHOOD

It is apparent that the motor development of children is dependent on a variety of developmental principles, involving factors such as the direction and the rate of growth, differentiation and integration of muscle systems, readiness for learning, individual differences, phylogenetic and ontogenetic behaviors, and the effects of both maturation and experience. We can now more fully appreciate the tremendous complexity of the process of motor development and view our role more objectively as a catalyst in this process, attempting to affect change through the interjection of developmentally appropriate movement experiences. No longer can we justify the view that free play, or recess time, provides ample opportunity and motivation for children to develop and refine their fundamental movement abilities.

The development and refinement of a wide variety of fundamental movement abilities is of great importance. Children need to learn more about their bodies. They need to learn how to effectively gain and maintain their equilibrium in relationship to constant alternations in the force of gravity (stability). They must learn how to move effectively through space using a variety of efficient patterns (locomotion). Children need to learn how to relate with other objects in their environment and to be able to give and receive force from these objects (manipulation). It is also important that they become adaptable and flexible in these movement responses rather than exhibit rigid or inflexible behaviors.

The process of developing movement abilities, as we have seen, is one in which gradual shifts or increments in the child's level of functioning occur in the stability, locomotor, and manipulative categories of movement behavior. During the first 2 years children are involved in developing rudimentary movement abilities in these three categories. They gain the very simplest controls over their movements in order that they may survive at the lowest level of motoric functioning. Preschool and primary-grade children are involved in developing and refining what have been termed fundamental movement abilities. Fundamental movement abilities are those basic movements of which all that we do are composed. The many complex movements found in sport and dance are no more than more highly elaborated forms of these fundamental movements developed and combined with one another at a more sophisticated level of functioning (see Figure 3.1). As was pointed out earlier in Chapter 1, fundamental movement abilities continue to be elaborated upon, more highly refined, and applied to increasingly complex patterns of movement as the individual develops. They are termed general movement abilities during middle childhood, (8–10 years), specific movement abilities during later childhood (11–13 years), and specialized movement abilities during adolescence and adulthood (14 years and over).

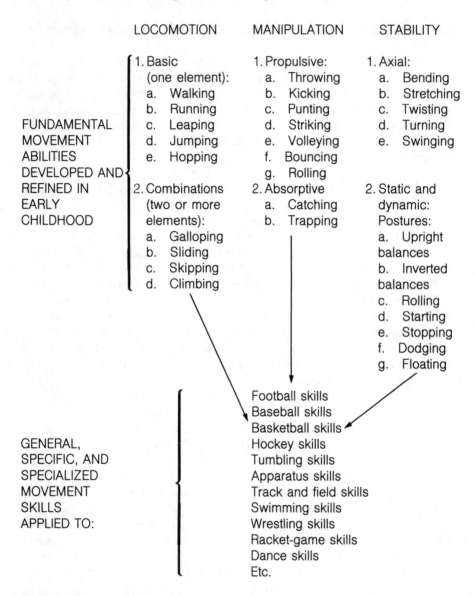

Figure 3.1 Fundamental Movement Abilities Must Be Developed and Refined Prior to the Introduction Of Sport and Dance Skills.

For many years we have made the assumption that children develop mature patterns of movement through the process of maturation only. It is true that various elements of numerous movement patterns can be expected to be present by certain ages. It is, however, erroneous to conclude that the maturational factor alone will ensure the development of mature patterns of movement that may be elaborated upon and more highly developed without the benefit of experience. A wide variety of meaningful movement experiences are necessary during the early years of life to help each child refine the many fundamental movements to a point where they are fluid and adaptable to a wide variety of movement situations. Then, and only then, should the individual be exposed to the more complex sport-type experiences found in the general, specific, and specialized stages of motor development. Witness, for example, the comments of children when the boys say, "she throws and runs just like a girl" or when the girls say, "boys can't jump rope or play hopscotch." Do comments like these really mean that girls cannot learn how to throw and run efficiently, or that boys cannot learn how to jump rope or play hopscotch proficiently? Certainly not. This situation is merely a reflection of cultural factors that often influence the different types of *experience* that boys and girls are encouraged to take part in. There are few physiological differences in the early years between boys and girls that would inhibit them from developing and refining efficient movement patterns in those skills often thought to be the exclusive domain of the opposite sex.

It is time that we realize the tremendous importance of motor–development programs during the preschool and primary-grade years. It is at this level that children should be exposed to a wide variety of fundamental movements and encouraged to refine these basic patterns of movement. Maturation alone will not account for the development of mature efficient patterns of movement. Meaningful experiences in each of the categories of movement are of vital importance to children. These are the years when children are learning to move.

All too often we find our best programs of physical education at the high-school and college levels. These programs often take the form of remedial programs in which many of the basic skills that could have, and should have, been developed earlier are practiced and learned for the first time. As parents and teachers it is necessary for us to realize that motor development should be an important part of children's lives. We must extend ourselves beyond the notion that swings and slides, along with free play and recess time, are all that is needed for children's optimum and balanced motor development. We must come to realize that a portion of each day should be spent in some form of guided movement experiences that encourage the child to develop and refine the many important fundamental movement abilities used throughout life. Chapters 12 and 13 take a detailed look at the place of movement in the education of young children and the role of toys, games, and play in the development of children's movement abilities. Tables 3.1, 3.2, and 3.3 present a list of the major rudimentary and fundamental movement abilities and the approximate age at which they

Rope jumping is an excellent conditioning and coordination activity that can be enjoyed by both boys and girls.

begin to emerge in children. These charts should serve as important indications of when children are generally maturationally ready to benefit from guided movement experiences. For an indepth discussion of each movement pattern found in these tables, the reader is referred to the work by Gallahue Werner, and Luedbe.[13] A *verbal description* and *visual description* of the mature movement pattern is provided along with *common problems* that children often encounter, *concepts* that they should know, and *suggested movement activities.*

[13] Gallahue, David L., Peter H. Werner, and George C. Luedke, *A Conceptual Approach to Moving and Learning*, New York: Wiley, 1975.

Table 3.1. Sequence of Emergence of Selected Locomotor Abilities.

MOVEMENT PATTERN	SELECTED ABILITIES	APPROXIMATE AGE OF ONSET
WALKING Walking involves placing one foot in front of the other while maintaining contact with the supporting surface	Rudimentary upright unaided gait Walks sideways Walks backward Walks upstairs with help Walks upstairs alone—follow step Walks downstairs alone—follow step	13 months 16 months 17 months 20 months 24 months 25 months
RUNNING Running involves a brief period of no contact with the supporting surface	Hurried walk (maintains contact) First true run (nonsupport phase) Efficient and refined run Speed of run increases	18 months 2–3 years 4–5 years 5 years
JUMPING Jumping takes three forms: (1) jumping for distance; (2) jumping for height; and (3) jumping from a height. It involves a one- or two-foot takeoff with a landing on both feet	Steps down from low objects Jumps down from object with both feet Jumps off floor with both feet Jumps for distance (about 3 feet) Jumps for height (about 1 foot)	18 months 2 years 28 months 5 years 5 years

HOPPING
Hopping involves
a one-foot takeoff
with a landing
on the same foot
	Hops up to three times on preferred foot
	Hops from four to six times on same foot
	Hops from eight to ten times on same foot
	Hops distance of 50 feet in about 11
	    seconds
	Hops skillfully with rhythmical
	    alteration
		3 years
		4 years
		5 years
		
		5 years
		
		6 years

GALLOPING The gallop combines a walk and a leap with the same foot leading throughout	Basic but inefficient gallop Gallops skillfully	4 years 6 years
SKIPPING Skipping combines a step and a hop in rhythmic alteration	One-footed skip Skillful skipping (about 20 percent) Skillful skipping for most	4 years 5 years 6 years

Table 3.2. Sequence of Emergence of Selected Manipulative Abilities

MOVEMENT PATTERN	SELECTED ABILITIES	APPROXIMATE AGE OF ONSET
REACH, GRASP, RELEASE Reaching, grasping, and releasing involve making successful contact with an object, retaining it in one's grasp and releasing it at will	Primitive reaching behaviors Corralling of objects Palmar grasp	2–4 months 2–4 months
THROWING Throwing involves inparting force to an object in the general direction of intent	Body faces target, feet remain stationary, ball thrown with forearm extension only. Same as above but with body rotation added. Steps forward with leg on same side as the throwing arm Mature throwing pattern Boys exhibit more mature pattern than girls	2–3 years 3.6–5 years 5–6 years 6.6 years 6 years and over
CATCHING Catching involves receiving force from an object with the hands, moving from large to progressively smaller balls	Chases ball; does not respond to aerial ball. Responds to aerial ball with delayed arm movements Needs to be told how to position arms. Fear reaction (turns head away). Basket catch using the body. Catches using the hands only with a small ball	2 years 2–3 years 2–3 years 3–4 years 3 years 5 years
KICKING Kicking involves imparting force to an object with the foot	Moves against ball. Does not actually kick it. Kicks with leg straight and little body movement (kicks *at* the ball) Flexes lower leg on backward lift. Greater backward and forward swing with definate arm opposition. Mature pattern (kicks *through* the ball).	18 months 2–3 years 3–4 years 4–5 years 5–6 years
STRIKING Striking involves imparting force to objects in an overarm, sidearm, or underhand pattern	Faces object and swings in a vertical plane Swings in a horizontal plane and stands to the side of the object. Rotates the trunk and hips and shifts body weight forward. Mature horizontal patterns	2–3 years 4–5 years 5 years 6–7 years

Stability is the most fundamental aspect of movement behavior and is developed through practice.

Table 3.3. Sequence of Emergence of Selected Stability Abilities

MOVEMENT PATTERN	SELECTED ABILITIES	APPROXIMATE AGE OF ONSET
DYNAMIC BALANCE Dynamic balance involves maintaining one's equilibrium as the center of gravity shifts	Walks 1-inch straight line	3 years
	Walks 1-inch circular line	4 years
	Stands on low balance beam	2 years
	Walks on 4-inch wide beam short distance	3 years
	Walks on same beam, alternating feet	3–4 years
	Walks on 2- or 3-inch beam	4 years
	Performs basic forward roll	2 years
	Performs mature forward roll	6–7 years
STATIC BALANCE Static balance involves maintaining one's equilibrium while the center of gravity remains stationary	Pulls to a standing position	10 months
	Stands without handholds	11 months
	Stands alone	12 months
	Balances on one foot 3–5 seconds	5 years
	Supports body in basic inverted positions	6 years
AXIAL MOVEMENTS Axial movements are static postures that involve bending, stretching, twisting, turning, and the like	Axial movement abilities begin to develop early in infancy and are progressively refined to a point where they are included in the emerging manipulative patterns of throwing, catching, kicking, striking, trapping, and other activities	2 months– 6 years

PHYSICAL ABILITIES OF CHILDREN

The physical fitness and motor fitness of children should be of great concern to all parents and teachers and not just the physical educator and physician. The fitness level of boys and girls in our North American society is of great concern to many. This concern was highlighted by a test of minimum muscular efficiency (the Kraus–Weber test) that was administered to several thousand American and European children. The results of this 1954 experiment indicated that the performance of American children was significantly poorer than that of their European counterparts. In fact, over 55 percent of the Americans failed the test, as compared to less than 10 percent of the European youths.[14] Although the comparison has been criti-

[14] Kraus, Hans and Ruth P. Hirschland, "Minimum Muscular Fitness Tests in Children," *The Research Quarterly 25*, 178, 1954.

cized for several reasons, it pointed out the important fact that American children are often found to be in poor physical condition.

As a result of the Kraus–Hirschand study, the President of the United States at that time, Dwight D. Eisenhower, established the President's Council on Youth Fitness in 1956. This council was established in an effort to promote the upgrading of the physical fitness of our children. Since that time the President's Council and others concerned with the fitness level of our youth have made many important contributions toward that goal. The A.A.H.P.E.R. (American Alliance for Health, Physical Education, and Recreation) Physical Fitness Test was developed for boys and girls in the fourth grade and above. The importance of gaining and maintaining a higher level of fitness has been promoted by the President's Council through publications, newspaper articles, and television spots. The importance of movement, motor development, and good physical education programs as means of enhancing the fitness level of children has also been promoted.

The fact remains, however, that a great many of our young children are still woefully unfit. There are two factors that have contributed greatly to this state of affairs. First, the impact of the importance and need for enhancing physical fitness has been centered on children in middle childhood through adolescence (fourth grade through high school) and into adulthood. Little attention has been paid to the fitness needs of children during the preschool and primary-grade years. As a result our knowledge of the fitness of young children is very limited. This has given rise to the second factor, namely the child's "heart myth" and other basically false assumptions concerning the fitness of children.

The child's heart myth has made the assumption that there is a discrepancy in the development of the heart and blood vessels in children and as a result vigorous exercise should be avoided at the risk of "straining" the heart. This widely believed myth has been disproven by Karpovich,[15] Astrand,[16] and others and is reflected in Corbin's statement that "barring injury, a healthy child cannot physiologically injure his heart permanently through physical exercise."[17] Other assumptions, namely that young children play all day and get plenty of vigorous activity, no longer hold true. The crowded conditions of apartment living and city dwelling for many along with the ever-present television set and its fascination for children (and adults as well) have created a sedentary society of children. Children need at least 3 or 4 hours of vigorous activity a day and the only way they

[15] Karpovitch, Peter V. "Textbook Fallacies Regarding the Development of the Child's Heart," *The Research Quarterly 8,* 1937.

[16] Astrand, Per-Olaf. *Experimental Studies of Working Capacity in Relation to Sex and Age,* Copenhagen: Munksgoaard, 1952.

[17] Corbin, Charles B. *Becoming Physically Educated in the Elementary School,* Philadelphia: Lea and Febiger, 1969, p. 22.

Upper arm and shoulder girdle strength can be enhanced through use of the horizontal ladder.

are going to get it is through a drastic reorganization of the daily routines of millions of youngsters. Vigorous exercise and activity have been shown to be important factors in normal healthy growth.

Physical Fitness

Although there has been extensive study in the area of physical fitness over the past several years, it is startling to note that very little has been done concerning the physical fitness of young children. A review of the literature on fitness reveals a marked lack of information on children under 8 years of age. The nature of most tests of physical fitness requires the individual to go "all out" and perform at his or her maximum. Anyone familiar with young children will readily recognize the difficulty of the situation. The problems lie in: (1) being able to sufficiently motivate the youngsters for maximum performance, (2) accurately determining if a maximum effort has been achieved, and (3) overcoming the fears of anxious parents. Qualified experts working with younger children have an almost untouched area for study. The problems of conducting investigation of this nature are many, but carefully controlled, patient research will yield much valuable information. Muscular strength, muscular endurance, circulatory–respiratory endurance, and flexibility are generally considered to be the components of physical fitness. Each is briefly discussed in the following paragraphs and summarized in Figure 3.2.

Muscular strength is the ability of the body to exert a maximum force against an external object on the body. In its purest sense it is the ability to exert *one* maximum effort. Children engaged in daily active play are doing much to enhance their leg strength by running and tricycling. Their arm strength is developed through such activities as lifting and carrying large toys, handling tools, and swinging on the monkey bars. Strength is measured by use of a dynamometer or tensiometer. These instruments are calibrated and designed to measure grip strength, leg strength, or back strength. The longitudinal studies conducted by Clark[18] in Medford Oregon clearly revealed yearly strength increments between ages 7 and 17 years. Girls tend to differ markedly from boys after age 12 or 13 in their strength. According to Corbin,[19] they tend to level off at this age but boys continue to gain in

[18] Clark, Harrison. *Physical Motor Tests in the Medford Boys Growth Study,* Englewood Cliffs, N. J.: Prentice–Hall, 1971.

[19] Corbin, Charles B. *A Textbook of Motor Development,* Dubuque, Iowa: W. C. Brown, 1973, pp. 90–95.

strength. It seems probable that the strength levels of preschool and primary-grade boys and girls is similar, with the edge being given to the boys based on their tendency to be slightly heavier and taller than their female counterparts.

Muscular endurance is the ability to exert force against an external object on the body for several repetitions. Muscular endurance is similar to muscular strength in the activities performed but differs in the emphasis. Strength-building activities require overloading the muscle or group of muscles to a greater extent than endurance activities. Endurance-building activities have less of an overload on the muscles but require a greater number of repetitions. Boys and girls performing several sit-ups, pull-ups, or push-ups are performing muscular-endurance activities. The daily play routine of youngsters when viewed in toto is an excellent example of endurance. Most of us would find it extremely difficult to match the endurance of an energetic 4- or 5-year-old in terms of relative body proportions.

When we speak of *relative* endurance we are referring to the child's fitness level adjusted for body weight. It stands to reason that the adult's gross level of fitness is greater than that of young children, but when we divide one's body weight into the total fitness score we find that the differences are much less pronounced.

Circulatory–respiratory endurance is an aspect of muscular endurance specific to the heart, lungs, and vascular system. It refers to the ability to perform numerous repetitions of an activity requiring considerable use of the circulatory and respiratory systems. To date little research has been conducted in this important area with preschool or primary-grade children. It is difficult to accurately measure the volume of oxygen utilized in aerobic (stress producing activities requiring considerable consumption of air) activities without the use of sophisticated scientific equipment. We may assume, however, that the aerobic working capacity of an individual begins to develop as early as the preschool years and is dependent in part on the lifestyle of the individual child. Children who are overly concerned with television and other sedentary activities will not develop the degree of circulatory–respiratory endurance as their active counterparts. Activities such as running, peddling a tricycle or bicycle, and swimming should be a part of the daily life experiences of children.

The research of Astrand[20] represents the most extensive study of aerobic working capacity in relationship to age and sex. The results of his comprehensive research with subjects ranging in age from 4 to 33 years old as reported by Corbin indicates that:

[20] Astrand, Per-Olaf. *Experimental Studies of Working Capacity in Relation to Sex and Age,* Copenhagen: Munksgoaard, 1952.

1. Children have, in relation to body weight, a smaller blood volume, but have a slightly higher maximal O_2 intake per liter of blood volume. Thus, as previously mentioned, children can achieve maximum O_2 values similar to adults when corrected for body weight.

2. While adults have an increased O_2 pulse with increased heart rate, children do not. This may explain the reason why maximal heart rates of children exceed those of adults.

3. Children are capable of lower maximal blood lactate levels during exercise. This might be a result of the child's "unwillingness to strain himself" in exhausting feats or a lower buffering capacity, of younger subjects. If children were able to "persist," thus building greater maximal loctate levels, it would follow that they would be capable of greater maximal O_2 intake than possible for the average child.[21]

Further investigations need to be conducted in the area of circulatory–respiratory endurance of children in order to more fully reveal the nature and extent of cardiovascular fitness in young children.

Flexibility is the fourth and final area of physical fitness to be considered. Flexibility is joint-specific and can be improved with practice. Improvement has been shown by Hupprich and Segerseth[22] to continue from ages 6 to 12 in girls but to decrease thereafter. The same is probably true for boys. Flexibility is the ability of the various joints of the body to move through their full range of motion. Most young children are involved in numerous flexibility-developing activities. Their constant bending, twisting, turning, and stretching, along with the natural elasticity of their bodies, accounts for much of their flexibility. We need only to look at the contorted positions that children sit in while watching television or listening to a story to realize that they have a good deal of flexibility in the hip and knee-joint area. All too often, however, the range of motion diminishes in later childhood and adolesence due to lack of activity. Flexibility activities, like each other component of fitness, must be a part of the daily lives of children.

Motor Fitness

Much has been said and done concerning the motor performance of the skilled performer and athlete. The literature is replete with information dealing with the performance levels, mechanics, and physiological capabilities of adolescents and adults, but very little work has been done with preschool and primary-age children. The situation is much the same as with physical fitness and only recently have investigators begun to more closely

---

[21] Corbin, Charles B. *A Textbook of Motor Development.* Dubuque, Iowa: W. C. Brown, 1973, pp. 87–88, used by permission.

[22] Hupprich, Florence L. and Peter Segerseth, "Specificity of Flexibility in Girls," *Research Quarterly 21;* 25, 1950.

MUSCULAR STRENGTH

The ability to perform one maximum effort

MUSCULAR ENDURANCE

The ability to perform a movement task over an extended period of time.

CIRCULATORY RESPIRATORY ENDURANCE

The ability of the heart, lungs and vascular system to function efficiently at a high rate for an extended period of time.

FLEXIBILITY

The range of motion of the various joints of the body.

Figure 3.2

analyze the motor abilities of young children. Keogh states that "currently there are no adequate tests or scales which may be used clinically or experimentally to assess motor development in the early school years."[23] The tests available have not been rigorously standardized and are inadequately constructed. The need for tests and scales of motor abilities has increased over the past several years because of the increasing interest in the relationship of motor performance to learning and other factors. Although the available tests of motor ability are inadequate in several ways, they do, upon further standardization and modification in the testing and scoring criteria, offer great potential.

The Lincoln–Oseretsky Motor Development Scale developed by Sloan[24] is an American revision of the original Oseretskey scale devised in Russia in 1923. It has been used extensively to evaluate the motor fitness of children and is outlined here in an effort to illustrate typical test items of motor fitness. The original version had age-graded tasks for six motor-ability areas and was organized on a Binet-like scale. Sloan's revision of the test reduced the number of items from the original 83 to 36. Thirteen of these items were gross motor tasks and the remainder were geared more to fine motor abilities. The deleted items were eliminated on the basis of unreliability and possible injury to the child being tested. This test appears to have adequate reliability and good discrimination between 6 and 14 years of age. The Lincoln–Osertsky scale has proved useful in research and in evaluating the motor development of children in special programs. The major limitations of the test is that it requires about 1 hour to administer and does not have a standardized scale that is readily usable. The following is a list of the gross motor items contained in the Sloan revision in order of difficulty as determined by the percentage passing:

1. Walk backward.
2. Crouch on tiptoe.
3. Stand on one foot.
4. Jump over a rope.
5. Stand heel to toe.
6. Catch a ball.
7. Jump, make a half turn, land on toes and hold (3 seconds).
8. Throw a ball.
9. Balance on toes.
10. Jump and touch heels.

[23] Keogh, Jack F. "Analysis of Individual Tasks, in the Stott Test of Motor Improvement," Technical Report 2-68 (U.S.P.H.S. Grant), Department of Physical Education, University of California, Los Angeles, 1968, p. 1.

[24] Sloan, W. "Lincoln–Oseretsky Motor Development Scale," *Genetic Psychology Monographs 52*, 1955 pp. 183–252.

11. Stand on one foot, eyes closed.
12. Jump and clap.
13. Balance on toes.

Motor fitness or ability is considered to be one's quality of performance of a movement task. The child that displays skill in activities such as bicycling, swimming, throwing, catching, and climbing is said to possess good motor fitness. The components of motor fitness are briefly discussed in the following paragraphs and diagrammed in Figure 3.3.

Coordination is the ability to integrate separate motor systems with varying sensory modalities into efficient movement. The harmonious working together of the synchrony, rhythm, and sequencing aspects of temporal awareness (see Chapter 9) are the predecessors of coordinated movement. Various parts of the body may be involved, such as eye–foot coordination as in kicking a ball or walking upstairs. Eye–hand coordination is evident in fine motor activities such as bead stringing, tracting, and modeling clay and gross motor activities such as catching, striking, or volleying a ball.

Speed is the ability to move from one point to another in the shortest time possible. It is influenced by one's reaction time (the amount of time elapsed from the signal "go" to the first movements of the body) and movement time (the time elapsed from the initial movement to completion of the activity. Reaction time is generally considered to be innate but movement time may be improved with practice. Children's speed of movement generally improves to around age 12–13 years in both boys and girls, at which time the girls often perform better than the boys. After this, however, the *present* tendency is for the girls to level off in performance and the boys to continue improving throughout their teenage years. In young children we may witness their speed of movement in such activities as crawling, running, climbing, and playing tag. We may foster its natural development by providing plenty of opportunity and open space in which to run and play.

Agility is the ability to change the direction of the body rapidly and accurately while it is moving from one point to another as fast as possible. It is the ability to make quick and accurate shifts in body position and direction of movement. Agility may be enhanced in young children through participation in tagging and dodging activities. Performing through mazes and obstacle courses are also aids to agility development.

Power is the ability to perform one maximum effort in as short a period as possible. It is sometimes referred to as "explosive strength" and represents the combination of strength times speed. This combination of strength and speed is exhibited in children by jumping, striking, and throwing for distance. The speed of contraction of the muscles involved, as well as the strength and coordinated use of these muscles, determines the degree of power.

COORDINATION

The rhymthmical integration of motor and sensory systems into a harmonious working together of the body parts.

SPEED

The ability to move from one point to another in the shortest time possible over a short distance.

AGILITY

The ability to move from point to point as rapidly as possible while making successive movements in different directions.

POWER

The ability to perform one maximum explosive force.

BALANCE

The ability to maintain one's equilibrium in relationship to the force of gravity in both static and dynamic movement situations.

Figure 3.3

Balance is a complex quality of motorfitness. It is influenced by vision, the inner ear, cerebellum, proprioceptors, and the skeletal muscles. Balance is the ability to maintain one's equilibrium in relation to the force of gravity. It is the ability to make minute alterations in one's body position when it is placed in various positions of balance. Balance may be subdivided into *static* and *dynamic* balance. Static balance is the ability to maintain one's equilibrium in a fixed position, such as when standing on one foot or on a balance board. Dynamic balance is the ability to maintain one's equilibrium while the body is in motion. Walking on a balance beam and bouncing on a trampoline are examples of dynamic balance activities.

In actuality all movement involves an element of either static or dynamic balance, because balance is a basic aspect of all movement. As such it is very important for young children to begin developing their balancing abilities at an early age. A motor development program that provides numerous opportunities for practice in balance is highly recommended.

CONCLUSION

The psychomotor development of children represents *one* aspect of the total developmental process. It is intricately interrelated with both the cognitive and affective domains of human behavior, particularly during the early childhood years. The importance of optimum motor development in children must not be minimized or thought of as being of secondary importance to these other developmental processes. The unity of man clearly demonstrates the integrated development of the mind and the body and the many subtle interrelationships of each.

Principles of motor development emerge from the study of children as they grow. These principles are general in nature and illustrate the gradual progression from relatively simple levels of functioning to more complex levels. Each of these principles are affected by the combined influences of maturation and experience.

Maturation and experience also influence the development of rudimentary and fundamental movement abilities. Rudimentary movement abilities are developed during the first 2 years of life. The term "fundamental movement abilities" is used here to refer to those patterns of movement that are developing and being refined during the early childhood years. They are developed in three areas, namely locomotion, manipulation, and stability and involve more than being able to perform a particular skill in a certain manner. An adequately developed movement pattern is one which is adaptable flexible and useable in a wide range of environmental situations.

Developing the many movement abilities characteristic of the preschool and primary years contributes markedly to the physical abilities of children. The physical fitness and motor fitness of today's children are of great concern to many because of the frequent lack of opportunity and/or motivation to be physically active. The motor-development program in the home, nursery school, or elementary school must provide many opportunities for large muscle activity and strive to increase the children's level of motivation for vigorous activity.

SUGGESTED READINGS

Cratty, Bryant J. *Perceptual and Motor Development in Infants and Children*, New York: Macmillan, 1970.

Corbin, Charles B. *A Textbook of Motor Development*, Dubuque, Iowa: W. C. Brown, 1973.

Drowatzky, John N. *Motor Learning: Principles and Practices*, Minneapolis: Burgess, 1975.

Engstrom, G. (ed.). *The Significance of the Young Child's Motor Development*, Washington, D. C.: National Association for the Education of Young Children, 1971.

Espenschade, Ann S. and Helen M. Eckert, *Motor Development*, Columbus, Ohio: Charles E. Merrill, 1967.

Flinchum, Betty M. *Motor Development In Early Childhood*, St. Louis: C. V. Mosby, 1975.

Gallahue, David L., Peter H., Werner, and George C. Luedke, *A Conceptual Approach to Moving and Learning*, New York: Wiley, 1975.

Godfrey, Barbara B. and Newell C. Kephart, *Movement Patterns and Motor Education*, New York: Appleton–Century–Crofts, 1969.

Oxendine, Joseph B. *Psychology of Motor Learning*, New York: Appleton–Century–Crofts, 1968.

Melograno, Vincent and James E. Klenging, *An Orientation to Total Fitness*, Dubuque, Iowa: Kendall–Hunt, 1974.

Prudden, Bonnie. *Your Baby Can Swim*, New York: Reader's Digest Press, 1974.

Sinclair, Caroline B. *Movement of the Young Child: Ages Two to Six*, Columbus, Ohio: Charles E. Merrill, 1972.

Wickstrom, Ralph L. *Fundamental Motor Patterns*, Philadelphia: Lea and Febiger, 1970.

Chapter 4

Psychomotor Development and the Cognitive Behavior of Young Children

CONTENTS

Introduction
Perceptual Development in Infancy
  Visual Perception
  Auditory, Olfactory and Gustatory Perception
Perceptual-Motor Development of Young Children
  Body Awareness
  Spatial Awareness
  Directional Awareness
  Temporal Awareness
Perceptual-Motor Training Programs
Readiness and Remediation
Evaluating Perceptual-Motor Development
  Checklist of Possible Perceptual-Motor Dysfunctions
Conclusion
Suggested Readings
Selected Tests of Perceptual-Motor Functioning

> *Sometimes, looking deep into the eyes of a child, you are conscious of meeting a glance full of wisdom. The child has known nothing yet but love and beauty—all this piled-up world knowledge you have acquired is unguessed at by him. And yet you meet this wonderful look that tells you in a moment more than all the years of experience have seemed to teach.*
> *Hildegarde Hawthorne*

INTRODUCTION

Perceptual development plays an important role in cognitive functioning and as a result one is complexly intertwined with the other. The greatest development of perceptual abilities occurs during the preschool and primary years. Movement activities have been shown to be an important facilitator of perceptual development in young children. As a result the term "perceptual–motor" has come into wide usage in recent years. Perceptual–motor abilities and readiness for learning are closely interrelated in young children. Perceptual–motor (movement) activities serve as an important mode through which fundamental readiness and academic concepts can be developed and reinforced. Based on this the perceptual–motor development of children and its influence on academic concept readiness is the primary focus of this chapter.

The development of perceptual-motor abilities involves the complex interaction of perceptual, motor, and cognitive processes. Depending on the orientation of the reader, perceptual–motor experiences may be considered primarily as psychomotor or cognitive in nature. The variance in perspective stems from the purpose for which perceptual–motor activities are being performed. It has been clearly documented that practice is perceptual–motor activities will enhance perceptual motor abilities (psychomotor perspective).[1] It has, however, been correspondingly demonstrated that practice in perceptual–motor activities will reinforce and aid in the development of academic concept development (cognitive perspective).[2] Piaget lends support to this position with his stress on the tremendous importance of the "sensory–motor" phase of development in cognitive functioning. Perceptual–motor development is an important aspect of the cognitive domain that is linked to academic concept readiness. We will look at perceptual development and the role of perceptual–motor behavior from the cognitive point of view and its contribution to the development of fundamental concepts basic to readiness for schoolwork.

PERCEPTUAL DEVELOPMENT DURING INFANCY

From the moment of birth the infant begins the process of learning how

---

[1] Smith, Hope. "Implications for Movement Education Experiences Drawn From Perceptual Motor Research," *Journal of Health, Physical Education and Recreation,* April 1970, pp. 30–33.

[2] Cratty, Bryant J., *Physical Expressions of Intelligence*, Englewood Cliffs, N. J.: Prentice–Hall, 1972.

to interact with his environment. This interaction is a perceptual as well as a motor process. For our purposes we will discuss perceptual development separately, but caution must be taken not to separate the two in your thinking. The dash in the term perceptual–motor signifies the dependency of voluntary motor activity on perception and the dependency, to a large degree, of development of perceptual capacities on motor activity. The dash signifies that there must be an integration of perceptual data with motor data in order that both abilities may develop adequately.

The newborn receives all sorts of sensory stimulation (visual, auditory, olfactory, gustatory, tactual, and kinesthetic) through the various sense modalities. He makes responses to these stimuli but they are limited in their utility and are more or less automatic. The newborn is unable to integrate these sensory impressions that impinge on the cortex with stored information in order for meaning to be attached to these sensations. Only when sensory stimuli can be integrated with stored data do these senesations take on meaning for the infant and warrant being called "perceptions."

The newborn attaches little or no meaning to sensory stimuli. The ability to integrate stored data with incoming data has not developed sufficiently. For example, light rays impinging on the eyes register on the retinas and are transmitted to appropriate nerve centers in the sensory areas of the cortex. The newborn's reaction is simple (sensation); if the light is dim the pupils dilate, and if the light is bright the pupils construct and some of the stimulation is shut out (consensual pupillary reflex). Soon the infant blinks and the stimulus approaches. These simple reflex actions persist throughout life, but after a while the infant begins to attach meaning to the visual stimuli received. Soon a certain face becomes "mother". A blob is identified as having either three or four sides. Later it is identified as a triangle or as a square. The youngster now attends to certain stimuli and begins to apply basic meaning to them. The powers of visual perception are now developing.

The development of perceptual abilities is of considerable importance. McCandless has stated that:

> An adult functions well or poorly, succeeds or fails, depending on the way he manages his behavior in terms of his perception of himself and the world around him, and on how his perceptions fit with those of the people among whom he lives. His sense organs, the meaning he gives to the sensations he receives and his responses to the stimuli determine this consonance or disconance.[3]

As with the development of motor abilities in the infant, the development of perceptual skills is a matter of experience as well as maturation. Matura-

---

[3]McCandless, Boyd R. *Children: Behavior and Development*, New York: Holt, Rinehart, and Winston, 1967, p. 22.

tion plays an important role in the development of increased acuity of perception, but most of it is due to experience. The learning opportunities that the child and the adult have primarily account for the sophistication of their perceptual modalities. Only through experience will the infant be able to acquire these capabilities. The infant's sensory–motor development and later perceptual–motor development is basic to later functioning. If early opportunities are severely inhibited or retarded we may expect later abilities to be limited also.

Visual Perception

At birth, the infant's eyes have all of the parts necessary for sight and are completely formed with the exception of the fovea, which is incompletely developed. There is also an immaturity of the ocular muscles. These two factors result in poor fixation, focusing, and coordination of eye movements. The blinking and lacrimal apparatuses are poorly developed at birth, and the neonate is unable to shed tears until one to seven weeks after birth. It is debatable whether the newborn possesses color vision because of the amount of rhodopsin (visual purple) present in the rods and cones of the eye. Fixation, tracking, acuity, color preference, and visual discrimination all develop rapidly during the early weeks and months of life. Table 4.1 presents a list of the major developmental aspects of infant visual perception, along with the approximate age at which they begin to emerge.

In order to obtain information about the infant's perceptual abilities, a variety of measures may be obtained. Changes in general motor activity, physiological changes, reflexive movements, and voluntary motor responses are the primary means by which the researcher is able to determine if the infant is responding to the experimental conditions. A change in one or more of these processes provides cues to the infant's developmental level and response to the experimentally produced situation.

Auditory, Olfactory, and Gustatory Perception

Available research data concerning the development of auditory, olfactory, and gustatory perceptions in the human infant is much less complete than for the visual modality. In the area of auditory perception we find that as with vision the development of auditory abilities does not unfold naturally without the influence of the environment. Environmental conditions influence the extent of development of audition. The *ear* is structurally complete at birth and the infant is capable of hearing just as soon as the amniotic fluid drains (usually within a day or two after birth). The fetus

Table 4.1 Developmental Aspects of Selected Infant Visual Perceptual Abilities.

VISUAL QUALITY	SELECTED ABILITIES	APPROXIMATE AGE OF ONSET
SENSITIVITY TO LIGHT[4]	Consensual pupillary reflex (contraction and dilation of the pupils)	birth 2–3 hours
The visual apparatus is complete in the newborn and is first put to use by adjusting to varying intensities of the light source	Strabismus Turns head toward light source Closes eyes if light is bright Tightens eyelids when asleep More active in dim light than bright light	birth–14 days birth birth birth 0–1 year
FIXATION[5] Fixation is probably monocular and essentially reflexive during first 6 weeks of life	Fixates one eye on bright objects Fixates both eyes on bright objects Turns head from one stationary bright surface to another Follows an object in motion keeping the head stationary Directs eyes toward an object	birth 2–3 days 11 days 23 days 10 weeks
TRACKING[6] Tracking forms the basis for later crucial avoidance and approach reactions, and develops far sooner than the motor component	Horizontal Vertical Diagonal Circular	Begins at birth. Time of onset is inconsistent, but the sequence is fixed

[4] Sherman, M. and I. C. Sherman, "Sensorimotor Responses in Infants," *Journal of Comparative Psychology 6,* pp. 53–68, 1925.

[5] Zubek, J. P. and Patricia Solberg, *Human Development,* New York: McGraw-Hill, 1954.

[6] Pratt. K. C. "The Neonate," in Carmichael, L. (ed.) *Manual of Child Psychology,* New York: Wiley, 1954, pp. 215–291.

Table 4.1 (Continued)

VISUAL QUALITY	SELECTED ABILITIES	APPROXIMATE AGE OF ONSET
COLOR DISCRIMINATION AND PREFERENCE[7]	Color vision	birth?
	Color preference	4 months
	Prefer shape to color	15 days
Inconsistent evidence. Color vision may or may not be present at birth depending on the amount of rhodopsin present.	React to color	4 months
FORM, SHAPE, AND PATTERN DISCRIMINATION[8]	Prefers patterned objects to plain	1 month
	Prefers human face to all other objects	1 month
Discrimination begins early and develops rapidly in complexity. The human face is the favorite of all objects.	Size and shape constancy	2 months
	Geometric shape discrimination	6 months
VISUAL ACUITY[9]	Organically complete visual apparatus	birth
The length of focus increase daily or the eye matures.	Length of focus 4–10 inches	birth to 1 week
	Length of focus about 36 inches	3 months
	Length of focus about 100 feet	1 year
	Depth perception	3 months

[7] Spears, W. C. Assessment of Visual Preference and Discrimination in the 4-month Old Infant," *Journal of Comparative Psychological Psychiatry* 57, pp. 381–386, 1964.

[8] Fantz, R. L. "Pattern Vision in Newborn Infants," *Science* 140, pp. 296–297, 1963.

[9] McCandless, Boyd R., Children: Behavior and Development, New York: Holt, Rinehart, and Winston, 1967, pp. 29–30.

responds to sound before birth and the neonate reacts primarily to the loudness and duration of sound.[10]

The research on olfactory and gustatory perception is much more sparse than on hearing. It is difficult to separate the developmental sequence of smell and taste simply because the nose and mouth are closely connected, and stimuli applied to one are likely to affect the other. The newborn does, however, appear to react to certain odors, although this may be due more to the pain caused by the pungent odors used rather than smell. Newborns react to taste, preferring sweet tastes to sour and sour tastes to bitter ones. Table 4.2 presents a list of the major developmental aspects of infant auditory, gustatory, and olfactory perception.

PERCEPTUAL–MOTOR DEVELOPMENT OF YOUNG CHILDREN

The role of the preschool and elementary motor development specialist has been one of chronic misuse, abuse, and misunderstanding. Physical education is nonexistent in most elementary school systems, and where it does exist it is usually on a superficial basis. Lip service has been paid to the values of the physical education profession for many years but in actuality little has been done until recently to institute sound motor development programs in our nation's elementary schools. A well-planned physical education program that stresses exposing children to high quality and large quantities of movement experience is important to the development of the total child.

The visual perceptual abilities of young children are not the same as in adults. Their visual world is in the developmental stages and thus restricted. The development of perceptual abilities significantly inhibits or enhances children's movement performance. The converse of this is also true; that is, movement performance significantly inhibits or enhances the development of the children's perceptual abilities. The child restricted in perceptual development often encounters difficulties in performing perceptual–motor tasks.

The realization that the process of perception is not entirely innate enables one to hypothesize that the quality and quantity of movement experiences afforded young children are related to the development of their perceptual

---

[10] Bernard, J. and L. W. Sontag, "Fetal Reactivity to Tonal Stimulation: A Preliminary Report," *Journal of Gentic Psychology 70*, 205–210, 1947.

Table 4.2 Developmental Aspect of Selected Infant Auditory,
Olfactory, and Gustatory Abilities

PERCEPTUAL QUALITY	SELECTED ABILITIES	APPROXIMATE AGE OF ONSET
AUDITORY PERCEPTION (HEARING)[11]	Responds to loud, sharp sounds	Prenatal
	Reacts primarily to loudness and duration	Birth
The ear is structurally complete at birth and the newborn can respond to sound	Crude pitch discrimination	1–4 days
	Ability to localize sounds	3–4 months
	Responds to tonal differences	3–6 months
	Reacts with pleasure to parent's voice	5–6 months
OLFACTORY PERCEPTION (SMELL)[12]	Responds to odors	Neonate
	Reduced sensitivity upon repeated application of the stimuli	Neonate
The olfactory mechanism is structurally complete at birth and the newborn responds crudely to various, odors	Does not distinguish between pleasant and unpleasant odors	Neonate
	Discrimination abilities improve with practice	Neonate
GUSTATORY PERCEPTION (TASTE)[13]	Shows preference for tastes (prefers sweet to sour, and sour to bitter)	Neonate
The newborn reacts to variation in sweet, sour and bitter tastes. Little research data are available on this modality		

[11] Leventhal, Alice and L. P. Lipsett, "Adaptation, Pitch Discrimination, and Sound Vocalization in the Neonate," *Child Development, 35,* 759–767, 1964.

[12] Engen, T., L. P. Lippsitt, and H. Kaye, "Olfactory Responses and Adaptation in the Human Neonate," *Journal of Comparative Physiological Psychology, 56,* 1963, 73–77, 1963.

[13] Pratt, K. C. "The Neonate," in Carmichael, L. (ed.), *Manual of Child Psychology,* New York: Wiley, 1954, pp. 215–291.

Opportunity for a variety of movement experiences is an important facilitator of readiness.

abilities. The initial responses of young children are motor responses, and all future perceptual and conceptual data are based, in part, on these initial responses. Young children must establish a broad base of motor experience in order for these higher learnings to develop properly. Meaningfulness is imposed upon perceptual stimulation through movement. The matching of perceptual and motor data is thought by many to be necessary for the child to establish a stable spatial world.[14,15] The more motor and perceptual learning experiences that children have the greater the opportunity to make this "perceptual-motor match" and develop a plasticity of response to various situations.

Unfortunately the complexity of our modern society often deters the development of many perceptual–motor abilities. The environment in which today's children are raised is so complicated and dangerous that they are constantly being warned not to touch or to stay away from situations that potentially offer great amounts of motor and perceptual information. Children often grow up in a large city, or in an apartment building, and seldom are given the opportunity to climb a tree, walk a fence, jump a stream, or ride a horse. They often miss out on many of the essential experiences that children ought to have as a part of their daily life experiences, in order to develop their movement abilities. The lack or absence of these movement experiences and the adaptability of response that comes with practice and repetition often deter perceptual development.

Artificial means must be devised to provide additional experiences and practice in the perceptual–motor activities that modern society is unable to. Providing children with substitute experiences that they are unable to get or fully explore on their own may have a positive effect on the development of their visual perceptual abilities. This would seem to support the position that the motor development specialist should be an essential person in the child's educational curriculum. A movement oriented physical education program will contribute to the development of children's perceptual–motor skills and help develop many of the basic readiness skills necessary for success in school.

Recent physical education literature is replete with developmental skills and activities. For several years, many physical education and classroom teachers have been promoting cognitive readiness development through physical activities. The majority have not been fully aware of the magnitude of the contribution that they have been making to children's cognitive devel-

---

[14] Kephart, Newell C. *The Slow Learner In the Classroom,* Columbus, Ohio: Charles E. Merrill, 1971.

[15] Barsch, Ray H. *Achieving Perceptual-Motor Efficiency,* Seattle: Special Child Publication, 1965.

opment as well as their psychomotor development. It is time that the physical education profession, rather than individuals, recognize the potential contribution of physical education to the cognitive development of young children. We must see that quality physical education is included as an integral portion of the total school curriculum for all children.

The development and refinement of children's *spatial world* and their *temporal world* are two of the primary objectives of perceptual–motor training programs. The jargon used in each of the numerous programs across North America varies greatly. There does seem, however, to be general agreement that the following perceptual–motor qualities are among the most important to be developed and reinforced in children by the motor development specialist. The terms used here are not universal among authorities but their meanings are.

Body Awareness

The term "body awareness" is often used in conjunction with the terms "body image" or "body schema." Each term refers to the developing capacity

Duplicating body positions is a basic body awareness activity.

of young children to accurately discriminate among their body parts. The ability to differentiate among one's body parts and to gain a greater understanding of the nature of the body occurs in three areas. The first of these is *knowledge of the body parts.* This means being able to accurately locate the numerous parts of the body on oneself and on others. Second is *knowledge of what the body parts can do.* This refers to the child's developing abilities to recognize the component parts of a given act and the body's actual potential for performing it. *Knowledge of how to make the body move efficiently* is the third component of body awareness. This refers to the ability to reorganize the body parts for a particular motor act and the actual performance of a movement task. The following is a brief summary of some movement activities that may be used to enhance the various components of body awareness. A more detailed presentation of body awareness activities is presented in Chapter 9 (see pages 261-271):

1.   Knowledge of the body parts:

Touch your————.
A. Head

i. Hair	vi. Nose	xi. Teeth
ii. Forehead	vii. Nostrils	xii. Chin
iii. Eyebrows	viii. Cheeks	xiii. Ears
iv. Eyelashes	ix. Lips	xiv. Earlobes
v. Eyes	x. Tongue	xv. Neck

b. Trunk
    i. Chest
   ii. Stomach
  iii. Hips
  iv. Waist
    v. Side

c. Arms

i. Shoulders	vi. Thumb
ii. Elbows	vii. Palm
iii. Forearms	viii. Wrist
iv. Hands	ix. Knuckles
v. Fingers	x. Fingernails

d. Legs

i. Thighs	v. Instep
ii. Knees	vi. Toes

iii. Calves   vii. Heels
iv. Ankles

2. Knowledge of what the body parts can do:

a. Head
   i. I see with my_____.
   ii. I hear with my_____.
   iii. I smell with my_____.
   iv. I taste with my_____.
   v. I lick with my_____.
   vi. I blink my_____.
   vii. I talk with my_____.
   viii. I kiss with my_____.
   ix. I wrinkle my_____.
   x. I wear earrings on my_____.

b. Trunk
   i. I carry a knapsack on my_____.
   ii. Food goes to my_____.
   iii. I wear a belt around my_____.
   iv. I fold my arms across my_____.
   v. I bend at the_____.

c. Arms
   i. I shrug my_____.
   ii. I bend at the_____.
   iii. I clap with my_____.
   iv. I snap my_____.
   v. I wave with my_____.
   vi. I point with my_____.
   vii. I grasp with my_____.
   viii. I carry heavy things on my_____.
   ix. I color with my_____.
   x. I throw with my_____.

d. Legs
   i. I kick with my_____.
   ii. I bend at the_____.
   iii. I squat on my_____.
   iv. I kneel on my_____.
   v. I stand on my_____.

3. Knowledge of how to make the parts move efficiently:

a. Coupling Movements

      i. Touch your nose to your shoulder.
     ii. Touch your ear to your knee.
    iii. Touch your knee to a toe.
    iv. Touch your elbow to your knee.
     v. Touch your forehead to your thigh.
    vi. Touch your elbow to your waist.
   vii. Touch your head to your thigh.
  viii. Touch your back to your heels.
    ix. Touch your forearms to your calves.
     x. Touch your toes to your ear.

  b. Specific body part movements
      i. Click your heels.
     ii. Pike at the hips.
    iii. Tuck your trunk.
    iv. Shrug your shoulders.
     v. Stick out your chest.
    vi. Arch your back.
   vii. Jut out your chin.
  viii. Pop your lips.
    ix. Snap your fingers
     x. Wriggle your nose.

Spatial Awareness

Spatial awareness is a basic component of perceptual–motor development that may be divided into two subcategories: (1) *knowledge of how much space the body occupies* and (2) *the ability to project the body effectively into external space*. Knowledge of how much space the body occupies and its relationship to external objects may be developed through a variety of movement activities. With practice and experience children progress from their egocentric world of locating everything in external space relative to themselves (egocentric localization) to the development of an objective frame of reference (objective localization). For example, preschoolers determine the location of an object relative to where they are standing. Older children are, however, able to locate an object relative to its proximity to other nearby objects without regard to the location of their body.

As adults our spatial awareness is generally adequate but we may still encounter difficulties in locating the relative position of various objects. For example, when reading a road map while traveling through unfamiliar territory many people become considerably confused as to whether they are traveling north, south, east, or west. Difficulty is often encountered in deciding to turn right or left while looking at the map, without almost literally placing oneself on the map in order to project a mental image of which direction to turn. The absence of familiar landmarks and the impersonality of the road map make it difficult for many to objectively localize themselves in space relative to this particular task. Young children encounter much the same difficulty but on a broader scale. They must first learn to orient themselves subjectively in space and then proceed ever so carefully to venture out into unfamiliar surroundings in which subjective clues are useless. Providing children with opportunities to develop spatial awareness is an important attribute of a good movement-education program that recognizes the importance of perceptual–motor development. The following is a list of examples of how spatial awareness may be enhanced in children. A more complete listing of activities may be located in Chapter 9 (see pages 271-278):

1. How much space does the body occupy?

    a. Walk between two chairs.
    b. Step over objects at various heights.
    c. Walk or crawl under an object.
    d. Crawl through a tunnel (inner tubes will do).
    e. Estimate the size of various body parts.
    f. Compare body-part size to other objects.
    g. Estimate your height on a chalkboard and then compare with actual height.
    h. Trace your body on a sheet of newsprint.
    i. Estimate how many steps it will take to get to the other end of the gymnasium and then see how close you came.
    j. Make yourself as small, tall, large, or skinny as you can.

2. Projecting the body into external space

    a. Follow one-step directions from points A to B using familiar objects in the room (desk, table, window, etc.).
    b. Follow two- and three-step directions from points A to B and then C and D using familiar objects in the room.
    c. Follow one-step directions outdoors from points A to B without the use of familiar landmarks.
    d. Follow two-and three-step directions outdoors from points A to B and then C and D without the use of familiar landmarks.
    e. Place a long rope on the floor in a certain configuration. Have the children walk on the rope with their eyes open. Repeat with the eyes closed.

f.   Draw a pattern on the floor. Have the children walk the pattern with their eyes open and then repeat with their eyes closed.

g.   Draw a simple pattern (circle, square, or triangle) on the board. Have the children walk the same pattern on the floor.

h.   Give the children a task card indicating the location of a hidden object through a series of cues that require objective localization.

i.   Teach the children how to use a compass and locate various objects.

j.   Using a compass, determine the location of certain areas on a map of your school, community, city, or state.

Directional Awareness

An area of great concern to many perceptual–motor specialists is that of directional awareness. It is through directional awareness that children are able to give dimension to objects in external space. The concepts of left–right, up–down, top–bottom, in–out, and front–back are all enhanced through movement activities that place emphasis on direction. Directional awareness is commonly divided into two subcategories, namely *laterality* and *directionality.*

Laterality refers to an *internal* awareness or *feel* for the various dimensions of the body with regard to their location and direction. Children that have adequately developed the concept of laterality do not need to rely on external cues for determining direction. They do not need, for example, to have a ribbon tied to their wrist to remind them which is their left and which is their right hand. They do not need to rely on cues such as the location of their watch or ring to provide information about direction. The concept of laterality seems so basic to most adults that it is difficult to conceive how anyone could possibly not develop laterality. However, we need only to look into the rear-view mirror of our car to have directions reversed and sometimes confused. Backing up a trailer hitched to a car or truck is an experience that most of us prefer to avoid because of the difficulty we encounter deciding whether to turn the wheel to the left or right. The pilot, astronaut, and deep-sea diver must possess a high degree of laterality or "feel" for determining up from down and left from right.

Directionality is an external projection of laterality. It gives dimension to objects in space. True directionality depends on adequately established laterality first. Directionality is important to parents and teachers because it is a basic component in learning how to read. Children who do not have fully established directionality will often encounter difficulties in discriminating between various letters of the alphabet. For example, the letters b, d, p, and q are all similar. The only difference lies in the direction of the ball and the line that make up the letters. As a result the child encounters considerable difficulty discriminating between several letters of the alphabet. Entire words may even be reversed for the child with a directionality problem. The word *cat* may be read as *tac* or *bad* may be read as *dab*. The only reason being the inability to project direction into external space. Some children encounter difficulty in the top–bottom dimension which is more basic than the left–right dimension. They may write and see words upside down and are totally confused when it comes to reading.

It should be pointed out that establishing directional awareness is a developmental process and relies on both maturation and experience. It is perfectly normal for the 4- and 5-year old to experience confusion in direction. We should, however, be concerned for the 6- and 7-year old child who is consistently experiencing these confusions because this is the time when most schools traditionally begin instruction in reading. Adequately developed directional awareness is one important readiness skill necessary for success in reading, and movement is one way in which this important perceptual–motor concept may be developed. The following is a list of suggested movement activities useful in helping children develop directional awareness. They have not been separated into laterality and directionality here because of the author's conviction that the two cannot be be effectively dealt with independently of one another in movement. A more complete listing of directional awareness activities may be found in Chapter 9 (see pages 278-284):

1. Movement commands utilizing directional clues:

    a. Stand in front (behind) Jennifer.
    b. Step out on your left (right) foot.
    c. Move clockwise (counterclockwise).
    d. Stand to the right (left) of _____.
    e. Run between (around) the chairs.

2. Moving in different directions:

a. Forward	d. Diagonally	g. Upward
b. Sideward	e. Left	h. Downward
c. Backward	f. Right	

3. Moving with other people:

    a. Stand in front of (behind)_____.
    b. Step under (over)_____.
    c. Stand near (far)_____.

   d. Stand to the left (right) of_____.
   e. Stand between_____and_____.

4. Moving with an object (hoop, wand, etc.):

   a. Left–right
   b. Top–bottom
   c. Over–under
   d. Front–back
   e. On –in

5. Moving on an object:

   a. Carpet squares can be used as stepping stones to teach left–right concepts of footedness.
   b. With footprints or handprints on the floor or wall, match left and right.
   c. Balance-beam activities performed in a unilateral or bilateral manner are beneficial.
   d. Moving through a mat maze made from folding type mats placed in such a way that left-right decisions have to be made is beneficial.
   e. Obstacle-course activities that require the use of left and right in a prescribed manner are beneficial.

Temporal Awareness

The preceding discussion of the various aspects of perceptual–motor development has dealt with the development of the young child's spatial world. Body awareness, spatial awareness, and directional awareness are all closely interrelated and combine to help children make sense out of their spatial world. Temporal awareness, on the other hand, is concerned with the development of an adequate time structure in children. It is developed and refined through both maturation and experience at the same time the child's spatial world is developing.

Temporal awareness is intricately related to the coordinated interaction of various muscular systems and sensory modalities. The terms "eye–hand coordination" and "eye–foot coordination" have been used for years to reflect the interrelationship of these processes. The individual with a well-developed time dimension is the one that we refer to as "coordinated." One who has not fully established this is often called "clumsy" or "awkward."

Everything that we do possesses an element of time. There is a beginning point and an end point, and no matter how minute, there is a measurable span of time between the two. It is important that children learn how to function efficiently in this time dimension as well as in the space dimension.

Without one the other cannot develop to its fullest potential.

Rhythm is the basic and most important aspect of developing a stable temporal world. The term has many meanings but is described here as the synchronous recurrence of events related in such a manner that they form recognizable patterns. Rhythmic movement involves the synchronous sequencing of events in time. Rhythm is crucial in the performance of any act in a coordinated manner. Cooper and Glassow[16] recorded the sounds of the movement pattern of selected sports skills in outstanding performers through the use of a tape recorder. The sounds made by these performers were transcribed into musical notation illustrating that a definite recordable rhythmical element was present. The recorded rhythm of these outstanding athletes were beaten out on a drum in several teaching situations with beginners. The results were startling in that the beginners learned the movements of the champions more rapidly when this techniques was used than in a standard teaching situation. Cooper and Andrews in their excellent article[17] concluded that "it appears that beginning performers can profit by listening to and emulating certain elements of the rhythmic pattern of the good performers. Teachers should take full advantage of this phenomenon." Surely this statement applies to children as well as athletes. We must recognize the rhythmic element in all efficient movement and in so doing be sure that we emphasize the rhythmic component of all movement.

Smith[18] indicated that children begin to make temporal discriminations through the auditory modality before the visual and that there is transfer from the auditory to the visual but not the reverse. Activities that require performing movement tasks to auditory rhythmic patterns should begin with young children and be a part of their daily lives. The activity possibilities are endless. Moving to various forms of musical accompaniment ranging from the beat of a drum to instrumental selections can be important contributors to temporal awareness.

The following is a partial list of activities that may be used with young children to help them develop a more efficient time structure. Chapter 9 contains a more complete listing of appropriate activities geared specifically to enhance temporal awareness (see pages 285–288).

1.   Rhythmic activities (with accompaniment):

   a.   Move to various tempos
   b.   Move to various accents

[16] Cooper, John M. and Ruth Glassow, *Kinesiology,* St. Louis: C. V. Mosby, 1972.

[17]Cooper, John M. and Wendy Andrews, "Rhythm as a Linguistic Art," *Quest,* 65, January 1975,

[18] Smith, Hope, "Implications for Movement Education Experiences Drawn from Perceptual–Motor Research," *Journal of Health, Physical Education and Recreation* April 1970, pp. 30–33.

   c. Move to various intensities
   d. Move to various rhythmic patterns
   e. Perform fundamental locomotor movements to music
   f. Singing rhythms
   g. Basic folk dances

2. Movement and drama (with accompaniment):

   a. Mimetics
   b. Finger plays
   c. Puppetry
   d. Creative dance

3. Ball activities:

   a. Tracking swinging ball
   b. Striking a stationary suspended ball
   c. Striking a swinging suspended ball
   d. Kicking a stationary ball
   e. Kicking a moving ball

4. Rhythmic ball activities:

   a. Bounce and catch to music
   b. Toss to self and catch to music
   c. Toss to partner and catch to music
   d. Volley to music (use a balloon)
   e. Combine bouncing, tossing, and catching to music

PERCEPTUAL–MOTOR TRAINING PROGRAMS

During the past several years numerous programs of perceptual–motor training have sprung up across North America. During the 1960's several of these programs were given considerable exposure in the popular press. Based on these articles and the claims of some, many people formed the impression that these programs were panaceas for the development of cognitive and psychomotor abilities. Considerable confusion and speculation developed over the values and purposes of perceptual–motor training programs. Programs adhering to one technique or another emerged almost overnight. All too often people were inadequately trained, ill informed, and frankly, not clear on just what they were trying to accomplish. The smoke is now beginning to clear and concerned educators are taking a closer, more objective look at perceptual–motor training programs and their role in the total educational spectrum. Rather than claiming panaceas or adhering to one training technique or another, many are viewing perceptual–motor

programs as important facilators of readiness development. Perceptual–
motor activities are being recognized as important contributors to the *general* readiness of children for learning. The contribution of perceptual–
motor activities to *specific* perceptual readiness skills is being closely reexamined.

Readiness programs may be classified as *concept developing* or *concept reinforcing* in nature. Concept developing programs are generally designed for children who for a variety of reasons have been limited or restricted in their experiential background (e.g., socioeconomic class, prolonged illness, ethnic background, television). Headstart programs and Frostig's[19] developmental program are examples of concept developing programs, in which a variety of multisensory experiences including perceptual–motor activies are used as a means of developing fundamental readiness skills.

Concept-reinforcing programs are those in which movement is used in *conjunction* with traditional classroom techniques to develop basic cognitive understandings. This type of program is one in which movement is used as an aid or vehicle for reinforcing cognitive concepts dealt with in the nursery school or primary grade classroom. Cratty,[20] Humphrey,[21] and others[22] have outlined a variety of concept reinforcing activities for use by young children.

Remedial training programs are the third and most controversial type of perceptual–motor training program. They have been established as a means of alleviating perceptual inadequacies and increasing academic achievement. Programs have been developed by Delacato,[23] Getman,[24] Kephart[25] and others in attempts to aid cognitive development through perceptual–motor remediation techniques. Figure 4.1 presents an overview of the various types of perceptual-motor training programs.

READINESS AND REMEDIATION

Research indicates that as children pass through the normal developmental stages their perceptual abilities become more acute and refined. This is

[19] Frostig, Marianne *Move, Grow & Learn*, Chicago: Follett, 1969.

[20] Cratty, Bryant. *Intelligence in Action*, Englewood Cliffs, N. J.: Prentice–Hall, 1973.

[21] Humphrey, James H. *Child Learning*, Dubuque, Iowa; W. C. Brown, 1974.

[22] Gallahue, David L., Peter H. Werner, and George C. Ludeke, *A Conceptual Approach to Moving and Learning*, New York: Wiley, 1975.

[23] Delacato, Carl, *Treatment and Prevention of Reading Problems,* Springfield, Illinois: Charles C. Thomas, 1959.

[24] Getman, G. N. *How to Develop Your Child's Intelligence,* A Research Publication, Lucerne, Minnesota; G. N. Getman, 1952.

[25] Kephart, Newell C. *The Slow Learner in the Classroom,* Columbus, Ohio: Charles E. Merrill, 1971.

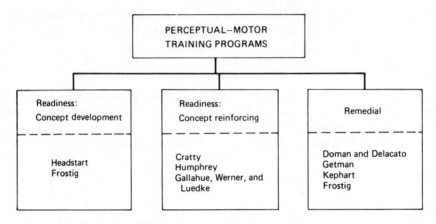

Figure 4.1 Three types of perceptual-motor training programs.

due to the increasing complexity of the neuromuscular apparatus and se-
nory receptors and partly due to the increasing of their ability to explore and
move throughout their environment. Piaget's work[26] has traced the gradual
development of perception from crude meaningless sensations to the perception of a stable spatial world (see pages 00-00). His stages of development rely
heavily on motor information as a primary information-gathering process.
As the perceptual world of children develops they try to construct it with
as much stability as they can in order to reduce variability as far as possible.
As a result they learn to differentiate between those things that can be
ignored, are easily predictable, or are wholly unforeseen and must be observed and examined in order to be understood. Movement plays an important role in this process of developing perceptual readiness for cognitive
tasks.

The majority of our perceptions, and visual perceptions in particular,
result from the elaboration and modification of these basic reactions by
experience and learning. When we speak of children being perceptually
ready to learn we are in fact referring to a point in time in which they have
sufficiently developed their basic perceptual and conceptual learning tasks.
Perceptual readiness for learning is a developmental process and perceptual–
motor activities play an important part in helping young children achieve
a *general* stage of readiness. *Specific* perceptual readiness skills, such as
visual perceptual readiness for reading, *may* be affected by the quality and
quantity of the perceptual–motor experiences engaged in by children.

The process of being able to read (as well as other important taks) involves

---

[26] Piaget, J., *The Construction of Reality and the Child.* New York: Basic Books, 1954.

a number of abilities of which visual perceptual ability is an important one. The reading process may be considered in terms of three basic areas; namely language, skill, and perception. Considerable research has been conducted in the first two areas but the third has only begun to be explored. The perceptual phase of reading involves the identification and recognition of words on a printed page. Form and shape perception may be enhanced through movement as well as directional awareness of up, down, left, and right. All are important factors associated with word identification and recognition.

The period of the greatest amount of perceptual–motor development is between ages 3 and 7 years. These are the crucial years preceding and during the time that children beging to learn to read. They are perceptually ready to read when they have developed a sufficient backlog of information which enables them to encode and decode sensory impressions at a given point in time with the benefit of previous learning experiences of high quality as well as quantity. A sufficient number of children enter the first grade with a lag in their perceptual abilities to warrant programs in readiness training that utilize perceptual–motor development activities. The movement education portion of the school day can play an important role in helping many of these children catch up with their peers.

EVALUATING PERCEPTUAL–MOTOR DEVELOPMENT

During the past several years numerous measures of perceptual–motor development have been constructed. Generally these tests were developed as measures for children who had been classified as "slow learners," "brain-damaged," or "neurologically impaired." They have been used with varying degrees of success by many. A list of selected tests of perceptual–motor functioning may be found at the conclusion of this chapter. The classroom teacher and physical education teacher is the first one to pick up "subjective" cues of possible perceptual–motor difficulties in preschool and primary-grade children. The validity of these subjective observations must not be discounted or minimized. On the contrary, the careful daily observation of children's behavior can be very valuable and reliable in detecting potential lags in development. It is suggested that the teacher refer students suspected of a developmental lag to the school psychologist for testing and specific delineation of the problem. The results of the testing should be shared with the parents and teachers with whom the child comes in contact. In this way they can form an effective team to eliminate or diminish the difficulty. The following is a checklist of possible perceptual–motor dysfunctions that may aid the classroom teacher in more accurately assessing children.

Checklist of Possible Perceptual–Motor Dysfunctions.

The following checklist is designed to serve only as a subjective indicator of *possible* perceptual–motor difficulties. Failure in several of these items may lead the teacher to seek further information through more objective evaluative procedures.

1. Has trouble holding or maintaining balance._____
2. Appears clumsy._____
3. Cannot carry himself well in motion._____
4. Appears to be generally awkward in activities requiring coordination. _____
5. Does not readily distinguish left from right._____
6. In locomotor skills, performs movements with more efficiency on one side than the other._____
7. Reverses letters and numbers with regularity._____
8. Is not able to hop or skip properly._____
9. Has difficulty making changes in movement._____
10. Has difficulty performing combinations of simple movements. _____
11. Has difficulty in gauging space with respect to his body, and bumps and collides with objects and other children._____
12. Tends to be accident-prone._____
13. Has poor hand–eye coordination._____
14. Has difficulty handling the simple tools of physical education (bean-bags, balls, and other objects that involve a visual–motor relationship)._____
15. Has persistent poor general appearance._____

    a. Shirt tail always out_____
    b. Shoes constantly untied_____
    c. Fly incessantly unzipped_____
    d. Socks bagged around ankles_____
    e. Hair uncombed_____

16. Is inattentive._____
17. Does not follow directions or is able to follow verbal but not written directions or vice versa._____
18. Has speech difficulties._____

    a. Talking too loudly_____
    b. Talking too softly_____
    c. Slurring words_____

19. Poor body posture._____

20. Has hearing difficulties._____

    a. Always turning head to one side_____
    b. Holding or prefering one ear over the other_____

21. Has difficulty negotiating stairs._____
22. Daydreams excessively._____
23. Is excessively messy in work._____

    a. Going out of the lines_____
    b. Inconsistency of letter size, etc._____
    c. General sloppiness_____

24. Is unable to copy objects, (words, numbers, letters, etc.)._____

SUGGESTED READINGS

American Alliance of Health, Physical Education and Recreation, *Approaches to Perceptual–Motor Experiences,* Washington, D. C., 1970.

American Alliance of Health, Physical Education and Recreation, *Foundation and Practices in Perceptual–Motor Learning—A Quest for Understanding,* Washington, D. C., 1971.

American Alliance for Health, Physical Education and Recreation, *Perceptual–Motor Foundations: A Multidisciplinary Concern,* Washington, D. C., 1969.

Bendick, Jeanne. *Space and Time,* New York: Franklin Watts, 1968.

Brown, Roscoe C. Jr. and Bryant J. Cratty (eds.), *New Perspectives of Man in Action,* Englewood Cliffs, N. J. Prentice–Hall, 1969.

Cratty, Bryant J. *Perceptual–Motor Behavior and Educational Processes,* Springfield, Illinois: Charles C. Thomas, 1969.

Cratty, *Perceptual–Motor Development in Infants and Children,* New York: MacMillan, 1970.

Cratty, Bryant J. and S. Margaret Mary Martin, *Perceptual–Motor Efficiency in Children,* Philadelphia: Lea and Febiger, 1969.

Gerhardt, Lydia A. *Moving and Knowing: The Young Child Orients Himself in Space,* Englewood Cliffs, N. J. Prentice–Hall, 1973.

Kephart, Newell C. *The Slow Learner in the Classroom,* Columbus, Ohio: Charles E. Merrill, 1971.

Werner, Peter H. and Lisa Rini, *Inexpensive Equipment Ideas and Activities for Perceptual–Motor Development,* New York: Wiley, 1975.

Williams, Harriet G., "Perceptual–Motor Development in Children," in *A Textbook of Motor Development,* Corbin, Charles C. (ed.), Dubuque, Iowa: W. C. Brown, 1973, pp. 111–148.

Wunderlich, Ray, *Kids, Brains and Learning,* St. Petersburg, Florida: Johnny Read, Inc., 1970.

SELECTED TESTS OF PERCEPTUAL–MOTOR FUNCTIONING

Ayres, Jean, *Southern California Perceptual–Motor Tests,* Western Psychological Services, Los Angeles, California.

Beery, K. E. *Developmental Test of Visual–Motor Integration,* Follett Educational Corporation, Chicago, Illinois.

Bender, Laura. *Bender Visual Motor Gestalt Test,* The Psychological Corporation, New York, New York.

Cheves, R. *Pupil Record of Educational Behavior,* Teaching Resources Corporation, Boston, Massachusetts.

Doll, E., *Oseretsky Motor Proficiency Tests,* American Guidance Service, Inc., Circle Pines, Minnesota.

Frostig, Marianne and D. Horne, *The Marianne Frostig Developmental Test of Visual Perception,* Consulting Psychologists Press, Palo Alto, California.

Katz, J. *Kindergarten Auditory Screening Test,* Follett Educational Corporation, Chicago, Illinois.

Kirk, Samuel, et al. *The Illinois Test of Psycholinguistic Abilities,* University of Illinois Press, Urbana, Illinois.

Perceptual Testing–Training Kit for Kindergarten Teachers, Winter Haven Lions Research Foundation, Inc., Winter Haven, Florida.

Perceptual Testing–Training Kit for First Grade Teachers, Winter Haven Lions Research Foundation, Inc., Winter Haven, Florida.

Roach, Edward and N. Kephart, *The Purdue Perceptual–Motor Survey,* Charles E. Merrill, Columbus, Ohio.

Semel, E. *Sound, Order, Sense,* Follett Educational Corporation, Chicago, Illinois.

Valett, Robert. *Valett Developmental Survey of Basic Learning Abilities,* Fearon Publishers, Palo Alto, California.

Wepman, J. *Auditory Discrimination Test,* Language Research Associates, Chicago, Illinois.

Chapter 5

Psychomotor Development and the Affective Behavior of Young Children

CONTENTS

Introduction
What is Self-Concept?
Social Status and Movement Skill
Possible Consequences of A Poor Self-Concept
The Influence of Movement on Self-Concept
Movement and the Developing Self
   Success
   Developmentally Appropriate Activities
   Adventure Activities
   Sequencing of Tasks
   Reasonable Expectations
   Encouragement
Conclusion
Suggested Readings

We have met the enemy, and he is us.
Pogo

INTRODUCTION

Do you remember when you were a child with nothing to do but play for hours and hours each day? Do you remember the excitement of that first climb to the top of the monkey bars, your first successful ride on your two-wheeler, or your first swim all the way down the pool? We can all remember as children how good it felt to succeed and can probably even remember a time or two when we did not. Those successes and failures of childhood may seem quite remote and meaningless to us now, but as a child they were important events in our lives. Events that had an influence on what we are and who we are today. Many of these events centered around our early play experiences because how children feel about themselves is greatly determined by play experiences, both successful and unsuccessful.

Children are active, energetic, and emerging beings. Much of their life is spent in play and active exploration of their ever-expanding world. The so-called play world of children occupies a large portion of their day and is of central importance to them. It is as an important avenue by which children come to learn more about themselves, their bodies, and their potential for movement. The development of many basic affective concepts have their roots in the carefree, exhilerating world of play.

Self-concept is an important aspect of children's affective behavior that is influenced through the world of games, play, and vigorous movement. Because the establishment of a stable positive self-concept is so crucial to effective functioning in our lives, its development is too crucial to be left to chance. The important contribution that movement and vigorous physical activity can make to forming a good self-concept should not be overlooked. As parents and teachers of young children we should be genuinely interested in the development of a good self-concept in our children. In the past the important link between physical activity and self-concept has often been given only lip service. In this chapter we will closely examine self-concept development and the potential for movement in enhancing self-concept. It should be recognized, however, that self-concept is only one aspect of affective behavior. Such things as creativity and appreciation of beauty are other important aspects of the affective domain that must be considered in the education of young children.

WHAT IS SELF-CONCEPT?

Self-image, self-esteem, self-respect, self confidence, and ego are terms used to describe essentially the same thing, namely one's inner estimate of personal worth or worthlessness. Although these terms have subtle differences in meaning, they are often used interchangeably and add up to the sum total of how we feel about ourselves and how we think others feel about us. It is that feeling of "I can" or "I can't," "I'm good," or "I'm bad," that we all possess.

Self-concept is that feeling of "I Can" or "I Can't."

Self-concept may be thought of as one's awareness of his or her personal characteristics, attributes, and limitations and the way in which their characteristics are both like and unlike others. The notion of self-esteem is also included in this definition, because it refers to the value one places on oneself and one's behavior. Self-esteem and self-concept are closely related and referred to interchangeably because value judgements are frequently involved in what children learn about themselves from other people.

What makes people different from each other and makes them uniquely themselves and not someone else is their self-concept and view of the world as *they* know it. The sum of their experiences and their feelings about these experiences contribute to this mental model. We find out about ourselves in many ways. By choosing, trying things out, experimenting, and exploring we discover who we are, what we can do, and what we cannot do. Not only do we *discover* who we are but through our experiences we contribute to the making or formation of our unique identity. For each new choice adds something to our backlog of experience and hence to our world and to ourselves.

Self-concept is *learned* and its development begins at least at birth. Some authorities argue that the emotional state of the expectant mother, ranging from a relaxed happy pregnancy, to a tension-filled traumatic pregnancy, may have a dramatic affect on the yet unborn child. Yamamoto states that "some studies have suggested that stress experiences by a pregnant mother can alter the movements of the fetus from normal to hyperactive—the mother should know that a physically healthy child has a greater chance for adequate psychological development, since the concept of a child's physical self plays an important part in the entirety of the self-concept."[1]

The early months of life mark the first tangible beginnings of self-concept development. The tenderness, warmth, and love displayed between parent and child conveys the first feeling of "I am loved" and "I am valued." The infant's sense of well-being is affected by the emotional state of the parent and attention to his or her physical needs. The fulfillment of psychological needs is just as important, for the infant needs to establish a sense of trust, security, recognition, and love. Trust is a basic issue to be resolved in the early mother–infant relationship. Mothers create a sense of trust in their children by combining sensitive care of their baby's individual needs with a firm sense of personal trustworthiness. Erikson was probably the first to recognize the establishment of a sense of trust during the early months of life. His stage of "trust versus mistrust" is rooted in the child developing a sense of being loved and valued in a world that has consistently and permanancy (see pages 29-32 for a discussion of Erikson's model of child development).

The toddler experiences the satisfaction of mastering the art of walking successfully or solving a problem with a new toy. This development of a sense of autonomy is an important facilitator of a positive self-concept, influenced greatly by parents, teachers, and other central adults in the life of the child. These individuals have a unique opportunity to selectively reinforce the child's learning about himself. This is done through consistent acceptance with both respect and concern and provision for freedom and independence within carefully defined limits. Much of what the young child learns is imitative, and this learning is not restricted to overt action. Feeling and attitudes can be learned also through imitation. As a result the type of model that central adults project determines many of the attitudes and feelings that the child develops.

[1]Yamamoto, Kaoru. *The Child and His Image,* Boston: Houghton–Mifflin, 1972, pp. 181–182.

The teenager feels good about the accomplishment of new and difficult tasks and the newly found sense of independence that accompanies performing meaningful work and earning money. The thoughtful parent recognizes the importance of the peer group at this level and the importance of assisting in the gradual establishment of a sense of mature independence. Self-concept can be enhanced continually throughout life through the pride of accomplishment and the sense of being needed, loved, and valued. When referring to the term "self" we find that it includes more than one's personal physical self. It also includes and is affected by all of those persons and groups with whom we identify. Our family, friends, acquaintances, church, school, and place of business are all persons or institutions with which we identify.

Our conviction of personal worth and effectiveness develops chiefly through successful experiences in coping, according to Maynard.[2] For one to have confidence in himself he must be able to cope. He must be willing to accept himself as well as others who are different. Children who can cope are adaptable rather than rigid in their behavior. They are diligent, can concentrate on a task, and work through difficulties. Confidence in oneself is developed through the joy of finding what one does well—of doing anything really well. Motor abilities and movement skills are one avenue by which self-image may be enhanced. It is, however, a very important one for most children, because so much of their daily life experiences are centered around the need for efficient and effective movement.

In short, self-concept is the sum total of our life's experiences. It is our personal estimate of self-worth based on what we think of ourselves and what we think others think of us. Self-concept is developed through successful experiences in coping throughout our daily lives and doing something well. Movement plays an important role in enhancing or limiting self-concept development in children because it is a central focus in their lives. High positive value is placed by both children and adults on successful performance in physical activities, as evidenced by the hero status of many college and professional athletes and the high positive peer-group acceptance of the skilled performer.

SOCIAL STATUS AND MOVEMENT SKILL

The relationship between children's social status and their performance in movement activities has been a subject of interest to researchers for many years. Numerous studies point out that there is indeed a link between high positive peer-group acceptance and ability in games and sports, especially

[2]Maynard, F. *Guiding Your Child to a More Creative Life,* New York: Doubleday, 1973.

in boys. Tuddenham points out that "probably central in the boys' constellation of values is athletic skill, predicated upon motor coordination, strength, size and physical maturity."[3]

Skill level is often controlled by factors that are outside the child's influence. Such things as physical stature, health-related conditions, and lack of experience and quality instruction make it impossible for many children to meet the values of their peer group. As a result they often suffer for it in terms of feelings of inferiority, rejection, and poor self-image. Tuddenham makes the statement that "personal insecurity and social maladjustment often have their roots in this area."

When considering the affect of skill level on the social status of young girls the available literature presents a somewhat different picture. The results of Tuddenham's classic study indicated that girls are "less dependent than boys upon possession of specific physical skills.[4]" Cratty does indicate, however, that it does seem important for girls to be moderately skillful in motor performance between the approximate ages of 5 and 14 years, but after that superior motor performance in other than a few acceptable sports (golf, tennis, horseback riding, etc.) can serve to *detract* from a girl's popularity.[5] It does appear that the tremendous changes we are presently witnessing in the role of women in our society and the recent surge of interest in all forms of competitive athletics for girls and women may soon prove Tuddenham's and Cratty's researches to be generally outdated. The upsurge of interest in participation in traditionally male activities such as Little League baseball and the Soap-Box Derby, along with increased intramural and interscholastic competition for girls, has clearly indicated a change in the social status of physical activity for females.

When applied to young children it is safe to hypothesize that boys and girls from about age 4 or 5 years onward are either positively or negatively affected by their performance abilities in games, sports, and dance activities. Although this is not the only avenue of influence on the child's self-concept, we must recognize that it is an important one, one that we should be sure to properly guide and nurture through concerned guidance and developmentally appropriate experiences.

[3] Tuddenham, R. S. "Studies in Reputation III, Correlates of Popularity Among Elementary School Children," *The Journal of Educational Psychology,* 272, May 1951.

[4] Tuddenham, R. S. "Studies in Reputation II, Correlates of Popularity Among Elementary School Children," *The Journal of Educational Psychology,* 272, May 1951.

[5] Cratty, Bryant, J. *Social Dimension of Physical Activity,* Englewood Cliffs, New Jersey: Prentice-Hall, 1967.

POSSIBLE CONSEQUENCES OF A POOR SELF-CONCEPT

A poor self-concept is reflected in the feelings of "I can't," "I'm always wrong," or "I'm worthless." Children who feel badly about themselves and the world they do know are not likely to feel better about the part of the world they do not know. As a result they often reflect the attitude of caring little to explore that world. This is simply because it does not look inviting and appears hostile, and full of possibilities for humiliation and defeat. Holt[6] makes the point that this hostile and threatening new world becomes one that does not lure the child out but thrusts in on him, invading those few fairly safe places where even a small sense of who and where he is are threatened. Children with a negative self-concept come to view the world they do not know as even worse than the world they are familiar with.

Children who feel themselves to be of little worth due to repeated failures often fall back on the protective strategy of deliberate failure. Deliberate failure serving as a self-protection device can be explained by the principle that you cannot fall out of bed when you are sleeping on the floor. In other words, children who view themselves as complete failures will not even be tempted to try. They avoid the "agony of defeat" because they feel that the "thrill of victory" is a hopeless cause.

Children with a poor self-concept are also negatively affected by what they think others think of them. Children, as well as adults, have a tendency to live up to the expectations of others, or at least what these expectations are perceived to be. Preschool and primary-grade teachers are of tremendous importance in shaping children's basic attitudes toward themselves in relation to school. During the elementary years a significant correlation exists between children's perception of their teacher's feelings toward them and their own self-image. Teachers who place a great deal of emphasis and value on self-concept tend to be associated with students who hold a positive view of themselves. The use of such terms as "stupid," "dumb," "always wrong," "bad boy (girl)," "trouble-maker," and "lousy" all have a tremendous impact on children. These spoken words, as well as our unspoken indications of disapproval, dismay, disgust, anger, and surprise all have an affect on what children think others think of them. Given enough negative information the child soon learns the role that he feels is expected of him. Children with a negative self-image tend to live up to their perceived negative role. As a result a cycle of failure and perceived expectation of failure is established.

Children with a poor self-image often are very little cheered when now and then they do succeed. Their perception of themselves as nonachievers

[6] Holt, J. *What Do I Do Monday?*, New York: E. P. Dutton, 1970, p. 34.

and the idea that others perceive them in the same manner is a difficult cycle to break when success is infrequent. This may be explained with the analogy of the person who is usually sick and suddenly starts to feel well. Unlike the usually healthy person who thinks he will soon be well, the sick person thinks that this good feeling surely cannot last. It is much the same with children. Even when the normal pattern of failure is broken occasionally with success they still have the feeling that it cannot last and things will certainly go awry soon.

The influence of a poor self-concept on the learning process can be tremendous. Brookover concluded from his extensive research on self-concept and achievement "that the assumption that human ability is the most important factor in achievement is questionable, and that the student's attitudes limit the level of achievement in school.[7] The student's perception of himself as a "learner" or "nonlearner" often has an affect on low academic achievement. Lecky[8] demonstrated that low achievement is often due to the child's definition of himself as a nonlearner because he resists learning when it is inconsistent for him, in his or her view, to learn. Children who feel that they cannot achieve experience a situation in with their actual ability to achieve is reduced or negated. On the other hand, children with a success-oriented outlook find that they can plunge into a project or take on a new challenge with little past experience and more often than not be successful. Watternbeg and Clifford[9] reported that the best single predictor of beginning reading achievement was children's perceptions of themselves in kindergarten.

In summary, the consequences of a poor self-concept can be devastating. Children with a poor self-image often display little interest in their expanding world. They often fail deliberately and perform poorly as both a protective device and an attempt to live up to perceived expectations. Children with a poor self-concept are little cheered by occasional successes. They often view themselves as nonlearners and perform poorly academically while possessing average or above-average intelligence. The consequences of negative feelings toward oneself are tremendous. They are associated with high anxiety, underachievement, behavioral problems, learning difficulties, and delinquency. The establishment of a stable positive self-concept is too important to be left to chance. The role of movement in self-concept development must be reexamined. We must pay more than lip service to its develop-

[7] Brookover, W. B., E. L. Erikson, and L. M. Joiser, "Self Concept of Ability and School Achievement," U. S. Office of Education, Cooperative Research Project, No. 2831 East Lansing: Office of Research and Publication, Michigan State University, 1967.

[8] Lecky, P. *Self Consistency: A Theory of Personality,* New York: Island Press, 1945.

[9] Wattenberg, W. and C. Clifford, "Relationship of Self-Concept to Beginning Achievement in Reading," Final Report, Wayne State University CRP, No. 377, U.S. Office of Education, 1962.

ment in children. Statements such as the following made recently by the American Alliance of Health, Physical Education and Recreation, although admirable, are vague and provide little insight into how movement has an impact on the developing self:

> Another prime goal in all physical education instruction is the development of a strong self concept or feeling of respect for the mind and body, and confidence in one's ability to function effectively. Individuals who feel good about themselves—who are active and involved, who can act effective and with grace—are more at ease socially and more self-assured in whatever they try to do.[10]

THE INFLUENCE OF MOVEMENT ON SELF-CONCEPT

The way children feel about their bodies and the ease and efficiency with which they move plays an important role in the types of activity they actively seek to engage in. If children are able to handle their bodies well, to move with a degree of success, they will experience positive reinforcement of their self-image. Cratty feels that almost without exception the children who have difficulty handling their bodies have a poor self-concept.[11]

The playground, gymnasium, and play environment of children provide excellent media for positive self-concept development. Although it is certainly not the only way in which self-concept may be influenced, research is beginning to show clearly that it is a very basic one for most children. Little research has been conducted in the area of movement and self-concept. It has long been considered a "sloppy" area in which to do study, for a variety of reasons. First, it is difficult to isolate the possible variables that influence the self. Second, the criterion measures of self-concept that are used are often suspect in terms of their validity. Third, the manner of construction of numerous tests has often been "weird," according to McCandless.[12] Research in the area of movement and self-concept is now beginning to reflect a concern for these difficulties and dealing effectively with them within the scope of the particular investigation. Quality investigations into the effects of movement on the self-concept of preschool and primary-grade children is virtually nonexistent. The following paragraphs summarize some significant research done in this area with other populations of children. The

[10] American Alliance for Health, Physical Education and Recreation, *What Every Parent Should Know About the New Physical Education,* Washington, D. C. 1968, p. 3.

[11] Cratty, Bryant, J. *Social Dimensions of Physical Activity,* Englewood Cliffs, N. J.: Prentice–Hall, 1967.

[12] McCandless, Boyd R. *Children: Behavior and Development,* New York: Holt, Rinehart, and Winston, 1967, p. 259.

reader is cautioned to be careful in making generalizations from these populations to young children.

Wallace and Stuff[13] administered a perceptual–motor training program conducted by classroom teachers over a 1-year period for 30 minutes per day. The most frequently reported change by the teachers was in behavioral areas. The data from the rating scales that were dispensed revealed a significant positive change in self-concept.

Exceptional children were studied by Johnson et al.[14] in a clinical physical education program. A specially constructed self-concept scale was administered before and after the 6-week hour-per-day program. The results of the experiment revealed that the discrepancy between ideal self and actual self decreased in several areas. The children showed a greater desire to work in groups and an increased willingness to be with certain family members.

Clifford and Clifford[15] reviewed the effects of the Outward Bound Program in Colorado. The stated purpose of the program was to build physical stamina and push each individual to his physical limit. Self-concept measures dealing with ideal self (what I would like to be) and actual self (what I am) were administered before and after the month-long program. At the conclusion of the program the gap between ideal self and actual self scores were lessened, with a positive change occurring in the actual self-concept.

Collingswood and Willett,[16] working with obese teenage boys, found that a specially constructed gymnasium and swimming program had positive affects on self-concept. Post-session scores of self-image were significantly increased and the ideal self versus actual self discrepancy significantly decreased.

In a study to investigate the influence of competitive and noncompetitive programs of physical education on body image and self-concept, Read[17] found significant differences in self-concept scores between those identified as consistent winners and consistent losers. The subjects that were consistent winners had significantly higher self-concept scores than did the consistent losers. The subjects who were neither consistent winners nor losers did not drastically change in body image or self-concept.

[13] Wallace, Richard N. and John Stuff, "A Perceptual Program for Classroom Teachers, Some Results," *Genetic Psychology Monographs 87*: (2), 253–288, May 1973.

[14] Johnson, W. R., B. R. Fretz, and Julian A. Johnson, "Changes in Self-Concept During a Physical Education Program," *Research Quarterly 39*: (3), 560–565, October 1968.

[15] Clifford, Edward and Miairam Clifford, "Self Concepts Before and After Survival Training," *British Journal of Social and Clinical Psychology, 6* (4), 241–248, December 1967.

[16] Collingswood, Thomas B. and Leonard Willett, "The Effects of Physical Training Upon Self-Concept and Body Attitude," *Journal of Consulting Psychology 2* (7), 411–412, July 1971.

[17] Read, Donald G. "The Influence of Competitive–Non Competitive Programs of Physical Education on Body Image and Self Concept," Unpublished doctoral dissertation, Boston University, 1968.

The implications gleaned from these few but important studies are that well-conceived and properly implemented movement programs can have an affect on self-concept development. Yamamoto feels that for the teacher interested in learning the feelings of pupils toward themselves, a very good first step is in the observation of gross and fine motor performance in the gym, on the playground, in competitive games, and when writing.[18]

MOVEMENT AND THE DEVELOPING SELF

Children who have difficulty performing the many fundamental skills basic to proficient performance in games and sports encounter repeated failure in their everyday play experiences. As a result they often encounter difficulties in establishing a stable view of themselves as valuable worthy beings. The question now becomes a matter of: (1) what can we do and (2) how can we utilize the movement activities of children and aid them in the formation of a stable positive self-concept?

During the past 3 years this writer has conducted a motor-development program designed to make positive contributions to the self-concept of children from ages 4 to 10 years. The "Challenger's" program, as it is called, caters to children that are experiencing difficulty in their everyday play world. Approximately 60 percent of the children are referred to the program because of problems in school adjustment, peer relations, self-confidence, and emotional instability. The remaining 40 percent do not possess any apparent difficulties in these areas. The results of the informal research with the children have shown positive increases in self-concept as measured by the Piers–Harris self-concept scale in a significant majority of the children taking part in the 2-day-per-week program. Throughout the operation of the Challenger's program a concentrated effort has been made to apply common-sense principles through movement to the enhancement of the developing self. The following paragraphs are a delineation of these principles. A film strip was developed by the author through a grant from Phi Delta Kappa, Phi Lambda Theata, and Delta Kappa Gamma Education organizations depicting the effort of the Challenger's program in enhancing self-concept.[19]

Success

The most important thing that we can do is to help children develop a proper perspective on success and failure in their daily lives. Because of the

---

[18]Yamamoto, Kaoru. *The Child and His Image,* Boston: Houghton–Mifflin, 1972, p. 117.

[19] Gallahue, David L. (Educational Consultant). *Yes I Can! Movement and the Developing Self,* Bloomington, Indiana, Pidelphi Productions (Film strip), 1974.

egocentric nature of children it is very difficult for them to accept both success *and* failure. Success is that feeling of "I can," "I did it," or "look at me" that we love to see in children. It is the sense of accomplishment that accompanies mastering a new skill, executing a good move, or making a basket. Failure is that feeling of "I can't," "I don't know how," or "I am always wrong." It is the feeling of frustration and hopelessness that often follows failure to master a skill or execution of a poor move.

We need to help children develop a balance between success and failure. We need to bolster their sense of self-worth so that when things do go poorly and they do fail to achieve at something they will not be completely defeated. This backlog of successful experiences will help develop that "I can" attitude. Success is very important, particularly at the initial stages of learning. Each of us need only look at ourselves and our tendency to continue those activities we are successful in. This basic principle of learning theory is applicable to both children and adults. We need to take the importance of success into consideration when working with young children by using teaching methods that emphasize success.

The use of a problem-solving or movement-exploration approach to the learning of new movement skills enables all children to experiment and explore their movement potentialities. It enables the children to become involved in the *process* of learning rather than being solely concerned with the *product*. In other words, it is a child-centered approach that allows for a variety of solutions or "correct" answers. Both the teacher and the children are more concerned about individual solutions to the problem than finding one best way. The astute teacher of young children recognizes the fact that there are no single best ways of performing at this level of development. The astute teacher is more interested in helping children gain greater knowledge of their bodies, how they move, and fostering more mature patterns of movement. For example, the teacher may structure a problem or challenge such as "how can you balance on three body parts?" or "who can balance on three body parts?" The number of possible solutions is great and so is the range of difficulty. As a result several solutions are possible and all children are gaining increased knowledge of how they can move and balance their bodies. The teacher, through a question or challenge, also avoids imposing a predetermined model of what the performance should be and how it should look.

Individualizing instruction is also another way of emphasizing success for each child. Individualized instruction takes into account the uniqueness of each learner and provides all with opportunities to achieve at their own particular level of ability. Although it is often difficult to put into practice because of large classes, limited staff, time, and facilities, teachers should try to individualize whenever possible. The typical nursery-school program does a tremendous job of individualizing instruction through incorporation of an open-classroom approach with a variety of interest centers. Too often, however, upon entering the first or second grade classroom, children are faced with the rigid structure of the traditional classroom and gymnasium program that assumes all children to be at the same level in their interests, abilities, and motivation for learning. The unquestionable fact is that all children are not "typical" first-graders. Within any given class the children can be functioning at levels passing through both ends of the spectrum of that particular grade level in cognitive, affective, and psychomotor abilities. Greater attention to recognizing individual needs and interests and abilities will do much to strengthen the success potential of each child.

Traditional methods of teaching movement are valuable, especially at higher skill levels, but the teacher often requires that all students perform at a certain level or emulate a particular model of performance. Some children may have considerable difficulty accomplishing the desired level of performance. Teacher-dominated methods are often limited in providing success-oriented experiences for everyone. Although these methods should be a part of the movement activity program, they should not be stressed too early in the learning process. They should attempt to allow for individual differences in readiness, rates, and abilities for learning new movement skills.

Motor development programs that make use of problem-solving approaches and recognize the value of individualizing instruction whenever possible are making positive contributions to self-concept development. However what actually is involved in using these success-oriented approaches?

Through the use of developmentally appropriate movement experiences that are challenging and properly sequenced we can help children. We can also help in the formation of a good self-image by helping them establish reasonable expectations of their abilities and through communication of our expectations (see Figure 5.1).

Developmentally Appropriate Activities

We must recognize that children are not miniature adults ready to be programmed to the whims and wishes of adults. They are growing, developing, and emerging beings with a set of needs, interests, and capabilities that are quite different from those of adults. Too often we fall into the trap of trying to develop miniature athletes out of 6- and 7-year-olds without first developing the children's fundamental movement abilities. Too often we force children to specialize in the development of their movement abilities at an early age. They become involved in competitive athletics before they

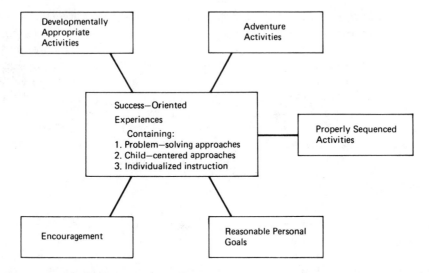

Figure 5.1 Five important factors to consider when utilizing success-oriented experiences to enhance self-concept developement.

are ready to handle the physical and emotional demands that competition can bring. Competition is not an evil or something to be excluded from the lives of children, but it must be kept within the proper perspective. Coaches and parents need to be fully cognizant of the children they are dealing with and the fact that winning is *not* everything, as proponents of that often quoted phrase, "winning isn't everything, it's the only thing," would have us believe. Parents and coaches must have as their objective the balanced, wholesome, and healthful development of children under wise leadership, through the avenue of competition. The needs, interests, and capabilities of each individual child must be carefully considered. Developmentally appropriate activites must be sought out as a means of aiding children in establishing a realistic concept of their abilities.

Adventure Activities

A second way in which we can have an impact on the self-concept of children is in the area of adventure or pseudodangerous activities. Children need to experience the thrill offered by climbing, balancing, and crawling through objects. They need the feeling of mastery that comes from succeeding at activities that challenge their courage and imagination. They need to experience the adventure of hanging by their knees, balancing on a beam, climbing a ladder, riding a horse, or crawling through a tunnel.

Activities must be geared to the development level of the child.

The teacher, through voice inflection and the use of the child's imagination, can also help to create an atmosphere of challenge and adventure. Imaginary obstacles may be put in the path of successful completion of an activity. Such things as "sharks" beneath the balance beam which has been transformed into a "narrow log" across a "shark-infested pond" or a story play depicting a bear hunt, or trip to the circus, stimulate children's imaginations. Through adventure-type activities, both real and imagined, children have an opportunity to learn more about their own bodies and the thrill of successfully overcoming a challenge.

Sequencing of Tasks

A third factor involved in using a success oriented approach to enhancing self-concept is the sequencing and difficulty of a movement task. The proper sequencing of movement activities is of crucial importance in determining a child's sense of success or failure. For example, it seems perfectly logical to first learn a tripod or frog stand followed by a headstand, and then to a

Adventure activities are important in self-concept development.

handstand rather than proceeding in the reverse order. Yet we often do just that when as adults we try to make miniature athletes out of 6- and 7-year old children. Too often parents and teachers neglect the development of fundamental movement abilities before proceeding to higher-level skills. Instead of looking at the development of movement skills from the point of view of the child, we all too often look at movement from our point of view, namely athletes. We skip the basics and go directly to high-level skill development. It is much better to begin at a lower level where the chances for experiencing success are greater and then proceed to develop skill upon skill in a logical sequential progression. Success at the initial stages of learning will not only encourage continued performance, but will have a tendency to generate success at later stages. Children who attempt a difficult task without the proper basic skills may not succeed and may give up entirely. It is important that we analyze movement activities that children engage in and determine logical sequences for accomplishing them.

Exactly scorable tasks such as archery or bowling may be difficult to deal with in the initial stages of learning unless modifications and provisions are made for success-oriented experiences. Cratty[20] states that "tasks which have performance limits, e.g., a bullseye in archery, will be more likely to produce feelings of failure when projected goals are not achieved." It would be better, in archery for example, to eliminate the target during the initial stages of learning, or to enlarge it or move it closer in order to maximize the opportunities for success.

Caution should also be taken not to introduce competition too early in the learning process. Because competition necessitates there being a winner and a loser, it gives too accurate an indication of relative success or failure during the early phases of learning. It may be better to postpone competitive situations until the child can make a sound appraisal of his ability.

Reasonable Expectations

A fourth area in which we can have an influence on children's developing self is helping them establish reasonable expectations of their abilities. This is especially true with young children because of their black and white world of good or bad, right or wrong, that allows little room for anything but these two extremes. It is important that we help children develop an attitude about personal success that is based on the extent to which they feel they have reached some goal, and not on the absolute scores obtained. Children need to learn how to set reasonable goals for themselves, and we can help them, by providing goals that are not so high that their obtainment is unrealistic, but high enough to ensure quality effort and a reasonable chance for success. For example, lowering the basketball goal or reducing the size of the ball will provide children with more opportunities for success rather than insisting on the use of a regulation ball and putting the standard at the regulation 10-foot height. It must be remembered, however, that once reasonable success through quality effort is ensured, new goals need to be established. This must be done in order to keep the activity challenging. Frost reinforces this statement by stating that "when tasks are too easy and success too cheap little development takes place. When tasks are too difficult and achievement impossible, frustration and reinforcement of a negative self-concept are likely to follow."[21]

[20] Cratty, Bryant J. *Psychology and Physical Activity.* Englewood Cliffs, N. J.: Prentice–Hall, 1968, p. 30.

[21] Frost, Reuben B. "Physical Education and Self-Concept," *Journal of Physical Education,* 36, January 1972.

Encouragement

A fifth area of influence that we have on the developing self is through communication of *our expectation* to the child. We must communicate how we feel about the child's accomplishments. Self-concept development is based in part on what we think others think of us. For children these significant "others" center around the home and school. It is important to use positive encouragement in order to communicate our feelings about their accomplishments, whether they be large or small. Praise and positive encouragement must be used judiciously because children will soon "read" it as being meaningless if it is inappropriately used. We can communicate our feelings to children by praise for a job well done with a pat on the back or a smile. We need to communicate the feeling of "you are loved" and "you are worthwile." One way to encourage these feelings is to recognize that it is often not so much what we say to children that influences their feelings about themselves as it is the way in which we treat them. Children value themselves to the degree that they are valued. The way we feel about our children actually builds in (or builds out) self-confidence and a sense of self-worth. Children build their picture of themselves from the words, attitudes, body language, and judgment of those around them.

By providing children with a nurturing climate of acceptance and experiences of success, negative attitudes can be changed to high self-esteem. It is important that when we do make a specific statement about something that disturbs us or that we do not like about a child's behavior, we should restrict our comments to the *behavior* instead of making generalized criticisms of the child *as a person.* For example, it is much better to say "I am worried about your difficulties with sharing" rather than "nobody likes a stingy person." Simarilarly, it is dangerous to label children as "stupid," "bad," or "motor moron." They often believe the labels that are attached to them and inadvertently act out their expected role. We should not link personal lack of worth with undesirable behavior. We should not make children feel that they are personally worthless just because their schoolwork, sports abilities, or something else does not meet our expectations.

There is no place for devastating remarks in teacher–child communication. A professional teacher shuns comments that casually destroy children's self-concept, The teacher's role is not to injure but to prevent injury and to heal. Positive encouragement on the playground, in the classroom, and at home plays an important role in helping children develop a stable positive self-concept.

CONCLUSION

Self-concept is an important aspect of the affective development of children. The concept that children have of themselves is based on their feelings about themselves and what they think others think of them. Their self-concept is in the developmental stages and profoundly influenced by all that happens to them is their daily life experiences. It is important that we as teachers and parents make an effort to ensure the development of a positive stable self-concept in our children, because once it is firmly established it becomes increasingly difficult to make radical changes. Combs and Snygg alluded to the stability of self-concept beyond its developmental stages:

> Once established in a given personality, the perceived self has a high degree of stability. The phenomenal self with the self-concept as its core represents our fundamental frame of reference, our anchor to reality; and even an unsatisfactory self-organization is likely to prove highly stable and resistant to change. This stability has been repeatedly demonstrated in modern research.[22]

Because of the importance of vigorous play in the lives of children and the high positive value placed on physical ability by children and adults, movement can serve as an important facilitator of a positive self-concept. We must, however, be sure to apply sound principles of growth and development to this important task. We need to provide children with *success-oriented experiences* that minimize the failure potential.

In order to do this we must be sure to employ *developmentally appropriate movement experiences* that are within the ability level of the individual. We must be sure that the learning of new movement tasks is *properly sequenced,* based on sound progressions from the simple to the complex. We must also help children *establish reasonable goals* for their performance within the limits of their abilities. We must be sure also to provide *positive encouragement* and to incorporate *adventure activities* into their lives.

Although movement is only one avenue by which a positive self-concept may be fostered, we must recognize that it is an important one for most children. The development of a positive self-concept is too important to be left to chance and we must do all that we can to assure its proper development.

SUGGESTED READINGS

Ames, Louise B., C. Gillespie, and John W. Streff, *Stop School Failure,* New York: Harper, 1972.
Briggs, Dorothy C. *Your Child: Self Esteem,* New York: Doubleday, 1970.

[22] Combs, Arthur W., and Snygg, Donald *Individual Behavior,* New York: Harper and Nov, 1959, p. 130.

Cratty, Bryant J. *Psychology and Physical Activity,* Englewood Cliffs, N. J.: Prentice–Hall, 1968.

Curry, Nancy L. "Self Concept and the Educational Experience in Physical Education," *The Physical Educator 31* (3), 116–119, 1974.

Felker, Donald W. *Building Positive Self-Concept,* Minneapolis: Burgess, 1974.

Fredelle, Maynard. *Guiding Your Child to a More Creative Life,* New York: Doubleday, 1973.

Frost, Reuben B. "Physical Education and Self-Concept," *Journal of Physical Education,* 35–37, January 1972.

Gallahue, David L. (Educational Consultant). *Yes I Can! Movement Experiences and the Developing Self,* Bloomington, Indiana, Phidelphi Publications (film strip), 1974.

Ginott, Haim G. *Teacher and Child,* New York: MacMillan, 1972.

Gordon, Ira J. "Children's Views of Themselves," *Association for Childhood Education International,* June 1971.

Holt, John. *What Do I Do Today?,* New York: E. P. Dutton, 1970.

Wallace, Richard N. and John Stuff, "A Perceptual Program for Classroom Teachers, Some Results," *Genetic Psychology Monographs, 87* (2), 253–288, May 1973.

Wylie, Ruth. *The Self Concept,* Lincoln, Nebraska: Nebraska U. P., 1961.

Yamamoto, Kaoru. *The Child and His Image,* Boston; Houghton–Mifflin, 1972.

Chapter 6

Individualized Movement Experiences for Enhancing Fundamental Movement Abilities

CONTENTS

Introduction
Methods of Instruction
Qualities of Movement
General Objectives
Activity Ideas for Enhancing Stability Abilities
  Problem Solving Stability Activities
    Specific Objectives
    Movement Experiences
  Stability Activities with Small Equipment
    Specific Objectives
    Movement Experiences
  Stability Activities with Large Equipment
    Specific Objectives
    Movement Experiences
Activity Ideas for Enhancing Locomotor Abilities
  Problem Solving Locomotor Activities
    Specific Objectives
    Movement Experiences
  Locomotor Activities with Small Equipment
    Specific Objectives
    Movement Experiences
Activity Ideas for Enhancing Manipulative Abilities
  Problem Solving Manipulative Activities
    Specific Objectives
    Movement Experiences

Manipulative Activities with Small Equipment
   Specific Objectives
   Movement Experiences
Suggested Readings
Suggested Records

To Move is to Be
JoAnn Seeker

INTRODUCTION

Although the activity ideas found in this and subsequent chapters are grouped according to their emphasis on a specific attribute of motor development, no movement experience in actuality contributes to only one aspect of movement behavior. On the contrary, the activity ideas found in this chapter and in the chapters to follow may contribute to a variety of developmental abilities. Equal emphasis may be given to more than one area at a time. For example, when exploring a variety of locomotor movements to the accompaniment of music we are in fact working in the areas of movement abilities (fundamental locomotor movements), rhythmic abilities (creative rhythms), and perceptual–motor development (temporal awareness and spatial awareness). As a result the wise teacher will carefully examine each activity in terms of its specific objectives and its contribution to the totality of the psychomotor, cognitive, and affective domains. Care should be taken not to reduce one's view on the scope of the potential contribution of any activity and to look at each activity in the context of its total potential contribution to the growth and development of the child.

The movement activities contained in this chapter are designed specifically to enhance children's fundamental movement abilities in the areas of stability, locomotion, and manipulation respectively. When working with preschool-age children it is generally wise to deal with specific skills (running, jumping, throwing, catching, etc.) in isolation prior to combining them with other skills into two or three part activities. In this way attention may be first focused on a particular pattern of movement, and then as the children begin to develop and refine this pattern it can be elaborated upon in such a way as to be beneficial in enhancing their adaptability to a variety of new movement situations.

METHODS OF INSTRUCTION

Through the use of a *movement exploration* approach the children have an opportunity to experiment with the movement task at hand under the careful guidance and verbal direction of the teacher. Movement problems or challenges are structured by the teacher and the children respond in the manner that they interpret these challenges. Each child is free to explore and no reasonable solution to the problem is rejected. The teacher *does not* establish a model for performance by demonstrating the correct solution of the problem. An exploratory approach, although time consuming and often limited in developing high degrees of movement skill, recognizes the individuality of each learner and permits them to solve movement problems within their own ability level.

It is suggested that with children an exploratory approach be utilized at the initial stages of involvement and learning of any new movement skill. It is, however, further recommended that both a *combination approach* and *traditional approach* be incorporated during subsequent and later stages of learning. The reason for this is that as children being to develop a level of proficiency in a given movement they will need problems and challenges stated in such a way that they lead to more efficient performance at a higher level.

The combination approach is one in which both the attributes of movement exploration (an indirect method) and the traditional method of teaching (a direct method) are combined into a workable whole. When utilizing a combination approach in the development of movement abilities the teacher first begins with loosely structured movement problems or challenges and as with the exploratory approach, children are permitted to solve these problems as they see fit. Now, however, the teacher gradually narrows down the response possibilities through the careful structuring of problems and challenges. In this manner the children are being exposed to the virtues of movement exploration: (1) individualization of instruction, (2) emphasis on involvement in the process of learning, and (3) success-oriented instruction. They are also being exposed to specific skill instruction: (1) quick and efficient means of presenting material, (2) emphasis on the product or performance level of learning, (3) ease of implementation, and (4) demonstration of correct performance. The children are exposed to a wide variety of movement situations and are continually challenged by the restructuring and rephrasing of questions. They are given an opportunity to view models of the product of their problem-solving through demonstrations of fellow students and/or the teacher. They are not, however, fully exposed to the "watch me," "do as I do" aspects of the traditional or direct method of teaching. Through use of an ecclectic combination approach to the teaching of movement patterns the children are encouraged to experiment and explore the movement potentialities of their bodies and are ensured of achieving a reasonable degree of success commensurate with their development level.

Qualities of Movement

Prior to implementing the movement activities contained in the following pages one should have a thorough understanding of the meanings and implications of the *qualities of movement.* The qualities of movement outlined below were originally proposed by Laban[1] and have since gained wide

---

[1]Laban, Rudolph. *Gymnastik und tang,* Oldenburg, Germany: Gerhard Stallings, Verlag, 1926.

acceptance by movement educators throughout Europe and North America. They offer an endless variety of opportunities for creative expressive movement in the performance of stability, locomotor, and manipulative movements.

1. FORCE is the degree of muscular tension required to move the body or its parts from place to place or to maintain its equilibrium. Force may be heavy or light or fall somewhere in between these two extremes.
2. TIME is the speed at which movement takes place. The movement may be fast or slow, erratic or sustained, gradual or sudden.
3. FLOW is the continuity or coordination of movements. Flow may be smooth or jerky, free or bound.
4. SPACE is the area that the body occupies as it moves through the environment. Space refers to the *levels, ranges,* and *directions* in which the body may move. The body level may be large, small, high, medium, or low. Its range may be wide, narrow, far, near, long, or short. Its direction may be forward, backward, sideward, diagonal, or form a straight, zig-zag, or curvy floor pattern.
5. ENVIRONMENT comprises of the actual sensations that the body or its parts directly experience. Different *surfaces, textures,* and *equipment* are utilizied. Wood, concrete, grass, water, and Astroturf are examples of different surfaces. Leather, plastic, rubber and the trampoline, balance beam, and jungle gym are examples of various textures and equipment in the environment.[2]

General Objectives

The general objectives of the movement experiences contained in the following pages are listed below. It must be remembered, however, that there is a great deal of overlap in these experiences with regard to the various psychomotor, cognitive, and affective contributions that they make to the growth and development of children; in order to enhance children's performance in a variety of fundamental: (1) stability abilities, (2) locomotor abilities, and (3) manipulative abilities.

ACTIVITY IDEAS FOR ENHANCING STABILITY ABILITIES

The development and refinement of basic stability abilities is the most fundamental aspect of learning to move. For without the ability to maintain

[2] Gallahue, David L., Peter H. Werner, and George C. Luedke, *A Conceptual Approach to Movement and Learning,* New York: Wiley, 1975, p. 18 (used with permission).

one's equilibrium, purposeful locomotor and manipulative movements are impossible. Preschool and primary-grade children who are exposed to a variety of movement situations generally develop stability abilities with little difficulty. On the other hand, children who do not have a varied background of movement experiences often lag behind in the development of their stability abilities.

When we use the term "stability," it goes beyond the notion of static and dynamic balance. Stability requires "the ability to sense a shift in the relationship of the body parts which alter one's balance . . . along with the ability to compensate rapidly and accurately for these changes with appropriate compensating movements."[3] Therefore stability encompasses non-locomotor or axial movements as they are often called, as well as static and dynamic body positions in which a *premium* is placed on the maintenance of equilibrium.

PROBLEM SOLVING STABILITY ACTIVITIES

Although the rudimentary stability abilities of infancy (control of the head, neck, and trunk; sitting and standing) are primarily maturationally determined, it would be a mistake to assume that the same is true with the development of fundamental stability abilities. Young children need exposure to a variety of movement situations in which they have ample opportunity to explore and experiment with the movement dimension of stability. The activities contained in the following pages are dedicated to that end.

Specific Objectives

1. To enhance nonlocomotor movement abilities.
2. To enhance dynamic balance.
3. To enhance static balance.
4. To develop increased abilities to gain and maintain one's equilibrium.

Movement Experiences

BENDING Bending involves bringing one body part to another with a curling action produced by the body's parts. The following is a sampling of problem-solving activities involving bending:

1. How many ways can you bend?

[3]Ibid.

Can you touch the ground with three body parts?

2. How many parts of your body can you bend down?
3. Bend the parts of your body up that you can.
4. Can you bend parts of your body when you are: (1) sitting down, (2) lying on your front, (3) lying on your back, (4) lying on your side, (5) kneeling, and (6) walking?
5. How many ways can you bend your head? What parts of your body can you touch by bending your head?
6. How many different ways can you bend your arms, wrist, fingers, legs, knees, ankles, and toes?
7. Can you bend up and down at the same time?
8. Can you bend to one side, to the other?

9. Can you connect parts of your body by hooking them together at the bends? Can you do that with a partner?
10. Can you make yourself smaller by bending?

STRETCHING Stretching is an unfolding motion at the joints. Stretching involves moving the joints in such a manner that there is a marked upward, outward, or downward movement of the body parts (extension). Stretching is the opposite of bending.

1. How many parts of your body can you stretch?
2. Can you stretch your arms up, down, and to the sides?
3. How far up can you stretch? (How tall can you make yourself?)
4. How wide can you make your arms, hands, and legs? (e.g., how big can you make your arms?)
5. How many different ways (directions) can your body stretch at the same time?
6. How much of the floor can you cover by stretching?
7. Can you make two parts of your body touch by stretching?
8. Can you combine stretching and bending movements to show how they differ?

TWISTING Twisting involves rotation of one body part in relation to another. The body parts are turned in opposite directions or partially rotated while the remainder of the body remains in a fixed position.

1. Can you twist your head without using anything else?
2. Can you twist your shoulders without moving your waist?
3. Can you twist the whole top part of your body and then the whole bottom part of the body?
5. Can you twist your arms, wrists, legs, ankles, fingers, and toes?
6. Can you twist your arms around each other? Can you twist your legs around each other? Can you twist your arms and legs around each other ?
7. Can you twist like a screwdriver?
8. Can you twist while standing on one foot? Can you twist while lying on your back, side, and front?
9. Can you twist the same body parts as a partner that is facing you?
10. Can you do the twist to music (fast or slow)?

TURNING Turning is a movement in which the entire body revolves around its vertical or horizontal axis while in an extended or flexed position. The head serves as the controlling factor for the body.

1. Can you turn your body to make a circle?

2. Can you turn and make half a circle?
3. Can you turn quickly? Can you turn slowly? Change the position of your arms what happens to your turn?
4. Can you turn without moving your head? Can you turn your head without moving your body?
5. Lying on the floor, how many different ways can you turn?
6. Kneeling on the floor, how many ways can you turn? Can your hands help?
7. Bend and turn your body to the right, to the left? Is one way easier?

SWINGING Swinging is a pendular motion in which one end of the body remains fixed while the other parts move freely back and forth, forming an arc.

1. How many parts of your body can you swing? Can you swing them in different directions?
2. Can you swing quickly? Can you swing slowly?
3. Swing one arm and one leg. Can you swing them in different directions?
4. Can you swing your body at different levels, standing up, and bending over?
5. Can you swing from a bar? How do your legs help?
6. Can you swing from a bar and drop off at the end of the arc?
7. Can you travel on a horizontal ladder while hanging and swinging?
8. Can you swing from a bar and drop off at the front part of your swing?

DODGING Dodging is a movement in which the body is moved quickly in a direction other than the original line of movement.

1. How can you get out of the way of a ball that is coming right at you? Can you do it by stretching, Bending, or jumping?
2. Can you dodge (change direction) with feet close together, wide apart, or on one foot? Which is easier?
3. Can you dodge as high as you can, then as low as you can?
4. Can you run and change directions when I clap?
5. Can you dodge around an obstacle (chair, cones, other students, etc.)?
6. Look into a large mirror and practice dodging.
7. Can you face a partner and move laterally or forward and backward in the direction she/he points?
8. Can you dodge a partner that is trying to tag you?

LANDING Landing is a movement that requires the individual to regain balance after a brief flight in the air. The force is taken on the balls of the feet, and ankles, knees, and hip joint bend upon impact.

1. How many ways can you land after jumping?

2. Can you land all the time without falling down?
3. Can you land with your feet together, apart? Which is easier?
4. Can you land without bending? Is it easier to bend?
5. Can you land and regain your balance with your arms at your sides, out straight, or up in the air? Which is easier?
6. Can you land on one foot and regain your balance?
7. Can you land on your feet and hands?
8. Can you make a turn in the air before landing?

STOPPING Stopping involves coming to a halt with the feet in a stride position and the knees slightly bent.

1. Run and then "freeze" with your arms, legs, and other body parts in various positions.
2. Run and stop when I clap.
3. How many positions can your feet be in when you stop? Which is the easiest?
4. Stop on your whole foot, on the toes, and on the heels.
5. Run with a partner and stop on command.
6. Play a game of red light–green light.

ROLLING Rolling involves moving through space in either a forward, backward, or sideward direction while the body is momentarily inverted. Rolling is considered to be a stability movement because of the premium placed on maintaining one's equilibrium.

1. How many ways can you roll (forward, backward, or sideward)?
2. Can you make yourself small and roll, or big and roll?
3. Can you roll with straight legs, bent legs, and legs apart?
4. Can you change your arm, leg, head, or body position when you finish your roll?
5. Can you stand up after your roll? Can you stand up and turn around after your roll?
6. Can you roll with a playground ball in your hand?
7. Can you perform consecutive rolls?
8. Can you roll in unison with a partner?
9. Can you combine forward, backward, and sideward rolls into a routine?

UPRIGHT SUPPORTS

Upright supports are static balance activities in which the body is required to balance in a variety of positions while the center of gravity remains stationary.

1. Can you balance on different body parts (feet, knees, seat, back, and front)?
2. Can you balance on different objects (see following section)?
3. Can you balance at different levels? Which is easiest or hardest? Why?
4. Can you balance with your eyes closed?
5. Can you balance with a partner?
6. Can you balance with various objects (see following section)?

INVERTED SUPPORTS   Inverted supports involve supporting the body in an upside-down position for at least 3 seconds. An inverted support is generally considered to be one in which the shoulders are above the base of support and the feet and legs above the shoulders.

1. Can you find ways to balance with your feet above your shoulders?
2. Can you perform a tripod (head and hands form a tripod and balance the body in a tucked position)?
3. Can you perform a tip-up (from a squat position, the elbows push out on the knees as the body tips forward and balances)?
4. Can you balance on your head and hands (headstand)?
5. Can you find different ways to do a headstand?
6. How many different ways can you balance in an inverted position?

Stability Activities With Small Equipment

There are a variety of pieces of small equipment that may be used to enhance stability abilities. Although some of this equipment (i.e., beanbags and ropes) is generally associated with manipulative and locomotor activities, it is possible to design numerous activities that place a great deal of emphasis on stability. The activity ideas that follow are a mere sampling of the almost endless variety possible. Keep in mind that it is important to first identify the specific movement abilities you desire to enhance and then to select appropriate activities, rather than proceeding in the reverse order.

Specific Objectives

1. To enhance fundamental stability abilities.
2. To enhance static balance abilities.
3. To enhance dynamic balance abilities.

Movement Experiences

BALANCE BOARDS   Balance boards are easily constructed and offer a variety of challenging activities. For young children a mat should be placed under the balance board to avoid slipping.

1. Balance on the board any way you can.
2. Can you balance with your feet apart?
3. Can you balance with your feet together?
4. Can you balance with your arms out from the side?
5. Can you balance with your arms at your sides?

The balance board is an excellent piece of equipment for enhancing static balance.

6. Can you balance with your eyes closed?
7. Can you squat down and balance?
8. Can you squat half-way down and balance?
9. Can you balance with a beanbag or eraser on your head?
10. Can you balance and catch a ball?
11. Can you toss a ball while balancing?
12. Can you throw at a target while balancing?
13. Can you balance on one foot?
14. Can you bounce a ball while balancing?
15. Can you touch various body parts while balancing?

16. Can you step from one balance board to another?
17. Can you balance with a partner on another board while holding hands?
18. Can you toss and catch a ball while balancing?
19. Can you turn around on the board?

BALANCE BLOCKS

Balance blocks may be cut to various sizes depending on the age and ability level of the children; they should be about 12 inches long and made out of 4 feet by 4 feet, 2 feet by 2 feet or 2 feet by 4 feet sections of board. They should be placed on a surface that is not slippery.

1. Can you balance on both feet?
2. Can you balance on one foot?
3. Can you touch various body parts while balancing?
4. Can you balance at various levels?
5. Can you balance and catch a ball?
6. Can you balance and bounce a ball?
7. Can you balance and toss and catch a ball to yourself?
8. Can you balance with a partner?
9. Can you turn around while balancing?
10. Can you find new ways to balance?

COFFEE-CAN STILTS

Coffee can stilts are easily made from metal coffee containers and a length of rope. They offer a new dimension to stability because the center of gravity is raised, thus making balancing more difficult.

1. Can you walk in various directions (forward, sideward, and backward)?
2. Can you step over a low object?
3. Can you step under objects?
4. Can you walk at various levels (high, low, and medium)?
5. Can you walk at various speeds?
6. Can you hop on one foot?
7. Can you jump forward?
8. Can you have races on the coffee can stilts?
9. Can you move a disk forward while walking on the stilts?

BARRELS

Barrels may be obtained from a janitorial supply company or oil distributor. They make an excellent piece of equipment for enhancing dynamic balance abilities and serve as containers for storing equipment. They must be closely supervised, however.

1. Can you sit on the barrel and balance?
2. Can you balance on your stomach, back, or knees?
3. Can you stand on the barrel and balance
4. Can you balance at different levels?
5. Can you touch various body parts while balancing?
6. Can you walk on the barrel, moving it forward or backward?
7. Can you stand on the barrel and bounce and catch a ball?
8. Can you and a partner balance on the barrel in any of the above ways?

WANDS

Wands can be easily made from ¾-foot dowling cut to 4-foot lengths. A variety of balance principles may be illustrated with wands as well as numerous challenging activities.

1. Can you balance the wand on the floor horizontally, then vertically? Which is easiest, or hardest? Why?
2. Can you balance your wand vertically, clap your hands, and grab it before it falls to the ground?
3. Can you run around your wand while it is balancing and catch it before falling to the ground?
4. Can you balance the wand horizontally on a variety of body parts (palm of hand, finger, foot, and forehead)?
5. Can you balance your wand vertically on a variety of body parts?
6. What do your eyes do when balancing the wand? Where do they look?
7. Can you move about while balancing your wand on various body parts?
8. Can you balance your wand while moving from a standing to a sitting position?
9. Who can balance their wand the longest?
10. Can you balance your wand either horizontally or vertically and transfer it from one body part to another?

BALANCE ROPES

When placed on the floor, ropes can serve as a simple means of developing knowledge about balancing without any fear on the part of the child. When balancing on ropes the children should perform in their bare feet in order to enhance the tactile stimulation. The ropes may be placed in a variety of configuarations and you may wish to heighten the interest by developing an appropriate story play such as one about a high-wire walker at the circus.

1. Can you walk in various directions (forward, backward, and sideward)?
2. Can you walk at various levels (high, medium, and low)?
3. Can you walk and step over objects?
4. Can you walk and step under objects?
5. Can you step from one rope to another?
6. Can you jump from one rope to another?
7. Can you walk the rope with your eyes closed?
8. Can you find new ways to walk and balance on the rope?

Inner tubes are an excellent means for developing dynamic balance.

INNER TUBES   Inner tubes may be obtained from tire-salvage stores. Use large truck tubes or airplane inner tubes if possible. Be sure to secure the valve and stem of each inner tube prior to use in order to avoid any safety hazards.

1. Can you walk around the tube?
2. Can you move in different directions, levels, and at different speeds while walking around the tube?
3. Can you jump up and down on the tube (spot carefully)?
4. Can you jump onto the tube, jump into the center, jump back on, and then off the opposite side?
5. Can you repeat the above activity using different variations?
6. Can you sit on the tube and bounce?
7. Can you balance on the tube while someone is bouncing it?
8. Can you do a knee bounce on the tube? From a standing position near the tube bounce, on the knees, returning to a controlled standing position. Repeat three or four times.
9. Can you do a feet bounce? From a standing position on the tube,

bounce on both feet, bending the knees slightly. To obtain height, raise the arms forward and upward. Do this at first with a spotter holding the wrist. Do in a series.

10. Can you do a seat drop? Stand 1–2 feet away from the tube with your back to the tube. Kick your legs out, landing on your seat supported by the hands near hips. Bounce back to a standing position.
11. Can you bounce with a partner? Partners, holding hands, stand on top of the tube facing each other. Partners bounce on both feet all the way around the tube to the right and then to the left.

BEANBAGS

Although generally thought of as a manipulative piece of equipment, beanbags serve as an excellent piece of equipment for enhancing stability abilities. Among the numerous possibilities for activity are the following:

1. What does it feel like? What is inside?
2. Can you drop it and pick it up without moving your feet?
3. Can you drop it and pick it up without bending your knees?
4. Can you drop it so you must stretch to pick it up? Without moving your feet?
5. Can you move it around your body without dropping it?
6. How many ways can you balance while the beanbag is on one part of your body, then on another part?
7. Can you keep it balanced while you are moving around the room?
8. Can you move the beanbag from one place to another and not drop it?
9. Can you move it with other parts of your body?
10. Can you move it from your feet to your hands?
11. Can you move it from your feet to your head, then shoulder?
12. Can you balance your beanbag on a body part and exchange it to the same body part on your partner without using your hands?

Stability Activities With Large Equipment

At the preschool and primary-grade levels the use of large equipment is often limited the cost of commerically purchased apparatus often makes it prohibitive for nursery and elementary schools to purchase traditional gymnastic equipment such as side horses, parallel bars, and turning bars. There are, however, a number of pieces of equipment particularly beneficial to young children. Some may be handmade but others must be purchased commercially. Among these pieces of equipment are the balance beam, benches, bounding board, trampoline, horizontal ladder, and "lind climber." The following is a compilation of numerous activities utilizing large equipment appropriate for use with preschool and primary-grade children.

Specific Objectives

1. To enhance fundamental stability abilities on a variety of large equipment.
2. To enhance dynamic balance abilities on a variety of large equipment.

Movement Experiences

BALANCE BEAM   The balance beam is an extremely useful piece of equipment. It may be purchased commercially or made in a variety of ways for only a few dollars.

1. Walking on a single beam:
   a. Walking forward and backward with arms at different positions (held forward, sideways, overhead, behind back, on head, etc.).
   b. Side-step with hands in various positions. Use for closing steps, crossing front and rear, alternating crossing.
   c. Walk forward, backward, using follow steps.
   d. Move forward with one step for halfway; complete the trip with another step.
   e. Perform dip walks from one end of the beam to the other.
   f. Walk forward and backward to middle of the beam, kneel on one knee; straighten leg forward until the heel is on the beam and knee is straight. Rise and walk to the end of the beam.
   g. Hop forward and backward on right or left foot the full length of beam. Variations: hop the length of the beam, then turn around and hop back. Hop to the middle of the beam, turn around on same foot, and hop backward to the end of the beam.
   h. Walk to the middle of the beam, balance on one foot, and walk backward to the end of the beam.
   i. Walk to the middle of the beam left sideways, turn around and walk to the other end right sideways.

The balance beam is a versatile piece of equipment.

j. With arms clasped about the body in the rear, walk forward to the middle, turn around once, and walk backward the remaining distance.

k. Place an eraser at the middle of the beam, walk out to it, kneel on one knee, place the eraser on top of the head, rise, turn around, and walk backward to the end of the beam. Variations: kneel on one knee, pick up the eraser, and place it on the beam behind the pupil, rise, and continue to the end. Walk beam left sideways, pick up the eraser, place it on the right side of the beam, turn around, and walk right sideways to the end of the beam.

l. Walk the beam backward with an eraser balanced on the back of each hand. At the center, turn around and walk backward to the end of the beam.

m. Walk to the middle of the beam, do a right-side or left-side support, rise, and walk to the end.

n. Walk to the middle of the beam, do a balance standing on one foot, arms held sideways with the trunk and free leg held horizontally.

o. Hold the wand 15 inches above the beam. Balance an eraser on the head, walk forward, backward, and sideways right or left, stepping over the wand.

p. Have the wand held at a height of 3 feet. Walk forward and backward with hands on the hips, and pass under it.

q. Fold a piece of paper at a right angle so it will stand on the beam at the middle. Walk to the paper, kneel, do a right-side or left-side support, pick it up with teeth, rise, and walk to the end of the beam.

r. Walk the beam forward, backward, and sideways, left or right, with the eyes closed.

s. Stand on the beam (feet side by side, one foot in advance of the other, on right or left foot) with the eyes closed.

t. Partners start at opposite ends, walk to the middle, pass each other, and continue to the end of the beam.

2. Partners on two parallel beams:

a. Walk forward, inside hands joined. Walk backward.
b. Walk sideways with both hands joined.
c. Walk sideways with both hands joined, using grapevine step.
d. Alternate crossing feet behind and in front while stepping.
e. Toss and catch a ball while balancing on the beam.

3. Throwing, catching, bouncing:

a. Roll a volleyball or playground ball across the beam.
b. Bounce the ball across
c. Dribble the ball across. Bend low for short dribbles.
d. Pass and receive from a partner at the head of the beam.
e. Hit the ball back to a partner.

BENCHES

Many schools have benches as part of their standard equipment. They may be used in a number of ways to enhance stability abilities.

1. Can you walk on the bench:

a. Forward, backward, sideways?
b. On hands and feet (cat walk)?
c. Duck walk.

    d. Using beanbag on the head for balancing.

    e. Boonce and toss a ball.

    f. Pass a partner without touching each other.

2. From a lying position, can you:

    a. Pull your body along, with your arms while in a prone position?

    b. From a back-lying position, balance with the body crosswise to the bench?

    c. From the above balance position, roll lengthwise along the bench?

3. From a sitting position on the bench can you:

    a. Swing on the seat?

    b. Sitting astride, reach as far sideways as possible to touch the floor without falling off?

    c. Support your weight on your hands?

4. Can you vault over the bench?
5. Can you do a forward roll on the bench?
6. Can you do a backward roll to a straddle seat on the bench?
7. Can you find many more ways to move and balance on the bench?

HORIZONTAL LADDER

An old wooden ladder makes an ideal piece of equipment for enhancing stability abilities. Here are some appropriate activities for use with young children.

1. From a position on the side supports can you:

    a. Walk forward?

    b. Walk backward?

    c. Bounce a ball between the rungs while walking?

    d. Walk forward on one support?

    e. Walk backward on one support?

    f. Walk sideways on one support using a step–close–step, or crossover step?

2. From a position on the rungs can you:

    a. Walk forward?
    b. Walk sideways using a follow step?
    c. Walk sideways using a crossover step?
    d. Walk backwards?

3. From a position between the rungs can you:

    a. Walk forward?
    b. Walk sideways using a follow step?
    c. Walk sideways using a crossover step?
    d. Walk backwards?

HORIZONTAL LADDER
(suspended)

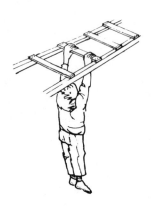

North American youth are often weak in the upper arms and shoulder girdle. Practice in activities on a suspended horizontal ladder are excellent for developing these groups of muscles. The following is a list of suggested activities that may be performed on a horizontal ladder, turning bar, or parallel bars.

1. Can you grab hold of one of the rungs with your thumbs around the bar and hang for 5 seconds?
2. Can you swing forward and backward?
3. Can you swing and drop off at the end of your swing? Where is it best to drop off?
4. Can you travel like a monkey from one end of the ladder to the other:

    a. Using a follow grasp?
    b. Using an alternating grasp?

5. Can you do a chin-up (palms facing child) or pull-up (palms facing away)?
6. Can you hook your knees on one bar and with your hands on the other do several pull-ups?

7. Can you hang by your knees?
8. Can you pull your knees and legs between your arms and turn over to a stand?
9. Can you "skin the cat" (same as above but return to the original hanging position without letting go)?
10. Can you get yourself up to the top of the bars and then jump off?
11. Can you travel from one end of the ladder to the other and pass a partner traveling in the opposite direction?

BOUNDING BOARD

A bounding board may be easily constructed with plywood and blocks of wood measuring 4 inches by 4 inches. It provides an opportunity for young children to experience alterations in the force of gravity. Here are some activities appropriate for preschool and primary-grade children:

1. Can you bounce on both feet?
2. Can you bounce on one foot?
3. Can you bounce with right foot, left foot combinations?
4. Can you bounce with quarter, half, and full turns?
5. Can you bounce from one board to another?
6. Can you begin at one end and bounce forward, backward, or sideward?
7. Can you bounce while visually fixating on an object?
8. Can you bounce and toss a ball?
9. Can you bounce while bouncing a ball?
10. Can you bounce and catch a ball?
11. Can you bounce and toss at a target?

TRAMPOLINE The trampoline is an expensive piece of equipment and rather limited in its use due to the fact that only one person at a time can be performing on it. It also requires close supervision. It can, however, be very beneficial in enhancing stability abilities.

1. Can you mount on the trampoline:

   a. Climbing up?
   b. Rolling forward?
   c. Vaulting up?

2. Can you walk around on the trampoline (get the "feel" of it)?
3. Can you bounce:

   a. In the center?
   b. Fixating on an object out in front without looking at the bed?
   c. Controlling your bounce?
   d. Moving the arms and legs in rhythmical coordination?
   e. Making a turn (quarter, half, three-quarters)?
   f. Touching various body parts?
   g. Tucking your knees up?
   h. Stopping on command by bending at the knees and hips?

3. Can you perform stunts on the trampoline with:

   a. Knee drop?
   b. Hands and knees drop?
   c. Seat drop?
   d. Front drop?
   e. Back drop?
   f. Back roller?
   g. Swivel hips?
   h. Combinations of these?

4. Can you toss and toss and catch a ball while bouncing?

ACTIVITY IDEAS FOR ENHANCING LOCOMOTOR ABILITIES

As the infant progresses through the rudimentary locomotor movements of infancy (creeping and crawling), she or he gradually begins to acquire a variety of higher order or fundamental locomotor movement abilities (walking, running, hopping, jumping, galloping, skipping, etc.). The development of these movements into mature patterns is both maturationally and experientially based. Most locomotor abilities have a maturational component, but will only develop to their fullest extent through practice and experience in a variety of movement activities.

Locomotor movements involve giving force to and receiving force from the body. Locomotor movements are generally considered to be those movements in which the body is transported from one point to another in either a horizontal, diagonal, or vertical direction and in which there is not an overriding balance component, as with a forward or backward roll.

Problem-Solving Locomotor Activities

An almost limitless number of problem-solving activities are possible in the area of locomotion. By simply varying the qualities of movement being dealt with (force, flow, time, space and environment), the teacher will be able to compose an extensive array of challenging and developmentally appropriate activities. It is a good idea to begin first with a specific locomotor skill such as running and then later on combine one or more other locomotor movements with it. For example "can you take four running steps and two jumping steps." Dealing with the various locomotor skills in isolation prior to combining them with other movements will facilitate efficient development of the pattern under consideration. As the child begins to move more efficiently, various combinations may be introduced. The age at which this should occur is variable and depends on the ability level of each individual child.

Specific Objectives

1. To enhance walking abilities.
2. To enhance running abilities.
3. To enhance hopping abilities.
4. To enhance jumping abilities.
5. To enhance galloping abilities.
6. To enhance skipping abilities.
7. To enhance leaping abilities.

Movement Experiences

WALKING Walking involves transferring the weight of body from the heel to the ball of the foot and then to the toes in an efficient alternating fashion.

1. While walking anywhere in the room without touching anyone:
   a. Keep your hands high while walking.
   b. Keep your hands low while walking.
   c. Change levels while walking.
   d. Walk as if you were happy or sad.
   e. Walk like a giant or a pixie.
   f. Walk forward, backward, sideward, diagonally.
   g. Walk at fast, slow, then medium pace.
   h. Walk turning your toes in different directions. Which ways can you do it? Which is the easiest way to do it? Which looks the nicest?
   i. Walk on different parts of your feet. Try walking fast on different parts of your feet. Walk slowly the same way.

    j. Walk as if it were icy underfoot.

    k. Walk while bending some part of the body.

    l. Follow a partner and walk as he does. In what ways can he change his walk? Reverse positions.

   m. Walk with a partner. Can you keep in step? Change partners. Now can you keep in step? How do people step differently?

2.	Animal walks:	Although not "walking" in the true sense of the word, animal walks provide a medium for learning how creatures move as compared with people. There are numerous types of walk, and the imaginations of the children will enable them to discover many new ways to move about in depicting various animals. The following is a compilation of a variety of animal walks appropriate for use with preschool and primary-grade children.
a.	*Bunny hop*	Raise the hands to the side of the head. Hop on both feet. The children wiggle the ears as they hop by moving the hands.
b.	*Bear walk*	Bend over from the waist and touch the floor with the hands. Keeps the legs stiff. Move forward, walking the hands and place the feet behind in a crosslateral fashion, keeping the head up.
c.	*Elephant walk*	Bend forward at the waist and allow the arms to hang limp. The children take big lumbering steps and sway from side to side as they walk, imitating an elephant and its trunk.
d.	*Ostrich walk*	Bend forward at the waist, and grasp the ankles. Keep the knees as stiff as you can. Children walk forward stretching their neck in and out.
e.	*Kangaroo jump*	Stand with feet together. Bend the elbows out from the body. Leave the hands to dangle limply. Do a deep bend with the knees and jump forward.
f.	*Prancing horses*	Standing, fold arms across the chest. Throw the head upward and back. Prance around, lifting the feet high and pointing toes.
g.	*Crane dive*	Standing, raise one leg off the floor, keeping the knees straight. At the same time raise both arms

out to the side to shoulder height. Hop on one foot in a circle turning to the left and then to the right.

h. *Stork stand*　　Stand on one foot and grasp the opposite foot in the back. Hop forward a few steps and then backward. Use the free arm to balance.

i. *Rabbit hop*　　Squat low on the heels. Place the hands palm down, fingers pointing toward the floor. In this position, move the hands forward and bring the feet forward between the hands with a little jump. Continue moving about in this fashion, imitating a rabbit.

j. *Crab walk*　　From a squatting position, the children reach backward with their arms and put both hands flat on the floor behind them. They raise up until the head, neck, and body are in a straight line. The head and back should be parallel with the floor. Walk or run in this inverted position.

k. *Puppy run*　　Run forward with both hands on the floor and the knees slightly bent.

l. *Galloping horse*　　Stand on the right foot and raise the left knee. Step forward on the left foot bringing the right foot to the heel of the left. Then raise the left knee and continue to step with this lead. Change and lead off with the right foot.

m. *Measuring worm*　　Support the body by the hands and toes. Hold the arms straight, shoulder width apart and directly under the shoulders. Keep the body in a straight line from head to toe. With the hands remaining stationary, walk the feet up to as close to the hands as possible taking tiny steps. The body should not sag. Next, keeping the feet stationary, walk the hands forward in tiny steps until the first position is reached.

n. *Seal walk*　　Assume a position flat on the floor. Push up the entire body with the arms, keeping the knees straight. Walk forward with the arms while the feet drag behind.

o. *Frog hop*　　From a squat position, place the hands on the floor outside of the feet. Leap forward several times and land on both feet.

p. *Caterpillar walk*   Lying face down on the floor, the children raise themselves up on their hands. Keep the elbows and knees stiff. Walk the feet two steps, walk the hands two steps; continue.

3. Walking like people, places, and things:

   a. Walk like someone you know or have seen.
   b. Pretend you are walking on ice, in mud, sand, snow, etc.
   c. Pretend to walk up a steep hill. How is your body position different? Why is it this way?
   d. Pretend you are walking against the wind.

4. Almost any play equipment can be incorporated into movement exploration with walking. Some of the equipment used is:

   a. Climbing ladder
   b. Horizontal ladder
   c. Stairs
   d. Tires
   e. Parachutes.

RUNNING   Running is similar to walking in many ways but differs primarily in that there is a momentary flight phase. The arms and legs are moved in rhythmical alterations with one another in a coordinated rhythmical manner.

1. Can You:

   a. Avoid bumping into people while running?
   b. Run and stop when I clap once?
   c. Pick one place in the room, run to it and back without touching anyone?
   d. Run as quietly as you can?
   e. Start very low and go to the highest running position
   f. Run in slow motion?
   g. Run around and between objects in the room?
   h. Run backward?
   i. Run with a partner?

2. Run like people, places, and things:

   a. Run like an animal that runs quickly
   b. Run like a character you have seen on television
   c. Pretend you are running at the beach
   d. Pretend you are running in the rain

3. Other equipment that can be used in movement exploration with running are:

a. Hoops
b. Playground balls
c. Ropes

JUMPING   Jumping is a movement that may be performed in a variety of ways. The vertical jump, jump for distance, and jump from a flight are the three primary patterns. A wide variety of problem-solving activities may be used to help further development of these abilities.

1.   Can you:

a. Jump in different ways around the room?
b. Jump in different directions?
c. Jump as far as you can?
d. Jump in place but at different speeds?
e. Jump and turn your body in the air?
f. Jump and move your legs in the air?
g. Jump with your legs crossed?
h. Jump with one foot forward and one backward?
i. Jump and land lightly? Where did you come down on what part of your foot?
j. Jump and land heavily? What part of your foot did you land on this time?
k. Jump as high as you can? Try again to go higher. How do you start when you want to go higher?
l. Jump and reach out?
m. Jump and reach up?
n. Jump backward without jumping into someone? How far?
o. Get a partner and jump together? Can you keep together?
p. Try it another way?

GALLOPING   In galloping, one foot leads and the other is brought up rapidly to it. The movement should be smooth and the hands may be held at the sides or swing alternately. The following suggested problem-solving activities involve galloping.

1.   Can you:

a. Gallop anywhere in the room without touching anyone?
b. Keep your hands low while galloping?
c. Keep your hands high while galloping?
d. Gallop fast and gallop slow?
e. Gallop high and gallop low?
f. Gallop sideways and backward? Which is easiest? Why?
g. Gallop with a partner?

h. Gallop in circles?
i. Gallop like a horse? Can you do it a different way?
j. Gallop and move in other ways that you know?

SKIPPING Skipping is a complex movement involving rhythmical altera- tion of the two sides of the body. It is a series of step-hops performed with alternate feet. Efficient skipping takes practice and can be taught by having the children take a step on one foot and then a small hop on the same foot. Repeat several times with one leg leading and then the other. Gradually work for alternate step-hops. The skip should be rhythmical and the arms should swing in opposition to the legs.

1. Can you:

a. Step and hop on one foot? Change feet? What movement have you discovered?
b. Try skipping in different directions?
c. Skip backward?
d. Skip sideways in both directions? How did your feet cross? Can you make them do it a different way?
e. Skip in a shape? What shape did you make? How many skips did it take you?
f. Skip high, and skip low?
g. Skip quickly and skip slowly?
h. Skip and bounce a ball?
i. Skip and jump rope?
j. Skip high? Look at your arms. How did you make yourself skip higher?
k. Skip fast? This time use tiny steps, but keep going fast.
l. Skip slowly? Use giant skips? When might you skip this way?
m. Skip with your arms above your head?
n. Skip with your arms at your sides?
o. Skip with your arms moving? Which is the easiest way of all? How does this way help you skip?
p. Skip with a partner?
q. Try some other movements while you are skipping?

LEAPING Leaping is an exaggerated run; however, the flight phase is longer. Leaping is usually combined with running due to the difficulty of maintaining the pattern.

1. Can you:

a. Leap into the air as high as you can? Do it on the other foot? What do you do before you leap?

b. Take a short leap? How did you land?
c. Run and take a long leap? What skill is something like this? How is it different from a run? How is it like a run?
d. Leap in slow motion?
e. Leap and move another part of your body?
f. Leap to the side?
g. Leap across two ropes (or lines) on the floor?
h. Leap over an object?
i. Leap and throw a ball?
j. Leap and catch a ball?
k. Run, then run and leap, repeating several times, leading first with one foot and then with the other?

LOCOMOTOR ACTIVITIES WITH SMALL EQUIPMENT

A variety of movement activities are possible with the use of small equipment. Ropes, hoops, carpet squares, and cones are among the pieces of equipment that may be effectively used to enhance fundamental locomotor abilities. Each of these pieces of equipment is inexpensive or may be easily constructed. The use of small equipment with the teaching of locomotor skills serves to add variety to the lesson, enhance interest, and provide new challenges.

Specific Objectives

1. To enhance fundamental locomotor abilities.
2. To enhance eye–hand and eye–foot coordination.
3. To enhance perceptual–motor functioning.

Movement Experiences

ROPES

Ropes provide a challenging and inexpensive piece of equipment for each child in the room. A variety of activities, ranging from movement exploration to rope jumping, may be performed with them.

1. Exploratory activities with ropes:

    a. Can you move the rope back and forth and jump over it?
    b. Can you move the rope around your body with one hand? With the other hand? Over your head? On your left side? Right side?
    c. Can you move the rope under your feet using just one hand?
    d. Can you support over the rope?
    e. Can you make a circle with your rope and move into the center and out again?
    f. Can you turn the rope and jump over it?
    g. Can you turn the rope, jump over it, and move around the floor?
    h. Can you turn the rope in a different direction and jump over it?
    i. Can you jump with both feet at the same time?
    j. Can you hop over the rope while it is turning?
    k. Can you hop on alternate feet while the rope is turning?
    l. Can you combine the jump and the hop while you are turning the rope?
    m. Can you cross your arms and still continue to jump?
    n. Can you jump more than once between turns of the rope?
    o. Can you combine jumps and hops over the rope with turning the rope around you with only one hand?
    p. How can you change your jumps and hops over the rope? Cross your feet? Spread your feet? Jump with one foot forward and the other foot backward?
    q. Can you move forward while combining steps? Backward? Sideways?
    r. Can you do a figure eight while going over the rope?
    s. Can you try many of the above movements with a partner?

2. Long stationary rope-jumping activities:

    a. Jump from one foot and land on both.
    b. Hop from one foot, land on same foot.
    c. Leap from one foot, land on opposite foot.
    d. Leap from one foot, land on same foot.
    e. Jump from both feet, land on both feet.
    f. Repeat by two's and three's.

3. Long pedulum-swinging rope activities:

    a. Follow the same progression as above.

4. Long rope-turning activities:

    a. Front swing—rope is turned away from the jumper after hitting the floor.

    b. Back swing—rope is turned toward the jumper after hitting the floor.

    c. Run through.

    d. Run in, take one jump, and run out the same side.

    e. Run in, take one jump, and run out the opposite side.

    f. Run in, take one jump with a half turn, and run out backward.

5. Individual rope-jumping activities:

    a. Skipping—stand on right foot, hop on right foot, and pass rope under it. Stand on left foot and pass rope under it.

    b. Running—run in place with no hop between steps.

    c. Double jump—with both feet together, jump the rope with an intervening step.

    d. Single jump—with both feet together, jump the rope with an intervening step.

    e. Hopping on one leg—hold one leg off the floor and hop on the other with an intervening step.

    f. Hop for distance on one leg—hold one leg off the floor and hop on the other without an intervening step.

    g. Rocking step—place one foot in front of the other. Jump on alternate feet with intervening step.

    h. Rocking step—place one foot in front of the other. Jump on alternate feet without intervening step.

    i. Backward skipping, hopping, and jumping—with the rope hold in front from a starting position any of the above may be used.

    j. Stiff leg kick forward—same as above except the raised leg is thrown forward on each step.

    k. Stiff leg kick backward—same as above except the raised leg is thrown backward on each step.

    l. Spread eagle—alternate between a closed step with an intervening step and a straddle step with an intervening step. Can be done without an intervening step.

    m. Double jump with arms crossed—execute a double jump, cross the arms as the rope is on the downswing, and jump over it. Then uncross them as it nears its completion of the upswing. Can be done while turning the rope backward.

    n. Double turn—turn the rope under the feet two times while in the air.

    o. Crossed and uncrossed legs—jump once with legs uncrossed, then cross legs and jump. Use an intervening step.

    p. Toe tap—skip on one foot, touch toe to the floor to the rear with the other foot.

    q. Lariat spin—hold ends of the rope with one hand. Circle the rope on the floor under the body and jump.

  r. Slide skip—place the rope at the side, bring the rope through the side instead of the front plane.

6. Chants for rope jumping*

  a. Hippity, Hoppity, Hop
   How many times before I stop
   1-2-3-4-5-6-etc. . . . .

  b. Mother, mother I am able
   To cook the food and set the table
   Daughter, daughter don't forget
   Salt, vinegar, mustard, pepper.

  c. I should worry, I should care,
   I should marry a millionaire,
   He should die and I should cry,
   And I should marry another guy.
   How many husbands shall I have?
   1-2-3-4-5-6, etc . . .

  d. House for sale,
   Inquire within,
   When I move out,
   Let (child's name) move in.

STRETCH ROPES

Stretch ropes are inexpensive to purchase† and offer practice in a variety of challenging locomotor activities.

1. With a single stretch rope:

  a. Can you walk along the rope?
  b. Can you run and step over the rope? (Vary the level.)

* An inexpensive booklet that contains Jump Rope Rhymes by Patricia Evans may be obtained from Porpoise Bookshop, 308 Clement Street, San Francisco, California (25¢).

† Stretch rope may be purchased from Physical Educator Supply Associates, Inc., P. O. Box 292, Trumbull, Connecticut 06611.

    c. Can you run and jump over the rope?

    d. Can you skip and crawl under the rope?

    e. Can you hop over the rope? Leap over?

    f. Can you go over the rope on four parts of your body?

    g. Can you support over the rope?

    h. Can you do a balance over the rope? Change your balance?

2. From two parallel ropes:

    a. Can you jump over the first rope and go under the second rope?

    b. Can you do the same and stay on your feet?

    c. Can you reach the first rope and bend under the second rope?

    d. Can you support over both ropes? (Support contact between the ropes.)

    e. Can you support over the ropes with only one part? Two parts?

    f. Can you support over the first rope and go under the second rope?

    g. Can you jump across both ropes?

    h. Can you jump over the first rope and roll under the second rope?

3. Standing lengthwise along the ropes:

    a. Can you move quickly from one side of the rope to the other?

    b. Can you move across both ropes without landing in the middle?

    c. Can you jump back and forth across the ropes?

    d. Can you run and jump alternately along the ropes?

    e. Can you jump and roll alternately?

4. With a circular rope (can be performed standing or sitting):

    a. Can you get into the center without letting go of the rope? Back outside?

    b. Can every other person jump over to get in and go under to get out?

    c. Can you move the rope high? Behind your head? Toward your toes?

    d. Move the rope to the parts of the body suggested in the song "Heads, Shoulders, Knees, and Toes?"

HOOPS Although generally thought of as a manipulative piece of equipment, provide opportunities for practice in a variety of locomotor activities.

1. Using a hoop alone:

    a. How many ways can you move with the hoop?

    b. Can you move through the hoop while it is moving?

    c. Can you move around the hoop while keeping it stationary? While the hoop is moving?

Use of the hoop requires coordination and timing.

    d. Can you support yourself in and out of the hoop?
    e. Can you roll the hoop and then move faster than the hoop?
    f. Can you roll the hoop and go through it while it is moving?
    g. Can you "jump rope" with the hoop?

2.   With a partner:

    a. With a partner holding the hoop, can you go in and out of the hoop?
    b. Can you go under a hoop held by a partner?
    c. Can you jump through a hoop by a partner?
    e. Can one partner roll the hoop and the other run through it?
    f. Can one partner roll the hoop and both go through it before it stops
        moving?
    g. Can you step over and under a line of hoops held by partners without
        touching them?

JUMP AND CRAWL STANDARDS

This piece of equipment may be easily made and provides practice in numerous locomotor activities. Among them are the following:

1. Place the standards upright with a broom or mop handle between them.

   a. Jump over.
   b. Leap over.
   c. Crawl under.
   d. Jump and turn.
   e. Jump over or crawl under in a variety of ways.

2. Place standards of various heights around the room (you may want to color-code them) so that all children will be able to succeed, and find a challenge at some level.

3. Lean a hoop up against a standard.

   a. Step over the hoop.
   b. Climb through the hoop.
   c. Go under the hoop.
   d. Jump over the hoop.
   e. Vary the way in which the above activities are performed.

BOXES AND STAIRS

A sturdy wooden box ranging in height from 1 to 3 feet from top to bottom or a set of low stairs make an excellent piece of equipment on which to practice a variety of jumping and landing skills.

1. Can you get up on the box (stairs)?

   a. Step up.
   b. Do a two footed jump up.
   c. Hop up.
   d. Jump up at different levels and speeds.

2. Can you jump off the box (stairs)?

   a. Step off the box.
   b. Jump and land in a squat position.
   c. Jump and land at different levels.
   d. Jump at various speeds.
   e. Jump and assume various body positions in the air.
   f. Jump and touch various body parts while in the air.
   g. Jump and turn (half, quarter, three-quarters).
   h. Jump, land, and do a forward or backward roll.
   i. Jump over an object.
   j. Jump through an object.

3. Can you jump with a partner?

   a. Jump and land at the same time from two different boxes.
   b. Jump and land at the same time while holding hands.
   c. Touch body part named by partner while jumping.
   d. Perform jump-turn to the direction named by partner.
   e. Toss a ball to a partner.
   f. Catch a ball tossed from a partner.

ACTIVITY IDEAS FOR ENHANCING MANIPULATIVE ABILITIES

The development of fundamental manipulative skills is the third aspect of children's developing movement abilities that needs to be stressed in the motor-development program. The development of mature manipulative patterns such as throwing, catching, kicking, and striking occurs somewhat later than in the area of locomotion and stability. Manipulative activities require considerable coordination between various limbs of the body and the eyes. The eye–hand or eye–foot coordination required of successful performance of a manipulative skill is considerably more than required of the other two movement categories.

Manipulative movements involve giving force to and absorbing force from objects by use of the hands or the feet. Giving force to objects (propulsive movements) involves activities in which the object moves away from the body, such as throwing, kicking, volleying, striking, and rolling. These movements are generally a combination of various locomotor movements such as turning, stepping, stretching, and swinging. Receiving force from objects (absorptive movements) involves positioning the body and parts of the body in such a way as to stop or deflect an object moving toward the body. The absorptive patterns of movement are considered to be catching and trapping and are generally the result of combining the movements of bending and stepping.

Participation in manipulation-type activities contributes to the development of more mature patterns of movement and increased eye–hand and eye–foot coordination. Through manipulative activities children can explore and discover objects moving in space in relation to their direction of travel, distance, rate of travel, accuracy, and size of the object. Children who experience a variety of movement activities that involve practice in giving force to objects and receiving force from objects have a better opportunity to develop manipulative patterns of movement.

As with the stability and locomotor activities outlined in the preceding lists it is strongly suggested that considerable time be spent in movement exploration and problem-solving involving the specific skills to be stressed. Only after the children have taken part in this portion of the lesson should games be played. The games to be played should be directly related to the movement pattern being dealt with in the earlier portion of the lesson.

Problem-Solving Manipulative Activities

When performing ball-handling activities with young children, care should be taken to select balls that are appropriate in size and weight. Large balls (8½-inch playground balls) are generally easier for young children to catch than smaller ones such as softballs and tennis balls. Balls that are lightweight (plastic type, balloons, beachballs, or yarn balls) are often much more readily handled by young children because they are not physically threatening. That is, there is much less chance of getting hurt if hit in the face by this type of ball. As a result the child will not develop an avoidance reaction to oncoming objects. The following list is a compilation of several problem-solving activities that may be used with preschool and primary-grade children in developing specific manipulative skills. The list of activity possibilities is almost limitless. Remember to think in terms of applying the activities to the various qualities of movement, namely force, time, flow, and direction. Remember also to provide experiences with a variety of types and sizes of balls as the children are ready.

Specific Objectives

1. To enhance ball-rolling abilities.
2. To enhance ball-bouncing and catching abilities.

3. To enhance throwing and catching abilities.
4. To enhance kicking and trapping abilities.
5. To enhance striking abilities.

Movement Experiences

ROLLING   Numerous challenge activities can be performed by young children.

1. Can you roll the ball from various body positions?

   a. Straddle seat
   b. Crosslegged seat
   c. Hands and knees position
   d. Squatting position
   e. Standing straddle
   f. Standing stide position

2. Can you bounce and catch from different body positions?

   a. Sitting
   b. Kneeling
   c. Squatting
   d. Bending forward
   e. Erect
   f. Tiptoes

3. Can you bounce at different levels?

   a. Low
   b. Medium
   c. High

4. Can you bounce from one level and catch at another?

   a. Bounce to medium height, catch in squat position
   b. Bounce to low height, catch in forward bending position
   c. Bounce to high height, catch in a sitting position (squatting or kneeling)

5. Can you bounce and catch while moving in different directions?

   a. Walking forward, backward, or sideward
   b. Jumping forward, backward, upward
   c. Hopping forward, backward
   d. Sliding, sideward
   e. Galloping or skipping forward, backward

6. Can you dribble the ball?

   a. In a defined area
   b. In place
   c. While moving forward, backward, or sideward
   d. While assuming different body positions
   e. With one hand then the other
   f. Without bumping into anyone
   g. Between objects
   h. Using various combinations with the left hand, then the right hand
   i. Around your body
   j. Ten, 20, 50 times without stopping

THROWING AND CATCHING   Throwing skills begin to develop as early as infancy but will not become mature patterns of movement unless there are ample opportunities for throwing experience. Throwing may be performed in an overhand and underhand motion. Mature catching skills often develop later than throwing to the coordination component. Catching may be performed in a variety of ways (depending on the size and orientation of the object). Here are some challenging activities that may be used with the various throwing and catching patterns.

1. Can you throw the ball in different ways?

   a. One hand
   b. Both hands
   c. Overhand
   d. Underhand
   e. Sidearm

2. Can you throw the ball from different levels and in different directions?

   a. Sitting
   b. Squatting
   c. Standing
   d. Forward
   e. Upward
   f. Sideward

3. Can you throw the ball at different speeds

   a. Slow

    b. Medium
    c. Fast

4. Can you throw different types of ball?

    a. Fleece ball
    b. Sponge ball
    c. Ping-pong ball
    d. Softball
    e. Playground ball
    f. Soccer ball

5. Can you toss the ball and catch it?

    a. From one hand to the other
    b. With both hands (large ball)
    c. With one hand

6. Can you throw the ball with different flows of movement?

    a. Smooth
    b. Like a robot
    c. Slow motion
    d. Rag doll

7. Can you catch the ball from different body positions?

    a. Seated
    b. Kneeling
    c. Squatting
    d. Standing

8. Can you catch the ball at different levels?

    a. Waist level
    b. Knee level
    c. Eye level
    d. Overhead

KICKING AND TRAPPING   Kicking skills develop somewhat later than throwing abilities due to the cephalocaudal principle of development and cultural factors in our North American society. Trapping involves stopping an object without the use of the hands or arms.

1. Can you kick with different parts of your foot?

    a. Toe
    b. Instep

   c. Inside of foot
   d. Outside of foot
   e. Heel

2. Can you kick in different directions?

   a. Forward
   b. Backward
   c. Sideward
   d. Diagonally

3. Can you kick from different levels?

   a. Standing
   b. Squatting
   c. Seated
   d. Crab position

4. Can you kick at various objects?

   a. Hit the wall
   b. Kick at a target
   c. Kick between two chairs
   d. Kick on a straight line

5. Can you kick different types of ball?

   a. Stationary
   b. Rolling
   c. Soccer ball
   d. Football
   e. Wiffle ball
   f. Sponge ball

6. Can you kick the ball?

   a. As hard (soft) as you can
   b. With one foot then the other
   c. As far as you can
   d. To a partner
   e. Using a drop-kicking pattern

7. Can you trap (stop) the ball with different body parts?

   a. Sole of foot
   b. Shins
   c. Stomach
   d. Chest
   e. Bottom

8. Can you trap the ball from different body positions?

   a. Hands and knees
   b. Crab position
   c. Seated

9. Can you trap a ball?

   a. That is bouncing
   b. Moving away from you
   c. Moving at various speeds
   d. Coming from various directions
   e. Coming at various levels

STRIKING Striking may be performed with the hand or arm or with the aid of an implement. The longer the length of the implement, the greater the arc of the swing. As a result a proportional greater amount of force be applied to the object. Efficient striking patterns are generally the last of the fundamental manipulative patterns to develop. This is due to the fine perceptual and motor adjustments that must be made by the child.

1. Can you strike a ball with your hand or fist?

   a. Balloon
   b. Beachball
   c. 8-Inch playground ball

2. Can you strike balls of various sizes with your hand or fist?

   a. Large beachball
   b. 8-Inch playground ball
   c. 5-Inch playground ball
   d. 6-Inch sponge ball
   e. Wiffle ball
   f. Yarn ball
   g. Ping-pong ball

3. Can you strike a ball with your hand or fist?

   a. From different body positions
   b. At different speeds
   c. From different directions

4. Can you strike a beachball with a ping-pong paddle or tennis racquets (cut the handle shot)?

   a. Use a sidearm, overarm, and underhand pattern

    b. Dribble the ball

    c. Bounce it repeatedly on the racquet

    d. Bounce the ball and hit it

    e. Hit the ball against the wall

    f. Hit the ball on the wall alternating with a partner

5. Can you repeat the above activities with different sizes of balls?

    a. Ping-pong ball

    b. Tennis ball

    c. Small playground ball

6. Can you strike a ball using an oversized bat or golf club (available in most toy departments)?

    a. Hit a ball off a batting tee

    b. Hit a pitched ball

    c. Hit a Stationary suspended ball

    d. Hit a swinging suspended ball

    e. Hit a stationary ground ball

    f. Hit a rolling ball

7. Can you stroke a balloon with the hands or an implement?

    a. Keep it up

    b. Use an overhand volleying pattern

    c. Use different body parts

    d. Strike it from different body positions

    e. Strike it with different body parts

    f. Strike it with various amounts of force

    g. Hit it to a partner

    h. Keep it up as long as you can

8. Can you strike a ball using regulation implements and balls?

    a. Table tennis

    b. Softball/baseball

    c. Tennis/badminton/racquetball

    d. Handball

    e. Golf/field hockey

Manipulative Activities with Small Equipment

A variety of small equipment may be used to enhance the manipulative abilities of young children. Each of the following pieces of equipment may be purchased commercially or homemade.

Specific Objectives

1. To enhance gross motor manipulative abilities with a variety of implements.
2. To enhance fine motor manipulative abilities with a variety of implements.
3. To enhance eye–hand coordination.

Movement Experiences

BEANBAGS

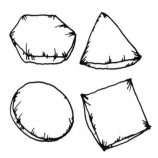

Beanbags are easy and inexpensive to make. They make an excellent implement for practicing basic throwing and catching skills. A sufficient number of beanbags should be available so that each child has one.

1. Can you toss the beanbag?

   a. Forward, backward, and to the side
   b. Straight up in the air
   c. Over a suspended rope
   d. At the wall
   e. High (or low) on the wall
   f. At a target
   g. Into a box or wastepaper can
   h. At different speeds
   i. With your opposite hand

2. Can you catch the beanbag?

   a. With both hands
   b. With one hand
   c. At different levels
   d. From different body positions
   e. At different speeds
   f. When it comes from different directions
   g. With various body parts.

3. Can you toss and catch the beanbag?

  a. Toss with one hand and catch with the other
  b. Toss and catch with the same hand
  c. Toss it high and catch it in a bucket
  d. Toss it high and catch it with your hands
  e. Toss it to a partner

HOOPS Hoops are a versatile piece of equipment. They are available commercially or may be easily made. They are excellent for enhancing gross and fine manipulative skills.

1. Can you roll the hoop?

  a. Forward, backward, and in a circle
  b. On a straight line
  c. To a partner
  d. So it comes back to you
  e. Using a wand to keep it rolling
  f. On a balance beam

2.   Can you twirl the hoop?

   a.   Around your wrist
   b.   Around your forearm
   c.   Around your waist
   d.   Around your neck
   e.   Around your foot
   f.   Around your foot and jump through with the other foot

3.   Can you toss and catch the hoop?

   a.   Toss high and catch it
   b.   Toss with one hand catch with the same hand
   c.   Toss with one hand, catch with the opposite
   d.   Toss to a partner
   e.   Toss to a partner while he/she tosses another to you
   f.   Toss and catch two hoops at a time

BALLOONS

Round balloons offer an excellent opportunity for young children to practice striking skills. Because of their lightness they are easier to contact than a regulation volleyball or playground ball. They are also inexpensive enough for each child to have his own, and may be used over and over if a rubber band is used to secure the inflated balloon instead of a knot.

1.   Can you toss the balloon and catch it?

   a.   Toss it to different heights and catch it
   b.   Toss it from various body positions and catch it
   c.   Toss it up and catch it with different body parts
   d.   Toss it to a partner
   e.   Toss two balloons with a partner

2.   Can you strike the balloon?

   a.   With your hands
   b.   At different levels
   c.   With various body parts
   d.   Keep it up in the air
   e.   Stay in one spot while you hit it
   f.   Move to the other side of the room while keeping it in the air

    g. Walk in a circle while hitting it

    h. Make a full turn and strike it again

3. Can you strike the balloon with an implement?

    a. Ping-pong paddle, tennis racquet, baseball bat

    b. Hit it as hard or soft as you can

    c. Hit it using different swinging motions sidearm, overarm, underhand

    d. Hit to to a partner

SCOOPS

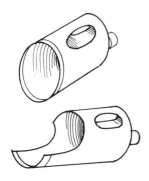

Scoops are easily made from old plastic bleach bottles or milk cartons. They offer a new and different medium for practicing throwing and catching skills.

1. Can you toss a ball using the scoop (a yarn ball or rubber ball will do nicely)?

    a. Underhand, overhand, sidearm

    b. High, low, waist level

    c. From various body positions

    d. To a partner

    e. At the wall

    f. At a target

2. Can you catch a ball using the scoop?

    a. From different levels

    b. From different body positions

    c. From different directions

    d. At various speeds

    e. From a partner

3. Can you play modified games using the scoop?

    a. Dodgeball

    b. Volleyball

    c. Softball

    d. Soccer

SUGGESTED READINGS

Barrett, Kate R. *Exploration, A Method of Teaching Movement,* Madison, Wisconsin: College Printing and Typing Co., 1965.

Bilbrough, A. and P. Jones, *Physical Education in the Primary School,* London: London U.P., 1964.

Fendeck, Ruth, *Classroom Capers, Movement Education in the Classroom,* Bellingham, Washington: Educational Designs and Consultants, 1971.

Hackett, Layne and Robert Jeason, *A Guide to Movement Exploration,* Palo Alto, California: Peek Publication, 1967.

Latchaw, Marjorie and Glen Egstrom, *Human Movement,* Englewood Cliffs, N. J.: Prentice–Hall, 1969.

Los Angeles City Schools, Learning to Move—Moving to Learn, Los Angeles City Schools, Division of Instructional Planning and Services, Publication No. E.C. 260, 1968.

North, Marion, *Body Movement for Children,* Boston: Plays, Inc., 1971.

Stanley, Sheila, *Physical Education: A Movement Orientation,* Toronto: McGraw–Hill, 1969.

SUGGESTED RECORDS

Corbin, Charles B. and Arabrace Brazelton, *Gymnastics,* Kimbo Records, Box 246, Deal, New Jersey, KEA6000.

Evans, Douglas and Gloria Evans, *Physical Funness and Exercise is Kid Stuff,* Kimbo Records, Box 246, Deal, New Jersey, KIM2060 and KIM2070.

Hallenbeck, Gertrude and Douglas Evans, *Fundamental Rhythms Movement Exploration,* Kimbo Records, Box 246, Deal, New Jersey, LP3090.

Lee, Karol, *Music for Movement Exploration,* Kimbo Records, Box 246, Deal, New Jersey, KEA5090.

Seeker, Jo Ann, *To Move Is To Be,* Kimbo Records, Box 246, Deal, New Jersey, LP8060.

Seeker, Jo Ann and George Jones, *Rhythmic Parachute Play,* Kimbo Records, Box 246, Deal, New Jersey, KEA6020.

Smith, Paul, *Movement Fun,* Kimbo Records, Box 246, Deal, New Jersey, EA21.

Riccione, Georgiana. *1 · 2 · 3 · Move,* Kimbo Records, Box 246, Deal, New Jersey, KIM9077.

Chapter 7

Active Games for Enhancing Fundamental Movement Abilities

CONTENTS

Introduction
  General Objectives
Games for Enhancing Locomotor Abilities
  Specific Objectives
  Movement Experiences
Games for Enhancing Manipulative Abilities
  Specific Objectives
  Movement Experiences

To Win the Game is Great
To Play the Game is Greater
To Love the Game is Greatest
Anonymous

INTRODUCTION

Games can play an important role in developing and refining a wide variety of fundamental movement abilities *if* they are properly incorporated into the motor development program. All too often teachers of young children include active games in their program simply for the sake of having fun or reinforcing certain social skills. Although these are certainly worthwhile objectives, they should not be viewed as the *primary* objectives of game activities.

Games, if they are to be of any real value, must be viewed from a developmental perspective. They must be carefully selected and implemented with regard to the particular locomotor, manipulative, and/or stability abilities that they reinforce. During the preschool and primary-grade years it is crucial that we assist children in learning how to move with greater efficiency and control. Therefore we must not take it for granted that they will develop and refine the numerous fundamental movement abilities necessary for successful performance in active games on their own. Children must first be provided with a variety of individualized movement experiences designed to enhance their movement abilities before emphasis can be placed on incorporating these skills into game activities.

It seems only logical that practice first be provided with specific movement patterns before they can be effectively incorporated into a game activity. We need only to look at football or basketball coaches and the emphasis that they place on "learning the fundamentals" through drill situations prior to the actual playing of the game of football or basketball. It should be much the same with preschoolers and primary-grade children. That is, a wide variety of movement experiences that incorporate movement exploration and problem solving should be practiced prior to the playing of games that utilize the particular movements practiced. In other words, games for young children should be viewed as *tools* for further enhancing and implementing the particular movement patterns dealt with during the individualized portion of the lesson. It is with this thought in mind that this chapter has been written.

Various locomotor and manipulative-type games are presented in this chapter. Many have been used for generations and may be found in numerous textbooks. They have been selected for inclusion here because they: (1) provide for maximum activity of all children, (2) promote inclusion rather than exclusion, (3) are easily modified and varied, (4) aid in the development of a variety of movement abilities, and (5) are fun for young children to play. Stability games have been omitted because they are few in number and many stability abilities are incorporated into the locomotor and manipulative games listed. A format is used in which each game is first viewed from the particular *movement skills* that it incorporates followed by the *desired outcomes, formation, equipment,* and *procedures* to be followed.

The general objectives of the movement experiences contained in this chapter are to: (1) enhance fundamental locomotor abilities, (2) enhance fundamental manipulative abilities, (3) contribute to the physical and motor fitness of children, (4) aid in developing and reinforcing a variety of social competencies, and (5) provide an avenue for implementing a variety of fundamental movement abilities.

Hide-and-seek is still a favorite game of today's children.

GAMES FOR ENHANCING LOCOMOTOR ABILITIES

There is an almost endless variety of locomotor games that young children enjoy playing. The vast majority of locomotor games, however, are designed around running as the primary mode of movement. The alert teacher will feel free to substitute other locomotor movements as they suit the nature of the lesson and the skills being stressed. Each of the games that follow may be modified in a variety of ways in order to suit the particular needs and age level of the children. Care should be taken to use these games after the children have had an opportunity to explore and experiment with the problem-solving activities contained in the preceding chapter.

Specific Objectives

1. To enhance fundamental locomotor abilities in running, jumping, skipping, and galloping.
2. To enhance agility and general body coordination.
3. To enhance rhythmic performance of locomotor movements.
4. To enhance ability to participate in a team effort.
5. To develop listening skills.
6. To enhance ability to follow directions and obey rules.

Movement Experiences

BROWNIES AND FAIRIES

Movement skills	Running, dodging, pivoting, starting, and stopping.
Desired outcomes:	1. To enhance a variety of fundamental movement abilities.
	2. To learn that sliding on one's knees is not a proper way to stop.
	3. To learn how to tag properly.
Formation	Two lines with the children facing each other.
Equipment	None.
Procedures	The class is divided into two groups. One group is called "brownies," the

other, "fairies." The groups line up at each end of the playing area facing each other. The "brownies" turn around and close their eyes and "fairies" quietly sneak up behind them. One of the brownies is designated to listen for the fairies and call "here come the fairies" when he feels they are too close. When he calls out, the fairies run to their goal and the brownies give chase. All persons tagged join the brownies. The game is repeated with the fairies being the chasers. Be sure to spend some time teaching proper tagging procedures and how to start and stop quickly and safely.

CROWS AND CRANES

Movement skills

Running, dodging, pivoting, starting, and stopping.

Desired outcomes

1. To enhance a variety of fundamental movement abilities.
2. To enhance listening skills.
3. To enhance auditory discrimination.

Formation

Two lines of children facing each other about 10 feet apart.

Equipment

None.

Procedures

The class is divided into two groups. One group is called the Crows and the other, the Cranes. The groups line up at each end of the playing area facing each other. On a signal, they will advance toward one another. The instructor either calls Crows or Cranes. If he calls Crows, they chase the Cranes back to their goal and all persons caught join the Crows. If he calls the Cranes, they become the chasers. The instructor calls various names beginning with "Cra . . . " before calling crows or Cranes (e.g., Cra . . . ckers, Cra . . . yfish, cra . . . yons).

SQUIRRELS IN THE TREES

Movement skills	Running, and dodging.
Desired outcomes	1. To enhance fundamental movement abilities. 2. To enhance dodging and agility. 3. To enhance listening skills.
Formation	Groups of threes. Two children stand with hands joined, third is in between.
Equipment	None.
Procedures	One player is designated as a fox, the others as squirrels. The remaining players scatter around in groups of "threes." Two of the players stand and hold hands above their head (tree): the others squat between them (squirrel). The game begins with the fox chasing the squirrel. To avoid being caught, the squirrel may run under a tree and the squirrel originally under the tree must flee from the fox. When tagged by the fox, the squirrel becomes the fox and the fox becomes a squirrel.

FROZEN TAG

Movement skills	Running, and dodging.
Desired outcomes	1. To enhance fundamental movement abilities. 2. To enhance agility.
Formation	Scatter.
Equipment	None.
Procedures	One person is designated as "it" and chases the other players. If a player is tagged, he becomes "it." A player may "freeze" to avoid being tagged.
Variations	Have players squat, stand on a line, and so on rather than "freeze."

RED LIGHT

Movement skills	Walking and stopping.
Desired outcomes	1. To enhance fundamental movement abilities. 2. To enhance starting and stopping abilities. 3. To enhance listening skills.
Formation	Players at one end of play area. "It" at the other end.
Equipment	None.
Procedures	The class lines up at the one end of the play area and one player, "it," stands in a line 50–60 feet away with his back to the group. The game begins with "it" calling "green light." When the other children hear their call, they begin to run toward the line where "it" is standing. "It" then calls "red Light"

and quickly turns to face the children. He calls the name of any children who have not completely stopped. These children must return to the starting line and the procedure is repeated. The first child to reach the line where "it" is standing becomes "it."

COLORS

Movement skills	Running.
Desired outcomes	1. To enhance fundamental movement abilities. 2. To enhance color naming and identification. 3. To enhance listening skills.
Formation	Two lines of players facing one another.
Equipment	None.
Procedures	The groups stand on opposite goals with the teacher in the middle. Each group chooses a color and then moves toward the center of the playing area until the two groups are about 5–10 feet apart. The teacher calls out a color. When she calls the color selected by either side, the players on that side run to their goal and the other group chases them. Those tagged before they reach their goal must join the other side. The teacher may call several colors before he calls one of the colors selected. The side having the most players at the end of the playing time wins the game.

MAGIC CARPET

Movement skills	Skipping, running, and walking.

Desired outcomes	1. To enhance fundamental movement abilities.
	2. To reinforce shape and color concepts.
Formation	Scatter formation with lines, circles, and spots on the floor.
Equipment	None.
Procedures	The entire play area is considered to be the "carpet." Spots, circles, and other markings on it represent the "magic spots." The class follows the leader in a simple file around the play area. When the leader stops, the children run to a "magic spot" and stand. Those that do not reach a spot are eliminated. The game ends when there are only as many "magic spots" as there are children.
Variations	Designate specific shapes or colors to go to.

FLOWERS AND THE WIND

Movement skills	Running and dodging.
Desired outcomes:	1. To enhance fundamental movement abilities.
	2. To enhance agility.
	3. To reinforce the ability to name flowers.

Formation	Two lines of children facing each other.
Equipment	None.

Procedures

The class divides into two groups, facing each other about 60 feet apart. One group is designated as flowers and the other as wind. The group designated as flowers decide upon a particular flower and advance toward the wind. While they are advancing, the other groups tries to guess what kind of flower they have selected. When the right flower is named, they chase the group back to their goal. All persons tagged join their group. The game is continued in this manner until all persons are caught or the groups can alternate roles.

MIDNIGHT

Movement skills

Running and dodging.

Desired outcomes

1. To enhance fundamental abilities.
2. To enhance the concepts of time.

Formation

Single line of children facing the leader ("fox").

Equipment

None.

Procedures

One player is the fox and he stands at one end of the gym (his den). The other players are sheep and go to the other end of the play area (the barn). On a signal, they walk toward the player that is the fox and call out, "What time is it, Mr. Fox?" If the fox answers "10 o'clock," "4 o'clock," and so on, the sheep are safe. Should the fox answer "Midnight" the sheep run back to the barn and the fox chases them. The game is repeated and all persons caught by the fox join him and help catch the remaining sheep.

STOP AND GO
Movement skills

Running, stopping, and starting.

Desired outcomes:

1. To enhance fundamental abilities.
2. To enhance agility and coordination.
3. To enhance listening skills.

Formation

Single line of children facing the teacher.

Equipment

None.

Procedures

Players stand side by side facing a line 50–60 feet away. The teacher blows a whistle and the children start to run toward the line. The whistle is blown again and the players must run in the opposite direction. They continue this procedure (i.e., blowing the whistle at irregular intervals) until somebody reaches the goal line.

RED ROVER
Movement skills

Running.

Desired outcomes

1. To enhance fundamental movement abilities.
2. To enhance agility and coordination.

Formation

Two lines facing each other with hands joined.

Equipment

None.

Procedures

The group is divided into two teams. They hold hands and line up side by side at a distance of about 20 feet from each other. On a signal, one team chants "Red Rover, Red Rover, we dare (call a name of a person on the other team) over." The person receiving the dare must try to run through the line of the other team. If he is successful, he may choose any member of that team to join his. If he does not break through, he must join the opposing team. This procedure is repeated with the other team uttering the chant.

AUTOMOBILES

Movement skills

Walking and stopping.

Desired outcomes

1. To enhance fundamental movement abilities.
2. To be able to follow directions of starting, stopping, and using caution from given signal.
3. To be able to manipulate a make-believe steering wheel.

Formation

Free formation according to manner in which the area is set up.

Equipment

Each child has a "steering wheel."

Procedures

Each child is to be a driver of an automobile and needs a "steering wheel." This can be a hoop, deck tennis ring, or something the child has made out of cardboard. The teacher has three flash cards colored red, green, and yellow. These are the traffic-control colors.

The children drive around the area, steering various paths, responding as the teacher raises the cards one at a time. The children follow the traffic directions: red—stop, green—go, and yellow—caution.

Variations

An ambulance station and fire station can be established with appropriate "cars." When one of these come forward with the characteristic siren noise (made by the driver), all other "cars" pull over to the side.

BACK-TO-BACK

Movement skills

Running, skipping, hopping, jumping, and sliding.

Desired outcomes

1. To be able to move quickly on signal.
2. To be able to perform correct directed movement.
3. To work successfully with a partner.
4. To enhance auditory perception.

Formation

Partners standing back-to-back with one extra child.

Equipment

None.

Procedures

The number of children should be uneven. On signal, each child stands back-to-back with another child. One child will be without a partner. This child can clap his hands for the next signal, such as face-to-face, side-to-side, and all children change partners with the extra player seeking a partner.

Variations

Other commands can be given such as "everybody run—or hop, skip, jump, slide" or "walk like an elephant." When the whistle is blown, they immediately find a partner and stand back-to-back.

HUNTSMAN

Movement skills	Running.

Desired outcomes

1. To enhance fundamental movement abilities.
2. To maneuver caller's position between the goal and the group.
3. To take off quickly on signal and run directly to the goal.
4. To run swiftly without falling down or colliding with others.

Formation

Scatter.

Equipment

None.

Procedures

One child is "huntsman" and says to the other children, "come with me to hunt tigers." The other children fall into line behind him and follow in his footsteps as he leads them away from the goal line.

When huntsman says, "bang!" the other children run to the goal as the huntsman tries to tag as many as possible. As each child is tagged, the huntsman calls out the child's name. The huntsman chooses a new huntsman from the players who reached the base safely.

Variations

Since the setting of this game is believed to be a jungle, and imitations of animal movements (e.g., bear-walk, kangaroo hop, elephant drag walk) could be used instead of running.

SPACE SHIP

Movement skills	Running, starting, and stopping.
Desired outcomes	1. To enhance fundamental movement abilities. 2. To run rapidly in a circle. 3. To start quickly. 4. To avoid collisions with other runners.

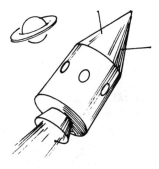

Formation	Scatter.
Equipment	An object to represent the earth (beanbag, tree, etc.).
Procedures	Children and teacher decide upon an object that will represent the Earth, such as a tree, beanbag, circle, base, and so on. Children are space ships, and on the countdown, "Five, four, three, two, ONE!" the rockets blast the space ships off the ground; they quickly pick up speed and go into orbit around the earth. After one or more orbits, space ships return and "splash down." The game may be repeated any number of times, with space ships flying any number of orbits. To improve endurance, children try to run longer and faster each time.

TOUCH AND FOLLOW

Movement skills	Walking, skipping, and galloping.
Desired outcomes	1. To enhance fundamental movement abilities. 2. To be able to imitate another child's activity.

3. To be able to stand in a circle with arms stretched outward.
4. To be able to lead a new activity if chosen by the previous "it."

Formation

Single circle facing in.

Equipment

None.

Procedures

The children stand in a large circle with their hands held out toward the center, palms upward. One child is chosen to be in the center of the circle. He moves about and then lightly touches the outstretched hand of some child. The child who is touched must follow the first child around the circle, imitating any activity chosen by him. They may skip, gallop, trot, or perform any other appropriate activity. They go around the circle and then the follower becomes the one in the center.

Variations

The game could be played in which the entire circle could imitate "it" rather than involve just one other child.

WALK, WALK, RUN
Movement skills

Running and walking.

Desired outcomes

1. To enhance fundamental movement abilities.
2. To move quickly to tag another and to avoid being tagged.
3. To assume responsibility for maintaining the vacant spot in the circle.
4. To accept defeat without argument.

Formation	Single circle facing in.
Equipment	None.
Procedures	Children stand in a circle, facing the center. One child is "it" and walks around outside the circle, chanting, "walk, walk, walk" touching each player gently on the shoulder as he passes them. When he touches a player and says "run!" the player touched chases him around the circle. If the chaser touches him before he can reach the chaser's place in the circle, he must go into the "mush pot," which is in the center of the circle, and stay there until another child enters the mush pot. If he is not tagged before reaching the chaser's place in the circle, he stays in the new circle position. In either instance, the chaser becomes the new "it," and the game continues.
Variations:	May be used for other types of locomotor skills; "it" may say, "Walk, walk, walk, skip!" or "Hop, gallop, slide," and so on.

WHERE'S MY PARTNER?

Movement skills	Skipping, galloping, walking, running, and hopping.
Desired outcomes	1. To enhance fundamental movement abilities.
	2. To move in the opposite direction than the facing circle.
	3. To be able to "halt" when the command is given.
	4. To know right from left.
Formation	Double circle of couples facing each other.

Equipment	None.
Procedures	The children are arranged in a double circle by couples, with partners facing each other. The inside circle has one more player than the outside. When the signal is given, the circles skip to the player's right. When the command "halt" is given, the circles face each other to find partners. The player left without a partner is in the "mush pot."
Variations	The game could be played with music. When the music stops, the players seek partners. The game could also be altered to a gallop, run, walk, or hop, rather than a skip.

WHISTLE STOP

Movement skills	Running, stopping, and chasing.
Desired outcomes	1. To enhance fundamental movement abilities. 2. To improve speed and time in running. 3. To stop and start quickly on signal. 4. To avoid running into others. 5. To respond appropriately to the sound of a whistle.
Formation	Scatter formation.
Equipment	Whistle.
Procedures	Children are scattered around the playing area. On the signal "run!" the children run in any direction until the whistle blows, then they stop immediately. They start again on the signal, "run!"

Children must be able to run and stop on appropriate signals, staying within the boundaries and avoiding other runners.

Variations

The game may be varied to explore directions, time, and movement:
1. Run in a circle and stop when whistle blows.
2. Walk like an elephant and stop when the whistle blows.
3. Run sideward.
4. Skip toward the teacher.
5. When whistle blows, stop and clap your hands.

FROG IN THE SEA

Movement skills

Running.

Desired outcomes

1. To move quickly to avoid being tagged.
2. To accept the challenge of the game.
3. To work together to tag others.

Equipment

None.

Procedures

One child is the frog and sits in the center of a circle. Other children dare the frog by running in close to him and saying, "Frog in the sea, can't catch me!"

If a child is tagged by the frog, he also becomes a frog and sits in the circle beside the first frog. Frogs must tag from a sitting position. The game continues until four players are tagged. Then the first frog chooses a new frog from the players who were not tagged.

Variations

Jumping like a frog could be performed rather than running.

CROSSING THE BROOK

Movement skills	Jumping and leaping.
Desired outcomes	1. To enhance fundamental movement abilities. 2. To promote agility.
Formation	File.
Equipment	Chalk or tape.
Procedures	Two lines are drawn to represent a brook. The children try to jump over. If they fall in they must return home and change shoes and socks. The width of the brook should vary from narrow to wide in order that all will find a degree of success.
Variations	Place an object in the brook to be jumped on as a stepping stone.

JUMP THE SHOT

Movement skills	Jumping and hopping.
Desired outcomes	1. To enhance fundamental movement abilities 2. To enhance eye-foot coordination 3. To enhance temporal awareness

Formation	Single circle facing in
Equipment	Beanbag on the end of 10-foot line
Procedures	The teacher squats down in the center of the circle and swings the rope

around at 3–6 inches off the ground. The end of the rope should be beyond the outside of the circle. The children jump to avoid being hit. Be sure to warn the children of the dangers of tripping and do not turn the rope too fast.

Variations | Have the children gallop, side hop or perform tricks over rope.

JACK BE NIMBLE
Movement skills

Desired outcomes

1. To enhance fundamental movement abilities.
2. To be able to learn a simple rhyme.

Formation | Lines of four or more

Equipment | Indian clubs to represent candles. One for each team.

Procedures | The following rhyme is recited by the children:

Jack (Jane) be nimble,
Jack be quick,
And Jack jump over the candlestick.

As the rhyme is repeated, the first player in each line runs forward and jumps over the candle. The others follow. Anyone knocking down the candle must set it up again. Caution the children to wait for the signal to "jump over the candlestick."

COME ALONG
Movement skills | Skipping.

Desired outcomes

1. To enhance fundamental movement abilities.

2. To reinforce concepts of working together.
3. To enhance listening skills.

Formation	Single circle, facing counterclockwise.
Equipment	None.
Procedures	One child is selected to start the game. He or she begins skipping around the outside of the circle and takes one other child by the hand and says, "come along!" as they continue to skip. When the teacher calls, "go home!" the youngsters drop hands and run to their places. The first one to reach his home position will begin a new game. Be sure that each child has an opportunity to be selected at least once.

SKIP FOR YOUR DINNER

Movement skills	Skipping
Desired outcomes	1. To enhance fundamental movement abilities. 2. To enhance directional concepts. 3. To enhance listening skills.
Formation	Single circle, facing in, hands joined, one player inside the circle.
Equipment	None.
Procedures	The player on the inside of the circle holds out his hands between any two players and says, "Skip for your dinner." These two players must then skip around the outside of the circle in a counterclockwise direction. The

one who returns to the vacant place first is "it" for the next game, the original "it" taking his place in the circle.

GAMES FOR ENHANCING MANIPULATIVE ABILITIES

There are several game activities that may be used to reinforce the development and refinement of fundamental manipulative abilities. It is suggested, however, that practice with individualized activities such as those presented in the preceding chapter proceed the games portion of the lesson.

Manipulative games can serve as an effective reinforcer of the particular skills being stressed. The teacher must keep in mind the desired outcomes of the game and feel free to modify it whenever necessary to ensure maximum participation and practice of the skills being stressed.

The following games are appropriate for use with primary—grade children and may in some instances be modified to include preschool children if different types of ball are used.

Specific Objectives

1. To enhance fundamental manipulative abilities in throwing, catching, kicking, trapping, volleying, striking, bouncing, and rolling.
2. To enhance eye–hand and eye–foot coordination.
3. To be able to work together in a group effort.
4. To enhance listening abilities.
5. To be able to follow directions and obey rules.

Movement Experiences

POISON BALL
Desired outcomes

1. To enhance fundamental manipulative abilities.
2. To enhance ability to grasp objects.
3. To enhance ability to follow directions.
4. To enhance fine motor coordination.

Fine motor activities need to be incorporated into the motor development program.

Movement skills	Tossing and catching.
Formation	Single circle facing in.
Equipment	Two yarn balls or beanbags.
Procedures	The balls are passed around the circle to either the left or to the right. The balls are handed rapidly to the next person and not thrown. A signal is given to stop and the children left holding the ball are "poisoned." They drop out of the circle and the game continues until only two players remain.

HOT POTATO

Movement skills	Tossing and catching
Desired outcomes	1. To enhance fundamental manipulative abilities. 2. To be able to follow direction. 3. To enhance fine motor coordination.
Formation	Single circle facing in.
Equipment	One 8-inch playground ball.
Procedures	The children sit in the circle an arm's length apart. On the command "go" the ball is passed around the circle until the signal to "stop" is given. The child left holding the ball drops out of the circle. The game continues until only two players remain.
Variations	To avoid the exclusion element of this and many other circle games, set up a point system. If a person gets three points against himself, for example, he has to sit in the "mush pot" in the center of the circle for one turn or perform a stunt for the class.

TEACHER BALL

Movement skills	Tossing and catching
Desired outcomes	1. To enhance fundamental manipulative abilities. 2. To enhance eye–hand coordination.
Formation	Several circles containing six to eight children each with the "teacher" in the center.
Equipment	One 8-inch playground ball for each group.
Procedures	One child stands in the center of the circle ("the teacher") and tosses the ball to each member of the circle. A new "teacher" then goes into the center. This game may be used as a practice drill or developed into a race between circles as the children's skill level increases.
Variations	Various sizes and types of ball may be used. Also various throwing, catching, kicking, trapping, and volleying skills may be developed this way.

GUESS WHO

Movement skills	Tossing and catching
Desired outcomes	1. To enhance fundamental manipulative abilities. 2. To enhance listening skills.
Formation	Single line of six to eight children per group, one child 10–20 feet away.
Equipment	Playground ball.

Procedures

The players line up about 10–20 feet from a player chosen to be "it," who turns his back as the ball is passed along the line of players. At a signal from a chosen leader, the player who is holding the ball throws the ball at "it" and tries to hit him below the waist. If the player who throws the ball misses, he has to change places with "it." If "it" is hit by the ball, he turns around and gets one guess as to who hit him. If he guesses correctly, he changes places with the player who threw the ball.

MOON SHOT
Movement skills

Throwing and catching

Desired outcomes

1. To enhance fundamental manipulative abilities.
2. To enhance ability to keep score.
3. To enhance ability to follow rules.

Formation

Single circle facing in with an outer circle also drawn on the floor, one child in the center.

Procedures

Each child stands on the inner circle and in turn tries to "shoot the moon" with the beanbag. "Moon" is a small circle inside two larger circles. If the child is successful he moves to the outer circle and shoots from there when his turn comes again.
When a child makes a successful throw, he moves to or remains on the outer circle. When he is unsuccessful he remains on or returns to the inner circle. Each successful

throw from the inner circle counts one point, and from the outer circle, two points.

The center player is retriever and throws beanbag to each player in turn, or each player may retrieve his own beanbag and pass to the next player. After the beanbag has gone around the circle once, the retriever (if one is used) chooses a player from the outer circle to be the new retriever and exchanges places with him.

CALL BALL

Movement skills

Vertical tossing and catching.

Desired outcomes

1. To enhance fundamental manipulative abilities.
2. To enhance eye–hand coordination.
3. To enhance ability to follow directions.

Formation

Single circle facing inward with a leader in the center.

Equipment

One playground ball for each circle of eight to ten players.

Procedures

The leader stands in the center of the circle and tosses the ball into the air while calling another player's name. The player called runs forward and attempts to catch the ball before it hits the ground or after one bounce. He becomes the new leader if he succeeds. Otherwise the original leader tosses the ball into the air again.

SPUD

Movement skills

Vertical tossing, throwing, and catching.

Desired outcomes	1. To enhance fundamental manipulative abilities. 2. To enhance eye–hand coordination. 3. To be able to follow directions.
Formation	Single circle facing in with the leader in the center.
Equipment	One playground ball for each circle of eight to ten players.
Procedures	The leader stands in the center of the circle and tosses the ball into the air and calls another player's name. The player called runs to the center of the circle and tries to catch the ball. At the same time the remaining players scatter. "It" catches the ball and says "stop" as soon as she gains control of it. The fleeing players freeze. "It" is permitted to take three "giant" steps in any direction. She then throws the ball at one of the players. If she hits that person, who is not permitted to move, he then becomes "it." If she misses, she remains "it" and begins the game again with a toss from the center of the circle.

CIRCLE DODGE BALL

Movement skills	Throwing, catching, and dodging.
Desired outcomes	1. To enhance fundamental manipulative abilities. 2. To enhance agility and coordination.
Formation	Single circle of 10–12 participants facing in, one child in center.
Equipment	Playground ball.

Procedures	The children form a circle and one child is placed in the center. The children in the circle attempt to throw the ball and hit the child in the center. If the child is hit, the thrower takes his place. (Do not permit throwing at the head.)
Variation	Use more than one ball. Divide the class in half. Place one team inside the circle while all others attempt to hit them. Reverse the procedures after a given amount of time or after all are hit.

KEEP AWAY

Movement skills	Throwing and catching.
Desired outcomes	1. To enhance fundamental manipulative abilities. 2. To enhance ability for teamwork. 3. To enhance eye–hand coordination. 4. To enhance agility.
Formation	Single circle of 10–15 participants facing in, one child in center.
Procedures	The children form a circle and one child is placed in the center. The remaining children attempt to pass the ball, keeping it away from the child in the center. If the child in the center catches the ball, the child who threw it takes his place in the center.

TUNNEL BALL

Movement skills	Rolling.
Desired outcomes	1. To enhance fundamental manipulative abilities. 2. To enhance eye–hand coordination.

Formation

Single circle of eight to ten players facing in, one child in center.

Equipment

Playground balls.

Procedures

Ten players form a circle with one player in the center of the circle. The players in the circle spread their feet apart and the player in the center tries to roll the ball through their legs or between the players. If he is successful in his attempt, he takes the place of the player in the circle. The player in the circle can block the ball with his hands but he can't move his feet.

ROLL AND CATCH

Movement skills

Rolling and catching.

Desired outcomes

1. To enhance fundamental manipulative abilities.
2. To enhance ability to identify balls of different sizes.
3. To enhance ability to tell why different balls roll at different speeds.

Formation

Double line, partners facing.

Equipment

Balls of various sizes.

Procedures

Give one ball to every couple. Players form double lines about 6 feet or more apart, partners facing each other. Partners roll the ball back and forth. If one of them misses the ball, have the pair sit. The couple remaining at the end of the game is the winner. Also have contests to see which pair can roll the ball the most times in a row without a miss.

ROLL IT OUT

Movement skills	Rolling
Desired outcomes	1. To enhance fundamental manipulative abilities.
	2. To enhance eye–hand coordination.
Formation	Single circle facing in, either seated or kneeling.
Equipment	One rubber playground ball per circle.
Procedures	A ball is rolled into the circle. When it comes near a child, he tries to roll it between two of the circle players by batting it with his hand. He may stop it first and then roll it. If he succeeds, he changes place with the circle player on whose right side the ball goes out.

I'LL ROLL IT TO . . .

Movement skills	Rolling.
Desired outcomes	1. To enhance fundamental manipulative abilities.
	2. To enhance ability to follow directions.
	3. To enhance eye–hand coordination.
Players	Single circle facing in, seated on the floor.
Equipment	Playground balls of different sizes.
Procedures	Teacher and children sit on floor in circle. Teacher has a rubber utility ball. He says, for example, "I'll roll the ball to Mary," and rolls the ball

to her. Child stops the ball with both hands, then rolls it with both hands to another child, saying first, "I'll roll the ball to . . ." Game continues until all have received the ball several times. Then teacher takes a different-sized ball and starts a new game, using only one hand to roll the ball. Children stop the ball with one hand, using the same hand to roll it.

KICK-AWAY

Movement skills	Kicking and trapping
Desired outcomes	1. To enhance fundamental manipulative abilities. 2. To enhance eye–foot coordination. 3. To enhance agility. 4. To enhance ability to follow directions.
Formation	Several circles with eight to twelve children per group.
Equipment	One 8-inch playground ball per group of 10–12 children.
Procedures	One player has ball on ground in front of him and his foot is resting on it. Kicks the ball across the circle, using the inside of his foot to avoid lofting it. The child receiving the ball traps it and kicks it quickly away from himself to another child. Children continue to kick ball until it goes outside of circle. The player who retrieves the ball brings it back to the circle and starts it again.

FREE BALL

Movement skills	Kicking and trapping

Desired outcomes	1. To enhance fundamental manipulative abilities. 2. To enhance eye–foot coordination. 3. To enhance ability to follow directions.
Formation	Two parallel lines (30 feet apart) with four to six players per group.
Equipment	One 8-inch playground ball per group
Procedures	Child who is "it" stands behind one line facing the other players, who stand behind the opposite line. "It" calls a player's name and kicks the ball toward the opposite line. Player whose name is called tries to trap the ball and kicks it back to "it." This continues until "it" has kicked it once to each player. Then "it" calls "free ball" and kicks toward the opposite line. Player who stops the ball is the new "it."

CROSS THE LINE

Movement skills	Kicking and trapping.
Desired outcomes	1. To enhance fundamental manipulative abilities. 2. To enhance eye–foot coordination. 3. To enhance ability to function as a team.
Formation	Five to eight players per group.
Equipment	One 8-inch playground ball per group.
Procedures	The "line" is a 25-foot line drawn a distance of 20–40 feet from the kick-

ing circle. Other players scatter in playing field in front of the wall. Kicker places the ball on the ground inside the kicking circle. He calls, "cross the line" and kicks toward the line. Any fielder who can trap the ball before it goes over the line is the new kicker. If the ball crosses the line, the original kicker kicks again. If no one stops the ball after he has kicked three times, he chooses a new kicker.

BALLOON VOLLEYING

Movement skills	Striking and volleying.

Desired outcomes

1. To enhance fundamental manipulative abilities.
2. To enhance eye–hand coordination.
3. To enhance temporal awareness.

Formation

Scatter.

Equipment

Enough round balloons and string for each child.

Procedures

Tie balloons around the children's wrist (left wrist if right-handed) an appropriate length to allow the child to volley it. The player who can keep it up the longest is the winner.

BOUNCE AND CATCH

Movement skills

Bouncing and catching.

Desired outcomes	1. To enhance fundamental manipulative abilities.
	2. To enhance eye–hand coordination.
	3. To be able to work with a partner.
Formation	Scatter.
Equipment	One playground ball per player.
Procedures	Each child has a rubber ball. He bounces it and catches it, using both hands, repeating the sequence several times. Then he tries to bounce his ball to a partner and catch the partner's return bounce.
	Children bounce a ball against a wall and catch it as it bounces back. Teacher places several children in a line and bounces to each in turn.

TEACHER'S CHOICE

Movement skills	Bouncing and catching
Desired outcomes	1. To enhance fundamental manipulative abilities.
	2. To enhance ability to toss and catch balls of various sizes.
	3. To enhance recognition of the functions of balls of different types.
Formation	Circle or line with six to eight players per group.
Equipment	Balls of different sizes.
Procedures	Children stand on a line facing the child who is "teacher." The "teacher" chooses any ball he wishes to use and throws or bounces it to each child in turn. When each child has

received the ball, the "teacher" goes to end of the line and child who is at head of line becomes the new "teacher," choosing the ball to be used. Game continues until each child has been "teacher."

SUGGESTED READINGS

Dauer, Victor P. *Essential Movement Experiences For Preschool and Primary Children,* Minneapolis: Burgess, 1972.

DeSantis, Gabriel, and Lester V. Smith, *Physical Education Programmed Activities For Grades K-6,* Columbus, Ohio: Charles E. Merrill, 1969.

Gallahue, David L., and William J. Meadors, *Let's Move: A Physical Education Program for Elementary School Teachers,* Dubuque, Iowa: Kendall–Hunt, 1974.

Rowen, Betty. *Learning Through Movement,* New York: Teachers College Press, Columbia University, 1963.

Wagner, Guy, et al. *Games and Activities For Early Childhood Education,* New York: MacMillan, 1967.

Chapter 8

Movement Experiences for Enhancing Fundamental Rhythmic Abilities

CONTENTS

Introduction
  General Objectives
Rhythm, Music and Movement
  Elements of Rhythm
Activity Ideas for Enhancing Creative Rhythmic Abilities
  Imitative Rhythms
    Specific Objectives
    Movement Experiences
  Interpretative Rhythms
    Specific Objectives
    Movement Experiences
Activity Ideas for Enhancing Auditory Rhythmic Abilities
  Finger Plays
    Specific Objectives
    Movement Experiences
  Nursery Rhymes and Poems
    Specific Objectives
    Movement Experiences
  Singing Rhythms
    Specific Objectives
    Movement Experiences

The Music in my heart I bore long after it was heard no more.
Wordsworth

INTRODUCTION

Rhythm plays an important role in the daily lives of preschool and primary-grade children. Responding to rhythm is one of the strongest and most basic urges of childhood. It is basic to the life process itself, as evidenced by the rhythmical functions of the body as in breathing, heart beat, and the performance of any movement in a coordinated manner. *Rhythm, therefore, is the measured release of energy made up of repeated units of time.*

Children begin developing their rhythmic abilities during infancy, as seen in the infant's cooing response to the soft rhythmical sounds of a lullabye, and by his attempt to make pleasurable rhythmic sights, sounds, and sensations last. As children grow they continue to explore and expand their environment. An internalized time structure is developed and refined (see chapter 4, pages 98–100 for a discussion of temporal awareness). This ability to respond rhythmically is developed and refined through practice and experience. As a result rhythmic activities play an important role in the preschool and primary-grade programs.

One avenue by which rhythmic abilities may be developed and refined is through movement. Rhythm is a basic component of all coordinated movement and as such the two may be effectively combined to enhance both of these interdependent areas. Movement activities designed to enhance rhythmic abilities of young children include creative experiences that are both imitative and interpretative in nature. They also include auditory rhythmic experiences that include finger plays, rhymes, and singing rhythms. Folk, square, and social dances are not appropriate for inclusion in the program at this level. This chapter will examine the role of rhythmic movement activities in enhancing fundamental rhythmic abilities.

The general objectives of the movement experiences contained in the following pages are: (1) to enhance children's fundamental locomotor and nonlocomotor abilities, (2) to enhance the child's ability to respond to variations in tempo, accent, intensity, underlying beat, and rhythmic pattern, (3) to enhance children's ability to imitate and interpret through creative rhythmic movement, and (4) to develop and refine children's auditory rhythmic abilities through participation in finger plays, nursery rhymes, poems, and singing rhythms.

RHYTHM, MUSIC, AND MOVEMENT

Rhythm is an element of movement. It is a distinctive and essential quality inherent in all coordinated movement. To be rhythmic there must be a presentation of a formed pattern in motion, sound, or design. Rhythm, music, and/or dance must possess the following qualities in order to be rhythmic. First, there must be a regulated flow of energy that is organized in both duration and intensity. Second, the time succession of events must result in balance and harmony. Third, there must be sufficient repetetion of regular symmetrical groupings in order to be rhythmical in nature.

A close parallel of rhythmics exists between music and movement. Rhythmic structure in music is allied with rhythmic structure in dance movements, and with rare exception children love both. They enjoy the melodic rhythmic succession of beats characteristic of music and the opportunity to express this through movement.

As children listen to music they respond to its rhythm in a variety of ways. They kick and laugh, jump and clap. They wiggle and giggle, twirl and skip. Sometimes they listen and relax, or simply burst into song and dance. They begin, in their own crude way, to make their own music. They hum, sing, and play a variety of improvised instruments in an effort to make music. The formation of a rhythm band utilizing a variety of homemade pieces of rhythmic equipment is an important first opportunity for young children to organize their efforts into an expressive whole. All children have music as a part of their being, and it is incumbent on the teacher to help each bring out his interest and to explore his own potential. Rhythmical music and movement is a vital part of the school program for preschool and primary-grade children, but how much depends on you, the teacher. You may not feel particularly adept at signing or playing a piano but you can:

1. Try an autoharp.
2. Play chords on a guitar.
3. Use a tape recorder.
4. Use records.*
5. Use a small xylophone.
6. Use a set of simple bells.
7. Use a drum.

Elements of Rhythm

Through listening and responding to music children begin to develop a knowledge and understanding of the elements of rhythm. Moving rhythmically is an excellent means by which children can begin to internalize the concepts of:

*Please refer to the end of this chapter for a list of selected record references listing appropriate record companies.

1. *Accent*—The emphasis given to any one beat (usually the first beat of every measure).
2. *Tempo*—the speed of the movement, music, or accompaniment.
3. *Intensity*—the loudness or softness of the movement or music.
4. *Underlying beat*—the steady, continuous sound of any rhythmical sequence.
5. *Rhythmic pattern*—a group of beats related to the underlying beat.

Participation in a variety of locomotor and nonlocomotor activities stressing the elements of rhythm serves as a means of practicing performance in a variety fundamental movement skills while learning about the elements of rhythm. For example, practice with running, jumping, and skipping to different tempos, intensities, and accents serves as a means of enhancing knowledge of fundamental elements of rhythm as well as developing skill in the movements themselves.

ACTIVITY IDEAS FOR ENHANCING CREATIVE RHYTHMIC ABILITIES

We often talk about creativity, but just what is it? When one creates something external, symbols or objects are manipulated in order to produce unusual events uncommon to the individual and/or environment. To create means to bring into existence, to make something out of a word or an idea for the first time, or to produce along new or unconventional lines. Generally speaking, we have not been trained to use our imagination to apply knowledge we already have and to extend it into creative behavior. Creativity hinges on the need for freedom to explore and experiment. It relies on a flexible schedule that permits time to explore, stand back and evaluate the results, and then continue on with the idea or project. Rhythm and dance constitute one avenue for enhancing creative expression.

Creative rhythmic activities require a flexible teacher and classroom techniques oriented toward creativity. The teacher needs to encourage the children to develop faith in themselves and others. The teacher must not leave creativity to chance, but must: (1) encourage curiosity, (2) ask questions that require thought, (3) reorganize original creative behavior, (4) be respectful of questions and unusual ideas (show them that their ideas have value), (5) provide opportunities for learning in creative ways, and (6) show a genuine interest in each child's efforts.

As humans we have the unique capacity to think and act creatively an ability that makes it possible to reach out for the unknown. All persons have the potential capacity to create, although some seem to have more innate ability than others. Highly creative individuals tend to possess characteristics such as openness to new experiences, the capacity to be puzzled, esthetic sensitivity, and imagination. However all children should be encouraged to develop their creative ability to its fullest. In order to develop they must have many opportunities to create and thus expand their insight, skill, and confidence.

Dance as an art experience is concerned with creativity. Even the beginner should be encouraged to make imaginative responses and to self-direct activity. The creative response can be attained through the process of exploration and improvisation, as well as through composition problems that provide opportunities for the children to think, feel, imagine, and create. Creative growth depends on experience and time to develop. Children must have the opportunity to progress from the simple to the complex and the demands of each creative rhythmic endeavor must be related to the developmental level of the individual.

Children are born with a natural drive for movement for it is a primary means by which they learn about their expanding world. They gradually expand their horizons through the cultivation of their inner impulses and urges for movement and learn to *think, act,* and *create* as they move. Creative rhythm is one avenue through which these desirable abilities can be developed and expanded in young children. Creative rhythmic experiences provide a means by which children can rhythmically *imitate* and *interpret* through movement.

Music and movement ideas that are used in creative rhythms must relate to the child's world in order to initiate spontaneity. The teacher serves as an essential catalyst in helping children develop and expand their powers of creativity and self-expression. As a result he or she should take the time necessary to carefully plan and execute lessons in creative rhythms.

Imitative Rhythms

Through imitative rhythms the children express themselves by trying to "be something." The teacher should be careful, however, to see to it that the children realize the movement potential of their own bodies prior to introducing imagery as a part of the rhythmic lesson. In their own mind the children take on the identity of what they are imitating. They interpret this identity with expressive movements to the accompaniment of a suitable rhythm. They are encouraged to explore and express themselves in varied and original movement as they react to the rhythm. There are three general approaches to imitation rhythms. In the first the teacher begins with a rhythm and lets the children decide what each one would like to be based on the characteristics of the rhythm. This approach is one of "what does this rhythm make you think of?" In the second method the teacher selects a piece of music and has the children make a choice of what they would select to imitate. All of the children imitate the same thing. Each child creates the selection as he or she wishes. If the choice were a "giant," each child would interpret his own individual concept of a giant. The third approach begins with a selection for imitation and thus choosing an apparopriate rhythm for movement. Listening to the musical accompaniment is important in all three approaches, as the children must "feel" the character of the music. The music (ranging from clapping or a drum beat to piano music or a recording) must be appropriate for the identity to be assumed in order to be effective; otherwise the movement becomes artificial. The movements of the children should also be in time with the music and reflect a basic understanding of the elements of rhythm.

Specific Objectives

Practice in creative imitative rhythmic activities with preschool and primary-grade children will contribute to their ability:

1. To think and act out creative movement sequences in response to rhythmic accompaniment.
2. To imitate the function of animate and inanimate objects through creative rhythmical movement.
3. To move efficiently through space in a controlled rhythmical manner.
4. To think and act creatively.

Movement Experiences

IMITATING LIVING CREATURES

There are many living creatures that children will enjoy imitating. These imitations may be done to the beat of a drum, piano, record, or without any form of accompaniment.

1. Animals:
   a. Elephant
   b. Giraffe
   c. Bear
   d. Lion
   e. Seal
   f. Snake
   g. Rabbit
   h. Kangaroo
   i. Puppy
   j. Duck
   k. Fish
   l. Bird

2. People:

a. Firefighter
b. Letter carrier
c. Doctor
d. Sailor
e. Soldier

f. Airplane pilot
g. Mountain climber
h. Ballerina
i. Cowboy
j. Carpenter

3. Pretend people and animals:

a. Witch
b. Gobblin
c. Elf
d. Dwarf
e. Giant

f. Fairy
g. Pixie
h. Dragon
i. Troll
j. Monster

IMITATING THINGS IN NATURE

Young children are rapidly expanding their knowledge and understanding of the world of nature. There are numerous things in nature that they will enjoy imitating and through these experiences will increase their knowledge and nature vocabulary.

1. Weather conditions:

a. Wind
b. Rain
c. Snow
d. Sleet
e. Hail

f. Hurricane
g. Tornado
h. Clouds
j. Storm
k. Sun

2. Climatic conditions:

a. Hot
b. Cold
c. Warm
d. Cool
e. Sunny

g. Summer
h. Autumn
i. Winter
j. Spring

3. Miscellaneous:

a. Smoke
b. Fire
c. Wave

d. Moon
e. Sun
f. Star

g. Flower
h. Water
i. Mineral

j. Soil

IMITATING OBJECTS

There are several play objects and machines that children enjoy imitating.

Imitating objects is an aspect of creative rythms.

1. Play objects:

   a. Swing
   b. Slide
   c. Seesaw
   d. Merry-go-round
   e. Ball
   f. Pull toy
   g. Yo-yo
   h. Frisbee
   i. Climbing tower
   j. Silly putty

2. Modes of transportation:

   a. Row boat
   b. Snowmobile
   c. Truck
   d. Car
   e. Canoe
   f. Rocket
   g. Bicycle
   h. Motorcycle
   i. Train

3. Machines:

   a. Elevator
   b. Tractor
   c. Bulldozer
   d. Crane
   e. Cement mixer
   f. Old-fashioned coffee grinder
   g. Pneumatic drill
   h. Lawn mower
   i. Record player

IMITATING EVENTS

As the world of children is expanding, so is their exposure to special events outside the home. The following is a list of suggested activities and events that may be imitated at strategic times during the year.

1. The circus:

   a. Clown
   b. Acrobat
   c. Juggler
   d. Trained animal
   e. High-wire walker
   f. Trapeze artist
   g. Lion trainer
   h. Marching band
   i. Barker
   j. Ring master

2. Sporting events (in slow motion, imitate the movements found in the following athletic events):

   a. Soccer
   b. Football
   c. Baseball
   d. Basketball
   e. Volleyball
   f. Track and field events
   g. Swimming and diving
   h. Fencing
   i. Tennis
   j. Bowling

Interpretative rhythms

Interpretative movements are the second form of creative rhythms. In interpretative rhythms the children act out an idea, a familiar event, or an ordinary procedure. They also express feelings, emotions, and moods through movement. The quality and direction of the interpretative movements rely on the mood, intelligence, and personal feelings of the children. In interpretative movement the teacher creates the atomsphere for the children to express themselves. There are three general approaches to this also. In the first the teacher begins with an idea, story, or other basis. As the story progresses, suitable rhythmic background can be used. Recordings, a piano selection, percussion rhythms, or even a rhythm band can be used. The teacher provides the verbal background and directions for the drama; however, the story can unfold without this.

The second approach begins with a piece of music, generally a recording, and develops an idea to fit the music. The piece of music selected should have sufficient changes in tempo and pattern to provide different kinds and qualities of background. A general idea or plan of action can be selected and fitted to the music. An idea such as "going to the fair" may be selected and an adaptable recording chosen.

In the third approach the children express moods or feelings. A piece of music may be played and the children act out how the music makes them feel. An alternative method is simply to give cue words that denote specific moods (happy, sad, etc.) and have the children express these words through movement.

Specific Objectives

Practice in creative interpretative rhythmic activities with preschool and primary-grade children will contribute to their ability:

1. To think through and act out creative movement sequences in response to rhythmic accompaniment.
2. To interpret moods, feelings, and ideas and to express them through creative rhythmic moves.
3. To solve rhythmic problems creatively through expressive movement.
4. To move efficiently through space in a coordinated rhythm.
5. To think and act creatively.
6. To "feel" auditory and visual symbols, and to be able to express these feelings through movement.

Movement Experiences

INTERPRETING ACTION WORDS

Numerous verbs provide opportunities for creative movement. Try several during the first few minutes of the lesson. The following represent only a few of the numerous possibilities:

1. Bang	8. Blow	15. Dart
2. Crack	9. Bump	16. Zoom
3. Spin	10. Tingle	17. Bop
4. Pop	11. Grab	18. Zip
5. Twinkle	12. Grumble	19. Boom
6. Glow	13. Punch	20. Pluck
7. Bubble	14. Float	

INTERPRETING FEELINGS AND MOODS

Children experience many feelings and moods during the course of their day. They will enjoy openly expressing them through expressive movement. Musical accompaniment may be used in order to enhance the experience.

1. Happiness	6. Gladness	11. Jealousy	16. Shyness
2. Sadness	7. Gayiety	12. Fear	17. Boredom
3. Bewilder- ment	8. Love	13. Hurt	18. Interest
4. Pride	9. Hate	14. Surprise	19. Laughter
5. Disappoint- ment	10. Friendship	15. Bravery	20. Tears

INTERPRETING ART THROUGH MOVEMENT

Art is an experience that may, through guided discovery, be successfully interpreted through movement. Various lines, forms, colors, and textures may be expressed through creative movement. Remember that the children should be encouraged to express how these things make them feel. Guessing games may be played with one group trying to guess what the other is imitating. Discuss the various art forms with the children before they show you their interpretation.

1. Line:

a. Straight	d. Dotted
b. Curved	e. Dashed
c. Zig-zagged	f. Broken

2. Form:

a. Circle
b. Square
c. Triangle

d. Rectangle
e. Hexagon

3. Color:

a. Red
b. White
c. Green
d. Blue

e. Yellow
f. Black
g. Purple
h. Pink

i. Brown
j. Orange

4. Texture:

a. Smooth
b. Slippery
c. Bumpy

d. Rough
e. Hard
f. Soft

g. Furry
h. Silky
i. Scratchy

j. Slick

INTERPRETING ACTION SEQUENCES

There is an innumerable number of action sequences that children enjoy interpreting. The following is a list of only a few of the possibilities that may be explored.

1. Move through molasses
2. Shoo the flies away
3. Floating in water
4. Hit the punching bag
5. Grow like a flower
6. Sway like a tree in the breeze
7. Build a house
8. Fight a fire
9. Rocket to the moon
10. Ride a bumpy road

INTERPRETATING PENDULAR MOVEMENTS

Have the children think of objects that swing. Let them move (clock, golfclub, baseball bat, swing, etc.) to each one. Use an object that has a pendular motion so they can keep time. Encourage them to swing with their eyes closed and then open to see if they are still in time with the beat. Encourage the children to also swing individual parts of their body one at a time.

INTERPETING SPECIAL HOLIDAYS

Discuss the meaning of various special holidays with the children, encouraging them to share their experiences with the class.

1. Christmas	6. Flag Day
2. Hanukah	7. Thanksgiving
3. Halloween	8. Fourth of July
4. Easter	9. Summer vacation
5. Valentine's Day	10. Snow days

ACTIVITY IDEAS FOR ENHANCING AUDITORY RHYTHMIC ABILITIES

Children should experience creative movement responses through as many different sensory modalities as possible. Singing rhythms, finger plays, and nursery rhymes offer opportunities for combining movement and socialization to rhythmic patterns. Singing rhythms are appealing to children because they: (1) tell a story, (2) develop an idea, (3) have pleasing rhythmic patterns, (4) stimulate use of one's imagination, or (5) have dramatic possibilities. Singing plays an important role in the life of children. They love repetition and will sing over and over again the songs they know. They enjoy hearing the same old songs and learning new ones. Children also like to respond to songs through movement. When responding to activity songs, they will usually join in the singing. This singing is important for it helps to internalize the rhythm of the song itself. When simple songs are utilized, children are given a variety of opportunities for repetition of movement and a chance to be creative and express themselves dramatically.

Singing and accompanying rhythmic responses are complex physical activities. Doll and Nelson have stated that: "They demand exacting functions of the small muscles. Well-planned rhythmic movements give one facet of the musical experience to the large and small muscles, generating a musical response throughout the total being."[1]

Young children need and enjoy singing rhythms and rhymes. Singing rhythms, finger plays, and rhymes are made up of actions that the children do as they sing or chant a particular song or repeat a particular rhyme. There may be a great deal of variation in the action patterns used in singing rhythms and finger rhymes. It will depend on how the children follow and interpret the action's suggested by the auditory cues, their willingness to express themselves freely, and the teaching cues used by the teachers.

The incorporation of action patterns with various songs, rhymes, and finger plays will do much to enhance young children's auditory rhythmic abilities. Developing and reinforcing an internal sensitivity to tempo, accent,

[1] Doll, Edna and Mary Nelson, *Rhythms Today,* Morristown, N. J.: Silver Burdette, 1967, 4.

Singing rhythms and rhymes are enjoyed by young children.

intensity, and rhythmic pattern will be by-products of successful participation in singing rhythms, rhymes, and finger plays that require a movement response.

The importance of developing the ability to express internally perceived rhythm motorically cannot be overemphasized. It is through the development of temporal awareness that children establish a meaningful and effective time structure. To see why the ability to interpret auditory rhythmic patterns is important, we need only look at how children first learn the alphabet or a new song. The "sing-song" rhythmic cadence used to recite the alphabet or song seems to make it easier to recall and retain. As adults we find it much easier to recall and remember the words to an old "long-forgotten" song than those uttered by your instructor just yesterday. For example, by listening to the melody of an old Beatles tune ("She Loves Me," "I Want to Hold Your Hand," etc.) will often trigger recollection of the words that accompany the tune. This would not be possible or would be considerably more difficult if our auditory rhythmic abilities were not adequately developed and refined. Hence from the standpoint of preschool and primary-grade children, practice and participation in singing, rhythms, rhymes and poems are important. Incorporation of the medium of movement serves as a means of making these experiences more enjoyable and increasing the number of sensory modalities involved.

The following pages present numerous examples of finger plays, rhymes, and singing rhythms that may be effectively used with young children. Finger plays are generally most appropriate for preschool children, along with most nursery rhymes. Singing rhyms are generally initiated during kindergarten through the second grade.

Finger Plays

Finger plays and nursery rhymes are generally the first versus committed to memory by preschool children. Finger plays are generally quite short and easy to learn. Many of them have been handed down from generation to generation. The small muscles of the hands and fingers are less well developed in preschool children than their other muscles. Practice in finger plays does much to aid in increasing their finger dexterity. They also provide children with an opportunity to being using movement to interpret specified rhythmical verses.

Specific Objectives

Practice in finger-play activities will contribute to children's:

1. Auditory rhythmic abilities.

2. Fine motor dexterity.
3. Auditory memory abilities.
4. Ability to combine rhythmical auditory and movement sequences into a coordinated whole.
5. Ability to utilize movement to interpret specified rhythmical sequence.

Movement Experiences

HERE IS THE BEEHIVE

Here is the beehive. (fold hands)*
But where are the bees? (puzzled look)
Hiding inside, where nobody sees. (peek inside)
They're coming out now. They're all alive. (show surprise)
One, two, three, four, five. (raise fingers one at a time)
Bzzzzzzzzzzzzzzzzz.

THIS LITTLE CLOWN

This little clown is fat and gay (hold up thumb)
This little clown does tricks all day (hold up forefinger)
This little clown is tall and strong (hold up middle finger)
This little clown sings a funny song (hold up ring finger)
This little clown is wee and small (hold up little finger)
But he can do anything at all.

I'M A LITTLE TEAPOT

I'm a little teapot short and stout
Here is my handle (place hand on waist, forming handle)
Here is my spout. (form spout with the other arm)
When I get all steamed up then I shout: (hiss)
Tip me over and pour me out. (pour the "tea" out the "spout")

*The words in parentheses indicate the suggested action pattern.

OVER THE HILLS

Over the hills and far away (pounding motion of hands)
We skip and run and laugh and play. (clap hands)
Smell the flowers and fish the streams, (sniff a flower—cast a line)
Lie in the sunshine and dream sweet dreams (sleep, cheek on hand)

ROW, ROW, ROW

Row, row, row your boat (rowing motion with both hands)
Gently down the stream (forward waving motion, one hand)
Merrily, merrily, merrily, merrily (clap hands in rhythm)
Life is but a dream. (sleep)

DIG A LITTLE HOLE

Dig a little hole, (dig)
Plant a little seed, (drop seed)
Pour a little water, (pour)
Pull a little weed. (pull up and throw away)
Chase a little bug (chasing motion with hands)
Height-ho, there he goes! (shade eyes)
Give a little sunshine, (cup hands, lift to the sun)
Grow a little rose. (small flower, eyes closed, smiling)

TEN FINGERS

I have ten little fingers (extend the 10 fingers)
They all belong to me.
I can make them do things,
Would you like to see?
I can open them up wide, (spread fingers apart)
Shut them up tight, (clench fists)
Put them out of sight, (place hands behind back)
Jump them up high, (raise hands)

Jump them down low, (lower hands)
Fold them quietly, and sit (fold them in lap)
Just so!

LITTLE FISH

I hold my fingers like a fish, (hold hands back-to-back with fingers
                                    spread, wave hands to the side as in
                                    swimming, continue to and fro)
and wave them as I go,
Through the water with a swish,
So gaily to and fro.

BUNNY

Hippity, hoppety, hop, hop, hop, (raise hands to side of head)
Here comes a little bunny, (children hop on both feet)
One ear is down, one ear is up, (press fingers of one hand against palm)
Oh, doesn't he look funny?

BIRDS

If I were a bird, I'd sing a song (entwine the two thumbs and so that
                                    palms of the hands are facing inward)
and fly about the whole day long, (flutter the hands)
And when the night came, go to rest (fold the hands and go to sleep)
up in my cozy little nest.

IF I WERE A BIRD

If I were a bird, I'd sing a song, (raise both arms, waving them as a bird
                                    flying)
And fly about the whole day long.
And when the night came, go to rest, (place both hands together on one
                                    side of face, like sleeping)

Up in my cozy little nest.
Oh look and see out—airplanes (raise both arms in horizontal positions,
as an airplane)
Away up in the sky.
Watch us gliding through the air, (fly about, as an airplane)
This is how we fly.

TWO LITTLE

Two little eyes that open and close, (children point to parts of the body
indicated by the verses)
Two little ears and one little nose,
Two little lips and one little chin,
Two little cheeks with the rose shut in,
Two little elbows so dimpled and sweet,
Two little shoes on two little feet.
Two little shoulders so chubby and strong,
Two little legs, running all day long.

FLOWERS

See the blue and yellow blossoms, (hold both hands above the head with
fingers touching, spread hands apart,
drop one hand)
In the flower bed.
The daisy spreads its petals wide,
The tulip bows its head.

LEFT AND RIGHT

This is my right hand, raise it up high, (raise right hand high)
This is my left hand, I'll touch the sky. (raise left hand high)
Right hand, left hand, whirl them 'round, (whirl hands before you)
Left hand, right hand, pound, pound, pound. (pound left fist with right)

This is my right foot, tap, tap, tap, (tap right foot three times)
This is my left foot, pat, pat, pat, (tap left foot three times)
Right foot, left foot, run, run, run, (run in place)
Right foot, left, foot, jump for fun. (lift right foot, and down
                                    (lift left foot, and down)
                                    (jump up and down)

Nursery Rhymes and Poems

There are numerous nursery rhymes and poems that have been passed from generation to generation that we are all familiar with. The following rhymes and poems may be less familiar but are equally suitable for adding action sequences. Nursery rhymes are particularly enjoyed by preschool and kindergarten-age children.

Specific Objectives

Practice in nursery rhymes and poems that incorporate action sequences will contribute to children's:

1. Auditory rhythmic abilities
2. Listening skills.
3. Auditory memory abilities.
4. Ability to combine rhythmical auditory sequences effectively with coordinated action patterns.
5. Ability to utilize movement to interpret specific rhythmical sequence.

Movement Experiences

MY HANDS

I raise my hands up high
Now on the floor they lie
Now high, now low
Now reach up to the sky.

I spread my hands out wide
Now behind my back they hide
Now wide, now hide
Now I put them at my side.

I give my head a shake, shake, shake,
Now, not a move I make
Now shake, shake, shake
Not a move I make
Now my whole self I shake

THE NOBLE DUKE OF YORK

The noble Duke of York
He had ten thousand men
He marched them up a hill
And marched them down again
So when you're up, you're up
And when you're down, you're down
And when you're only half way up
You're neither up nor down. (children stand and sit in response to the
words "up" and "down")

CHOO-CHOO

"Choo-choo" we hear the train
"Choo-Choo" it goes again
It pulls a heavy load all day. (pull self while sliding; use arm and feet
movements).

WINDY WEATHER

Life a leaf or a feather
In the windy, windy weather;

We will whirl around
And twirl around
And all sink down together.

FUNNY CLOWN

I am a funny clown
I move like a funny clown
I jump, I skip and run.
I stop and have a lot of fun.

MY LITTLE PUPPY

My little puppy's name is Rags,
He eats so much that his tummy sags.
His ears flip flp, his tail wig wags,
And when he walks, he zigs and zags.

HOW CREATURES MOVE

The lion walks on padded paws,
The squirrel leaps from limb to limb
While flies can crawl straight up a wall,
And seals can dive and swim.
The worm, he wiggles all around,
The monkey swings by his tail,
And birds may hop upon the ground
Or spread their wings and sail
But boys and girls have much more fun;
They leap and dance and walk and run.

JACK-IN-THE-BOX

Jack-in-the-box
All shut up tight,
Not a breath of air,

Not a peep of light,
How tired he must be
All in a heap
I'll open the box
And up he'll leap

STORMY DAYS

On stormy days
When the wind is high
Tall trees are brooms
Sweeping the sky.

They swish their branches
In buckets of rain
And swish and sweep it
Blue again.

FOLLOW THE LEADER RHYMES

Who feels happy? Who feels gay?
All who do clap your hands
    this way.
Who feels happy? Who feels gay?
All who do tap your feet
    this way.
Who feels happy? Who feels gay?
All who skip around this way.
(Add other activities as desired.)

I'll touch my hair, my eyes,
I'll sit up straight, then
    I'll rise
I'll touch my ears, my nose, my chin
Then quietly I'll sit down again.

The elephant walks just so
Swaying to and fro—
He liefts up his turnk to the trees
Then slowly gets down on his knees

Tip-toe, tip-toe, little feet,
Tip-toe, tip-toe, little feet,
Now fast, now slow
Now very softly—
Tip-toe, tip-toe little feet
(Add other activities as desired.)

Shall we go for a walk today?
A walk today, a walk today?
Repeat—use—pick flowers,
Smell flowers.
Shall we pick flowers today, etc.
Shall we smell flowers today, etc.
(Use any other ideas to incorporate bending, jumping, etc. to the above verses.)

DRAWING NUMERALS IN SPACE

A line straight down, and that is all (repeat twice)
To make the numeral 1
Around and down and to the right (repeat twice)
To make the numeral 2
Curve around and curve again (3)
Down, across, than all the way down (4)
Down, curve around a line at the top, (5)
Curve down, and all the way around (6)
A line across and then slant down (7)
Curve around and then back up (8)
Curve around and then straight down (9)
A straight line down and circle around (10)

(Have the children sit or stand and perform the actions of the words as they are sung through.)

HEAD, SHOULDERS BABY

Head, shoulders, baby 1, 2, 3. (repeat)
Head, shoulders, head, shoulders, head, shoulders, baby, 1, 2, 3
Chest, stomach, baby 1, 2, 3. (repeat)
Chest, stomach, chest, stomach, chest, stomach, baby, 1, 2, 3
Knees, ankles
Ankles, knees
Stomach, chest
Shoulders head

MISS MARY MACK

Teacher: Miss Mary Mack
Pupils: Mack, Mack
Teacher: All dressed in black
Pupils: Black, black
Teacher: With silver buttons
Pupils: Buttons, buttons
Teacher: She asked her mother
Pupils: Mother, Mother
Teacher: For fifteen cents
Pupils: Cents, cents
Teacher: To see the elephants
Pupils: Elephants, elephants
Teacher: Jump the fence
Pupils: Fence, fence
Teacher: They jumped so high
Pupils: High, high
Teacher: They touched the sky
Pupils: Sky, sky
Teacher: And they never came down

Pupils: Down, down
Teacher: Till the Fourth of July
Pupils: ly, ly.

(Standing in a circle, the children sing the song and respond to the beat by jumping.)

Singing Rhythms

A singing rhythm is a dance in which the children sing verses to a song that provides cues as to how to move. The children will first need to learn the words to the song. If musical accompaniment is used they should listen to it often. They have a general grasp of the words. The action phase of the activity should be added lastly.

Specific Objectives

Practice in singing rhythmic activities will aid children in the development of:

1. Auditory memory skills.
2. Listening skills
3. Auditory rhythmic abilities.
4. Fundamental movement abilities.

Movement Experiences

BINGO

Desired outcomes	1. To develop auditory memory and sequencing abilities.
	2. To perform rhythmic clapping to a prescribed rhythmic pattern.
Formation	Single circle facing the center.
Number of participants	Any number.

Song There was a farmer who had a dog,
    And Bingo was his name
    B-I-N-G-O, B-I-N-G-O, B-I-N-G-O
    And Bingo was his name-O

Procedures

Begin by singing whole song and then repeating the song, dropping the "o" in Bingo, substituting a clap. Next time drop the "g" and substitute two claps for the missing letters. Continue until each letter of Bingo is dropped and the whole word is clapped. (This may be done in a circle, standing or sitting.)

Variations

Select a "Bingo" and let him or her perform the actions of a dog while the others are singing.

DID YOU FEED MY COW?

Teacher: Did you feed my cow?
Pupils: Yes Ma'am.
Teacher: Could you tell me how?
Pupils: Yes Ma'am.
Teacher: What did you feed her?
Pupils: Corn and hay.
Teacher: What did you feed her?
Pupils: Corn and hay.

Teacher: Did you milk her good?
Pupils: Yes Ma'am.
Teacher: Did you milk her like you should?
Pupils: Yes Ma'am.
Teacher: Well, how did you milk her?
Pupils: Squish, squish, squish.

Teacher: How did you milk her?
Pupils: Squish, squish squish.
Teacher: Did my cow get sick?
Pupils: Yes Ma'am.
Teacher: Was she covered with ticks?
Pupils: Yes Ma'am.
Teacher: How did she die?
Pupils: Um um um!
Teacher: How did she die?
Pupils: Um um um!

Teacher: Did the buzzards come?
Pupils: Yes Ma'am.
Teacher: Did the buzzards come?
Pupils: Yes Ma'am.
Teacher: How did they come?
Pupils: Flop! Flop! Flop!
Teacher: How did they come?
Pupils: Flop! Flop! Flop!

Teacher: How did they come?
Pupils: Flop! Flop! Flop!

HEY, BETTY MARTIN

Desired Outcomes	1. To increase knowledge of the function of various body parts.
	2. To move rhythmically to a prescribed rhythmic pattern
Formation	Single circle facing in
Number of participants	Six children per circle

Song Hey, Betty Martin, tip toe, tip toe,
     Hey Betty Martin, tipe toe, fine;
     Hey Betty Martin, tip toe, tip toe,
     Hey Betty Martin, tip toe fine.

Can't get a boy, a boy to please her,
Can't get a boy to please her mind;
She wants to find a boy to please her,
She wants to find a certain kind.

Procedures

First verse:
With children sitting or standing in a circle, one child (Betty Martin") tiptoes around the inside of the circle looking for someone to "please her mind."

Second verse:
Continue as above until the end of the second verse, at which time "Betty" chooses someone by tapping his shoulder. She then takes the place of the child chosen.

The song is repeated, with the new "Betty Martin" (or Johnny Martin) tiptoeing around the circle. Several circles should be used, limited to six children, so that each child may participate.

Variation
The children may sing this verse after "Betty" or "Johnny" finds that "special one":

I found a boy, a boy to please me,
I found a boy to please my mind;
I found a boy, a boy to please me,
I found a boy, a certain kind.

(After the verse is sung the new "Betty" or "Johnny" repeats the original cycle of the game.)

LITTLE RED CABOOSE

Desired outcomes
1. To reinforce awareness of "red" as an color word, and the functions of a train.
2. To perform brisk walking movements to a prescribed rhythmic pattern.

Formation

Single line with both hands on the shoulders of the person in front.

Number of participants

ten to 15 per line.

Song Little red caboose, little red caboose,
   Little red caboose behind the train.
   Smoke stack on its back, rumblin' down the track,
   Little red caboose behind the train. Toot!"

   "Little red caboose, little red caboose,
   Little red caboose behind the train.
   Coming round the bend, hanging on the end,
   Little red caboose behind the train. Toot!

Procedures

While singing the song, groups of children can form a line with hands on the shoulders or waist of the child ahead. As some of them sing and move in time with the music, others chant the words "choo, choo, choo, choo."

Variations

Make up other verses to the song about trains as they rumble down the tracks.

MULBERRY BUSH

Desired outcome:

1. To perform rhythmic pantomining motions in time to the song.
2. To skip and move in other ways in time to the music.

Formation

Single circle facing in with one child at the center of the circle.

Song Here we go round the mulberry bush, the mulberry bush, the mulberry bush,
Here we go round the mulberry bush so early in the morning.

This is the way we wash our clothes, we wash our clothes, we wash our clothes
This is the way we wash our clothes, so early in the morning.

(Continue with:)
This is the way we hang our clothes.
This is the way we iron our clothes.
This is the way we fold our clothes.
This is the way we rake the leaves.
This is the way we sweep the floor.

Number of participants	Any number.
Procedure	Children may form a circle; one child designated as the mulberry bush stands in the center. Let them skip around the circle holding hands as they sing the chorus, and stopping to perform the action of the verses.
Variation	Make up other words to the songs, such as when doing a circus unit. (the words might be, "this is the way the elephant walks," "this is the way the seals clap," etc.)

TEN LITTLE JINGLE BELLS

Desired outcomes	1. To reinforce counting skills and increase small-muscle dexterity. 2. To perform galloping and pantomining skills to a prescribed rhythmic pattern.

Formation

Double row of 10 children in each row behind the leader (horse).

Number of participants

Twenty-one children.

Song Ten little jingle bells hung in a row,
 Ten little jingle bells helped the horse go.
 Merrily, merrily over the snow
 Merrily, merrily sleighing we go.

 One little jingle bell fell in the snow
 Nine little jingle bells helped the horse go.
 Merrily, merrily over the snow
 Merrily, merrily sleighing we go.

 (Continue subtracting bells until one is left.)

 "One little jingle bell fell in the snow (sing slowly)
 No little jingle bells help the horse go.
 Slowly, so slowly the bells are all gone.
 We'll get some new ones and put them right on."

Procedures

One child may be the horse and 10 children, the jingle bells in a double row behind the horse. One jingle bell drops off during each verse until only the horse is left. They should carry sleigh or jingle bells and ring them as they move to the rhythm.

Variations

Have two or three teams of horses so that full participation of all class members is going on.

LOBBY LOO

Desired outcomes

1. To reinforce left-right concepts of directional awareness through a rhythmic activity.

2. To perform turning, skipping, jumping, and shaking movements.

Formation

Single circle, all facing center with hands joined.

Number of participants:

Any number

Song Here we dance looby loo
Here we dance looby light
Here we dance looby loo
All on a Saturday night.

1. "I put my right hand in
I take my right hand out
I give my right hand a shake, shake, shake
And turn myself about."
2. "I put my left hand in, etc. . . . "
3. I put my right foot in, etc . . . "
4. I put my left foot in, etc . . . "
5. I put my head way in, etc . . . "
6. I put my whole self in, etc . . "

Procedures

On the verse part of the dance, the children stand still facing the center and follow the directions of the words. On the words "and turn myself about," they make a complete turn in place and get ready to skip around the circle. On the last verse, the children jump forward and then backward, shaking themselves vigorously, and then turning about.

Variation

This is an excellent activity to help children with left–right concepts. Be sure to use it as such.

BLUE BIRD

Desired outcomes

1. To remember a song and melody and to be able to perform pantomime movements while singing it.
2. To be able to walk in time to a prescribed rhythmic pattern.

Formation

Single circle facing inward.

Number of Participants

About 10 per circle

Song Blue bird, blue bird, in and out my windows,
   Blue bird, blue bird in and out my windows,
   Oh! Johnny, I am tired.

   Take a boy (girl) and tap him (her) on the shoulders (repeat two more times)

Procedures

The boys and girls form a circle facing inward, with hands joined raised to form arches. One child (the blue bird) stands outside the circle. Sing the words of the song as the bird goes in and out of the arches.

The child who has been tapped becomes the new bluebird while the former one takes the vacant place in the circle. Repeat until every one has been the bluebird. (You may need more than one circle.)

Variations

Let the children form a chain of bluebirds until all of the children become birds and there are no windows left.

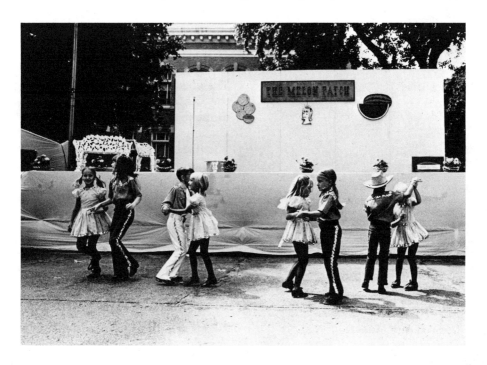

Simple folk dances are often enjoyed by first and second graders.

TEN LITTLE INDIANS

Desired outcomes	To enhance rhythmical expression and pattern.
Formation	Single circle facing inward.
Number of participants:	Ten per group.

Song

First verse: 1 little, 2 little, 3 little Indians,
    4 little, 5 little, 6 little Indians,
    7 little, 8 little, 9 little Indians,
    10 little Indian boys.

Second verse: 10 little, 9 little, 8 little Indians,
    7 little, 6 little, 5 little Indians,

4 little, 3 little, 2 little Indians,
1 little Indian boy.

| Procedures | The children stand in a circle facing the center. Each child is given a number from 1 to ten. As the first verse is sung, the children squat when their number is called. During the second verse they stand when their number is called. The song is repeated with the children hopping and whooping, Indian fashion, counterclockwise during the first verse and clockwise during the second verse. |

FARMER IN THE DELL

Desired outcomes	To enhance auditory memory and rhythmical sequencing.
Formation	Single circle facing inward.
Number of participants	Sixteen to 20 per circle.

Song
First verse The farmer in the dell,
The farmer in the dell,
Heigh-ho the dairy, oh,
The farmer in the dell.

Second verse: The farmer takes a wife—
(repeat first verse except for farmer in the dell.)
Third verse: The wife takes a child—
Fourth verse: The child takes a nurse—
Fifth verse: The nurse takes a cat—
Sixth verse: The cat takes a mouse—
Seventh verse: The mouse takes the cheese—
Eighth verse: The cheese stands alone—

Procedures

The children form a circle, holding hands with one child (i.e., farmer) in the center of the circle. The children walk or skip counterclockwise as they sing the song. As they sing the second verse, the farmer chooses somebody to be his wife, and during the singing of the third verse, the wife chooses somebody to be her child. Each time a new verse is sung, a child is chosen to play the role of the character about whom they are singing. The last child selected always chooses the next child. When the children finish the last verse, the "cheese" chases the children about the room. The child tagged becomes the farmer for the next time the dance is performed.

HOW DO YOU DO, MY PARTNER

Desired outcomes

To develop an understanding of rhythmical sequencing and enhance spatial awareness.

Formation

Single circle facing inward.

Number of participants

Any number.

Song How do you do, my partner?
 How do you do today?
 Will you dance in a circle?
 I will show you the way.

 Chorus: Tra-la-la-la-la-la.

Procedures:

One child is stationed in the middle of the circle. He faces a member of the circle and shakes hands while the children sing the song. As the song ends, the two skip around the circle as everyone sings, "Tra-la-la-la-la-la." When the chorus ends, the two face new partners and the song begins again. Continue this procedure until all children are dancing.

ROUND AND ROUND THE VILLAGE.

Desired outcomes

To develop an understanding of rhythmical sequencing and enhance spatial awareness.

Formation:

Single circle facing inward with one child on the outside.

Number of participants:

ten to 20

Song
 Chorus: Go round and round the village,
     Go round and round the village,
     Go round and round the village,
     As we have done before.

First verse: "Go in and out the windows—

Second verse: Now stand and face your partner,—

Third verse: Now follow me to London—

Procedures

The children stand in a circle with hands joined and one child stands outside the circle. The children walk counterclockwise singing the chorus (the child outside the circle skips clockwise). After the chorus, the children stop and raise their arms to make "windows" while singing the first verse. The child on the outside of the circle goes in and out of the windows. As the circle sings the second verse, the child selects a partner. The partners skip around on the outside of the circle while the other children sing the third verse. Repeat this procedure until all children have a partner.

I SEE YOU

Desired outcomes

To enhance rhythmic sequencing abilities.

Formation

Double circles facing inward, one behind the other.

Number of participants

Any number.

Song

First verse: "I see you, I see you
Tra la, la-la, la.
I see you, I see you
Tra la, la-la, la.

Second verse: "You see me and I'll see you,
You swing me and I'll swing you,
You see me and I'll see you,
You swing me and I'll swing you."

Procedures

The children form a circle with the girls standing behind the boys with their hands on the boys' shoulders. They then proceed to play "peek-a-boo" over the boys' shoulders on the first verse in tempo with the verse on each "see" and each "tra-la," "la-la," and "la." On the second verse, the boys face their partners, hook elbows, and skip around in a circle. The boys then change places with their partners and play "peek-a-boo" as the song begins again.

A HUNTING WE WILL GO

Desired outcomes:	To enhance rhythmical sequencing and body awareness.
Formation:	Two parallel lines facing one another.
Number of participants:	Six to eight per line.

Song A hunting we will go,
    A hunting we will go,
    We'll catch a fox and put him in a box
    And then we'll let him go.

Procedures	The head couple hold hands and slide down the line with eight fast steps and back again as the song is sung the first time. As the song is repeated, they lead a "parade" of all of the couples skipping in a circular pattern to the foot of the set. The head couple then forms an arch while the other children take the person's hand across from them and walk through the arch and back to their places. The entire verse is sung while doing this. The dance is repeated until all have had an opportunity to be the head couple.

DID YOU EVER SEE A LASSIE?

Desired outcomes	To develop an understanding of rhythmical sequencing

Formation   Single circle facing inward.

Number of participants   Ten to 12 per circle.

Song
    Chorus: Did you ever see a Lassie, a Lassie, a Lassie.
              Did you ever see a Lassie go this way and that?
              Go this way and that way, go this way and that way;
              Did you ever see a Lassie go this way and that?

Procedures: The children join hands and form a
                                              circle. One child is placed in the cen-
                                              ter of the circle and is designated to
                                              be a Lassie (or Laddie). The other
                                              children are also given character
                                              names such as farmer, soldier, fire-
                                              man, cowboy, and so on. When the
                                              verse is sung, the child in the center
                                              performs various movements to the
                                              rhythm of the song and the children
                                              in the circle try to imitate these
                                              movements.
                                              Each time the verse is sung another
                                              name is substituted for Lassie and
                                              the above procedure is repeated.

JOLLY IS THE MILLER

Desired outcomes   To enhance fundamental rhythmi-
                                              cal sequencing abilities.

Formation   Double circle facing counterclock-
                                              wise.

Number of participants   Twenty-one to 25.
Song Oh, jolly is the miller who lives by the mill
        The wheel turns round with a right good will.
        One hand in the hopper and the other in the sack
        The girl steps forward and the boy steps back.

Procedures

The children form a double circle facing counterclockwise and hold their partner's hand. One child is placed in the center of the inner circle (i.e., the miller). The children move counterclockwise as they sing the song. They change partners on the words "the girl steps forward . . . " At this time the "miller" attempts to get a partner and the child left without a partner becomes the "miller."

SUGGESTED READINGS

Arbuckle, Wanda, Eleanor Ball, and George Cornwell, *Learning to Move and Moving to Learn*, Columbus, Ohio: Charles E. Merrill, 1969.

Boorman, Joyce. *Creative Dance in the First Three Grades*, New York: David McKay Company, 1969.

Doll, Edna, and Mary Nelson, *Rhythms Today*, Morristown, N.J.: Silver Burdett, 1965.

Joyce, Mary. *First Steps in Teaching Creative Dance*, Palo Alto, Calif.: National Press Books, 1973.

Murray, Ruth. *Dance in Elementary Education*, 3rd edition, New York: Harper 1975.

Russell, Joan. *Creative Dance in the Elementary School*, London MacDonald and Evans, 1965.

Stanley, Sheila. *Physical Education: A Movement Orientation*, Toronto: McGraw–Hill, 1969.

Winters, Shirley J. *Creative Rhythmic Movement: For Children of Elementary School Age*, Dubuque, Iowa: W. C. Brown, 1975.

SUGGESTED RECORDS

Congdon, Paul. *Fun Dances for Children*, Kimbo Records, Deal, New Jersey, Box 246, KEA1134.

Herman, Michael. *First Fold Dances*, RCA Victor, New York, LPM6625.

Janiak, William. *Everyday Skills for Early Childhood and Special Education*, Kimbo Records, Deal, New Jersey, Box 246, KIM7016-7021.

Palmer, Hap. *Creative Movement and Rhythmic Exploration*, Educational Activities, Freeport, New York, Box 392, AR533.

Palmer, Hap. *Folk Song Carnival*, Educational Activities, Freeport, New York, Box 392, AR524.

Palmer, Hap. *Holiday Songs and Rhythms*, Educational Activities, Freeport, New York, Box 392, AR538.

Palmer, Hap. *Homemade Band*, Educational Activities, Freeport, New York, Box 392, AR545.

Palmer, Hap. *Mod Marches*, Educational Activities, Freeport, New York, Box 392, AR527.

Palmer, Hap. *Simplified Folk Songs*, Educational Activities, Freeport, New York, Box 392, AR518.

Seyler, Anita, *We Move to Poetry*, Bridges, 310 W. Jefferson, Dallas, Texas, 75208.

Zeitlin, Patty and Pearce, Marcia, *Won't You Be My Friend,* Bridges, 310 W. Jefferson, Dallas, Texas, 75208, AR544.

Music for Creative Movement, Bridges, 310 W. Jefferson, Dallas, Texas, 75208 (2 volumes), LP6070, LP6080.

Rhythmic Activity Songs for Primary Grades, Bridges, 310 W. Jefferson, Dallas, Texas 75208 (4 volumes), LP1055, LP1066, LP1077, LP1088.

Singing Action Games, Bridges, 310 W. Jefferson, Dallas, Texas 75208, HYP507.

Action Songs and Sounds, Bridges, 310 W. Jefferson, Dallas, Texas 75208, HYP508.

Chapter 9

Movement Experiences for Enhancing Perceptual-Motor Abilities

CONTENTS

Introduction
  General Objectives
Activity Ideas for Enhancing Body Awareness
  Specific Objectives
  Movement Experiences
Activity Ideas for Enhancing Spatial Awareness
  Specific Objectives
  Movement Experiences
Activity Ideas for Enhancing Directional Awareness
  Specific Objectives
  Movement Experiences
Activity Ideas for Enhancing Temporal Awareness
  Specific Objectives
  Movement Experiences
Suggested Readings
Suggested Records

*Happy is the Child that has for a friend an old, sympathetic,
encouraging mind, one eager to develop, slow to
rebuke or discourage.*
Arthur Bruisbane

INTRODUCTION

Every man, woman, and child is constantly being bombarded with stimuli from the environment. The ability to recognize these stimuli, absorb them into the flow of mental processes, and store them for future use is referred to as perception. Being able to absorb, assimilate, and react to the incoming data when needed falls into the area of perceptual–motor ability. Because the very essence of physical education is movement, perceptual–motor skills can easily be introduced, practiced, and refined in a well-organized and sensitive program. Indeed the physical education program is not the sole place where this type of learning can occur. Programs of this type can and should be carried out by the classroom teacher as well. The need for programs of perceptual–motor learning are important, and they should be viewed as an essential part of the curriculum of every preschool and primary-grade child.

The physical education curriculum affords a natural teaching base for perceptual–motor skills because in reality all voluntary motor acts are perceptual–motor acts and in actuality movement education programs are perceptual–motor programs. Interaction with our environment is a perceptual as well as a motor process. There is a dependency of voluntary motor processes on perceptual information. Conversely the perceptual stimuli received by the organism rely on the development of one's voluntary motor abilities.

What we have, then, is a process of stimulation and reaction that is essential to human life. This characteristic must be learned and the best time and place for this learning to occur is when children are *young.* During the early years, children are open to a wide variety of new and different situations that can enhance their perceptual–motor abilities.

Perceptual–motor activities help children achieve a *general* stage of readiness that helps prepares them for academic work. These activities provide a foundation for future perceptually and conceptually based learnings. Through a program of perceptual–motor skill development children can develop and refine their movement abilities as well as their perceptual–motor abilities.

Learning disabilities in academics are sometimes linked to perceptual–motor problems. Integrating and organizing information is related to visual and motor capabilities. If these capabilities are below normal the child *may* experience problems in the classroom that may or may not be permanent. Introduction to a program of perceptual–motor training, however, *may* contribute to the improvement of the condition. Perceptual–motor programs and activities are not intended as a panacea for remediation of all learning disabilities or developmental lags. They should, however, be viewed as important *contributors* to the remediation of perceptual problems. The opportunities afforded by a well-organized, well-taught physical education program geared to the individual's needs and capabilities provide an ideal avenue for helping children with perceptual and motor deficiencies as well as those who do not display any problem. Programs that stress the development of fundamental locomotor, manipulative, and stability abilities have a direct affect on enhancing the perceptual–motor functioning of young children.

The general objectives of the movement experiences contained in this chapter are designed to enhance the perceptual–motor components of: (1) body awareness, (2) spatial awareness, (3) directional awareness, and (4) temporal awareness.

ACTIVITY IDEAS FOR ENHANCING BODY AWARENESS

Young children are continually exploring the movement potentials of their bodies. They are in the process of gaining increased information about the body parts, what the body parts can do, and how to make them do it. The teacher of young children can assist in this exploratory process by structuring informal learning experiences that maximize children's opportunities for using a variety of body parts in a multitude of activities. The following is a compilation of some activities that will be helpful in enhancing body awareness.

Specific Objectives

Through participation in body awareness activities the children will learn:

1. The location of the various parts of the body.
2. The names of these parts.
3. The relationship of one body part to another.
4. The importance of a single body part in leading movement.
5. How to move the body more efficiently.
6. To be aware of the body and its parts at all times.
7. To be able to contract and relax specific muscles.

Movement Experiences

LOCATING THE LARGE BODY PARTS

1. Have the children find the location of their large body parts. Have

them see how quickly and accurately they can touch each part as you name it. See how quickly can they touch their:

a. Head
b. Neck
c. Chest
d. Waist
e. Stomach
f. Hips
g. Legs
h. Elbows
i. Shoulders
j. Back
k. Spine
m. Front

2. Repeat the above activity, this time reversing the procedure. That is, point to the body parts and have the children name them. The body parts may be as general or as specific as you wish, depending on the children's abilities.

3. Have the children find out how large their body parts are. For example:

   a. Move your hand down the length of your arm; where does it start, and where does it stop?
   b. Place two hands around your waist . . . how big is it . . . how can you move at the waist? Try bending forward, backward, and sideward . . . can you twist at the waist?

4. Help the children discover all about the sides of their bodies. For example, you may request that they:

   a. Move one hand down the sides of their bodies.
   b. Find the side of the head . . . shoulder . . . chest . . . waist . . . hip . . . knee . . . ankle . . . foot.
   c. Repeat the same procedure on the opposite side of the body.

LOCATING THE SMALL BODY PARTS

1. While the children are standing, the teacher may have the children

   a. Put their elbows together.
   b. Put their feet apart.
   c. Touch one elbow.
   d. Put their knees together.

   e. Touch their noses.

   f. Touch their toes with their arms crossed.

   g. Touch one knee and one foot.

   h. Place their palms together.

   i. Touch their heels.

   j. Touch their eyelashes, eyebrows.

2.   Use other body parts in place of or in addition to those mentioned above.

MOVE AND LISTEN

1.   Have the children perform a locomotor task but have them stop and position themselves on your command. For example, you may have them moving about the room and tell them to stop on:

   a. One foot

   b. Both feet

   c. One hand

   d. Seat and both feet

   e. Feet and fingers

   f. Head, hands, and feet

   g. Hands and knees

   h. Back

   i. One foot and one hand

   j. One foot, two hands, and head

2.   Permit the children to choose their own way of stopping and positioning themselves on your command of "freeze."

PARTNER PRACTICE

1.   Have the children move around the floor to a different person each time and touch the following body parts with their hands to another person as directed by the teacher:

a. Spine	f. Arms	k. Toes	p. Back
b. Ears	g. Elbows	l. Hands	q. Knees
c. Neck	h. Legs	m. Fingers	r. Hips
d. Chin	i. Ankles	n. Chest	s. Feet
e. Shoulders	j. Wrists	o. Stomach	t. Heels

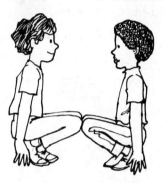

2.   Repeat the above activity with the children using the body parts you named to touch the corresponding body part of another child.

BODY-PART DIFFERENTIATION

1.   Hip movement with bending at the knee:

a.   Draw the knees up to the chest, then thrust them out straight while on the back.

b.   Do the same thing as above, but with continuous circular thrusting movements.

c.   While lying on the stomach, draw both knees up under the stomach and then extend them both outward.

d.   While on the stomach bend one knee and draw it up alongside the body, on the floor, until it is in line with the hip.

2. While lying on their backs have the children:

   a. Lift one leg and lower it.
   b. Move the leg out to the side along the floor, then return it to the midposition beside the other leg.
   c. Swing the leg out to the side and back.
   d. Rotate the leg back and forth on the heel.
   e. Lift one leg and cross it over the other leg and touch floor if possible.
   f. Swing one leg over the other.
   g. Lift the leg and rotate it at the hip, making circles in the air with the foot.
   h. Place an object between the child's knees and tell him to hold it tightly.

3. Repeat the above activities while on the stomach.

4. While standing have the children perform the following shoulder movements:

   a. Move a hand up alongside the body, extend it over the head, and lower it in the same way.
   b. Extend an arm out at the side, then lower it.
   c. Extend an arm over the head, then down.
   d. Extend an arm out in front, then lower.
   e. Extend an arm out in front, then move it from the center out to the side and then back again.
   f. Hunch the shoulders up and down with the arms at the sides, then swing them forward and backward.
   g. Swing the arms in a circle in front of the body.
   h. Swing the arms in a full circle at the side.
   i. Extend the arms out at the sides and swing them in circles of various sizes.
   j. Move just the shoulders forward and backward.
   k. Move the shoulders in a circle.

5. While seated have the children perform the following hand and finger movements:

   a. Make a fist.
   b. Spread the fingers apart, then move them back together.
   c. Bring the tip of the thumb and all of the fingers together.
   d. Bring the tip of the thumb and the "pointer" finger (forefinger) together.
   e. Extend the fingers and thumb to maximum and then relax.

f. Move the thumb across the four fingers and back.
g. Touch each fingertip with the tip of the thumb. Begin with the "pointer" finger and move to the little finger then back.
h. Grasp a ball in one hand, then lift one finger at a time.
i. Close the hand to a fist, and then release one finger at a time.
j. Extend the hands, then lower one finger at a time to form a fist.

WHERE CAN YOU BEND?

1. Permit the children to experiment with a still dowel and with a jointed "Barbie" doll to see where the body parts bend. If possible, a paper skeleton or a real one, and a dentist's jaw could be used to graphically portray the body parts that bend.

2. Encourage the children to move the following joints in as many ways as possible:

a. Jaw
b. Neck
c. Shoulders
d. Elbow
e. Wrist

f. Fingers
g. Waist
h. Hip
i. Knee
j. Ankle
k. Toes

3. Experiment with what movement is like *without* one of the above items at a time.

PAIRED PARTS

1. Have the children touch one body part to another. The following is a list of examples:

a. Touch your ear to a shoulder.
b. Touch your cheek to a shoulder.
c. Touch your shoulder to a knee.
d. Touch your nose to a knee.
e. Touch your elbow to a thigh.
f. Touch your thigh to a knee.
g. Touch your knee to an ankle.
h. Touch your toe to a knee.
i. Touch your toe to the chin.

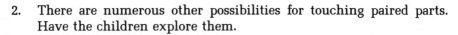

2. There are numerous other possibilities for touching paired parts. Have the children explore them.

RHYMES FOR ENHANCING BODY AWARENESS

The following is a compilation of several rhymes that may be used to enhance body awareness. A variety of body action can easily be set to these rhymes.

1. Caterpillar

Caterpillar crawling around
Where green and juicy leaves are found
Soon a silk cocoon you'll spin
Winding threads 'til you're within
When the spring comes by and by
Flutter out a butterfly.

2. Hands

Hands on your shoulders
Hands on your knees
Hands behind you—if you please
Touch your tummy, now your toes
Now your head, now your nose,
Hands up high in the air,
Now down to your side, then touch your hair.
Hands up as high as before
Now clap your hands, 1–2–3–4
And now—if you please, sit on the floor.

3. You're a tree

You're a tree, and so am I
With branches reaching to the sky
Our trunk is wrinkly, rough and brown

Our feet planted deep within the
ground
But our leaves the colors of pump-
kins and berries
Are preparing to fly as gaily dressed
fairies
Who love to play on a windy day
(And that's a secret I've been told)
We swing and sway in a gentle
breeze
But winter nears so the wind is cold
And we shiver and shake, shudder
and sneeze
And look! What's happened to all our
leaves
What lovely costumes the fairies
wear
As they glide donned in leaves
through the air
Down, downy
  Slowly
    down downy
Where they'll leave their gowns
  To paint the ground. . . .

4. Jack-in-the box

Down in the box, still as still can be
Lift up the lid, what do you see?
Jumping jacks, jumping jacks, high
as we go
Jumping jacks, jumping jacks, this is
how we go!
             (or)
Jack-in-the-box is out of sight
When the cover is fastened tight
Lift the lock and up he goes,
Jack-in-the-box with his hopping
toes!

5. Monkey on a string

I can climb so very high,
I can almost reach the sky,
I can climb most anything
I'm a monkey on a string!

6. Snowman

We're building a snowman big and round
And when the sun shines
He'll melt to the ground.

FINGER PLAYS FOR ENHANCING BODY AWARENESS

The following is a compilation of several finger plays that contribute to the development of body awareness.

1. Eensy weensy spider

Eensy Weensy Spider
Went up the water spout
Down came the rain
and washed the spider out
Out came the sun
and dried up all the rain
So the eensy weensy spider
Crawled up the spout again.

2. Where is thumbkin?

Where is thumbkin?
Where is thumbkin?

Here I am
How are you today sir?
Very fine, I thank you
Run a way
Run a way

(Repeat for pointer)
(Repeat for tall man)
(Repeat for ring man)
(Repeat for pinkie)

3. Two little firemen

Two little firemen sleeping in a row.
Ding dong goes the bell down the pole they go.
Off on their engines red they go-go go-go go.
Fighting the blazing fire so-o so-o so.
When all the fire is out home sooooo slooooow.
Back to bed they go—all in a row.

4. Three blue pigeons

Three blue pigeons, sitting on a wall
Three blue pigeons, sitting on a wall

One flew away, OHHHHH!
Two blue pigeons sitting on a wall
Two blue pigeons sitting on a wall
Another one flew away, OHHHH!
One blue pigeon sitting on a wall
One blue pigeon sitting on a wall
And one came back, hooray!
Two blue pigeons sitting on a wall
(etc.)

5. In a cabin

In a cabin in the woods
Little man by the window stood
Saw a rabbit hopping by,
Knocking at his door.
Help me, help me, help me he cried!
Else the hunter shoot me dead
Little rabbit come inside
Happy we will be!

6. Five little squirrels

Five little squirrels sat upon a tree
The first said, "What do I see?"
second said, "I smell a gun."
third said, "Come one! Let's run."
fourth said, "Let's hide in the shade."
fifth said, "I'm not afraid."
Bang, bang! Went the hunter's gun.
And, away they ran, everyone.

PUT-TOGETHER PEOPLE

1. Have the children make a life-sized figure by crushing single pieces of newspaper and stuffing them into long underwear. After the underwear is completely stuffed, dress the figure and have the children each draw a head and features from a paper bag. The hands and feet may be made with gloves and an old pair of shoes. The stuffed figure may be representative of a particular time of the year or theme.

    a. Cut out the body parts of a "person" using construction paper or poster board. Have the children assemble the legs, arms, head, and torso of the figures. Hook the pieces together with brads, or tape the pieces together to complete the figure.

    b. Cut out the body parts of two or more "people." Give each child in the group one body part. See if they can assemble the figure. The same activity may be repeated but as a relay.

c. Using a doll with moveable joints, have the children bend it into various positions and then see if they can reproduce these positions with their bodies.

d. Giants: The children sit in a circle around two giant paper cut-out parts of two bodies, one a boy, the other a girl. Two children are chosen to compete in putting the parts together; the one completing the giant figure first is the winner.

MIRROR ACTIVITIES

1. One child stands in front of a full-length mirror. The other children give directions to locate his body parts. The child can only look at his reflection in the mirror when touching the designated part. Upon making a mistake, the child giving the last instruction takes the mirror position.

2. Repeat the above activity but having the mirror child using both hands to touch his body.

3. Repeat the above activities but indicating the right or left parts of the body in the mirror reflection.

4. The teacher serves as the mirror. The children imitate the movements of the "mirror."

MISCELLANEOUS BODY-AWARENESS ACTIVITIES:

1. Balance-beam activities (see pages 144–146)
2. Balance-board activities (see pages 137–139)
3. Trampoline-type activities (see pages 149–150).

ACTIVITY IDEAS FOR ENHANCING SPATIAL AWARENESS

Specific Objectives

Through practice in spatial awareness activities the children will:

The trampoline is an excellent piece of equipment for enhancing perceptual–motor abilities.

1. Learn how much space their bodies occupy.
2. Be able to project their bodies into external space.
3. Be able to locate objects in space from a personal frame of reference (egocentric localization).
4. Be able to locate objects in space independent of one another (objective localization).
5. Improve their fundamental movement abilities.
6. Enhance their efficiency of movement.

Movement Experiences

BIG AND SMALL

1. Have the children find a place on the area where they are free from contact with others. Ask them to make themselves as small as possible. Point out that as small "balls," each child takes up very little room and so does not bother his neighbor.

2. Now have the children make themselves as big as possible. Now point out that as they get bigger so do their neighbors. This means that each needs more room for himself and to keep from bumping someone else. The children become familiar with their spatial relationships to others.
3. The children can be asked to assume different shapes such as a "tree," "rock," or "telephone pole." Have the children assume the new positions at varying rates of speed. Assuming the shapes of letters and numbers may also be performed.

MAZE WALK

1. Children walk through a maze of chairs and tables without touching.

   a. Walk between objects
   b. Step over objects
   c. Crawl under objects
   d. Walk around objects
   e. Step on objects

2. Perform the maze activities using a variety of locomotor activities

   a. Jumping
   b. Hopping
   c. Skipping
   d. Crawling

ROPE WALKING

1. Place ropes in various patterns and geometric shapes on the floor. Have the children walk the rope forward.

    a. Wavy lines
    b. Circle
    c. Square
    d. Triangle
    e. Step over and through objects

2. Repeat the activities as above but moving forward while blindfolded. Have children tell you about the shape of the line they are walking on.

BACK SPACE

1. Walk a rope placed on the floor going backward. Place the rope in various patterns.
2. Throw objects backward to a visualized goal.
3. Sit down on an object without visually monitoring it.

    a. Chair
    b. Beanbag chair
    c. Inner tube
    d. Trampoline

4. Walk backward through a simple obstacle course that the child has had an opportunity to visually memorize.
5. Count the number of steps to a point on the floor while walking forward. Repeat while walking backwards and see how close the children come to the predetermined point.

OBSTACLE COURSE

1. Use tasks such as:

   a. "Footsteps" placed on the floor
   b. Carpet squares on the floor
   c. Climbing and sliding ropes
   d. Crawling over and under and
      through objects
   e. Stepping into shoe boxes

2. Map.

   a. Follow yarn line through the obstacle course.

BODY SPACE

1. Outline the children's bodies on a sheet of newsprint while they are
   lying on their backs. Have the children:

   a. Cut out their bodies
   b. Color their bodies
   c. Dress their bodies
   d. Hang their bodies up
   e. Compare sizes

2. Gross motor activities:

   a. Have the children roll over and see how much space they occupied.
   b. Have the children spread out and see how much space they can
      occupy.
   c. Have the children see how little space they can occupy.
   d. Have them crawl under a table and other objects of different heights
      and see how well they fit without touching.
   e. Count steps, jumps, and so on taken to go from one point to another.

OTHER SPACE

1. Using empty milk cartons:

   a. Compare different-sized milk cartons (half pint to gallon containers).
   b. Compare the water-holding capacity of the containers. Compare size by pouring from carton to carton.
   c. Fill different-sized containers with sand. Compare the weights of the containers.
   d. Compare the volumes of sand held by each container.

NEAR AND FAR

1. Egocentric localization:

   a. Have the children estimate the distance from where they are standing to a specific point by the number of steps that it will take to get there.
   b. Measure the distance in steps. Compare estimates.

2. Objective localization:

   a. Have the children estimate the distance between two independent points, for example, the doll house and the carpentry bench.
   b. Step off the distance and compare.

TWISTER ACTIVITIES

1. Have the children first play the game individually in order to develop free body control.
2. Have them play the game with a partner.

MAP ACTIVITIES

1. Map reading:

   a. Place a large map of the classroom, school, community, or state on the floor. Give them a route to follow indicating specific points that they must visit before proceeding to the next point.

b. Give each child a map with clues to the "treasure." Indicate in precise terms where they should go and the procedures to be followed. (Second grade and up).

Exploring space in an important means of developing spatial awareness.

MISCELLANEOUS SPATIAL AWARENESS ACTIVITIES

1. Locomotor movements:

   a. Crawling
   b. Leaping
   c. Jumping

2. Axial movements:

   a. Bending
   b. Rising

    c. Stretching
    d. Reaching
    e. Twisting
    f. Falling

3. Following objects:

    a. Following colors
    b. Following arrows
    c. Following words
    d. Tunnel crawling

4. Exploring space:

    a. Self-space
    b. Common space
    c. Moving at different levels
    d. Moving in different floor patterns

ACTIVITY IDEAS FOR ENHANCING DIRECTIONAL AWARENESS

Directional awareness is of considerable concern to the classroom teacher and children who are beginning formal instruction in reading. Directional awareness involves both an internal and external sensitivity for sidedness. Activities designed to enhance directional awareness may have an influence on perceptual readiness for reading.

Specific Objectives

Practice in movement activities that emphasize the directional aspect of the task will:

1. Contribute to the development of laterality (internal awareness of direction).
2. Contribute to the development of directional (external projection of laterality).
3. Aid in establishing readiness for reading.
4. Contribute to the development of fundamental movement abilities.
5. Enhance one's ability to move efficiently through space.

Movement Experiences

CLOCK GAMES

1. Make a clock on a chalkboard about 18 inches in diameter. Instruct the children to place their right hand on one of the numbers and their left

hand on a second number, holding a piece of chalk in each hand. Ask them to move their left hand to a different number and their right hand to a different number on your command. Both hands should move at the same time and arrive at their goals at the same time.

2. Variations:

    a. Toward the center: Place hands on the circumference of circle and bring both to center. Place hands on 1 and 5 and bring to zero, then 6 and 2 to zero.
    b. Away from center: Begin with both hands on zero and move out to specified numbers.
    c. Parallel movements: Put the left hand on 7 and right hand on zero, then move the left hand to zero and right hand to 3. Change directions.
    d. Crossed midline movements. Place the left hand on 7 and right hand on 1, then move both hands to zero. Change directions.
    e. Left to right: Place the left hand at 7 and right hand at zero, then move the left hand to zero and right hand to 1.

DIRECTIONAL SWINGING-BALL ACTIVITIES

1. Attach a ball to a string. Move it in different directions and in different orientations to the child.

    a. Tap it, then catch it.
    b. Swing it with one hand, then the other, then both.

2. Swinging activities:

    a. Swing ball to the left and to the right.
    b. Swing ball forward and backward.
    c. Swing ball in circles around the child.
    d. Swing ball in circles in front of the child.
    e. Swing ball in different planes above the child as he lies on his back.
    f. While he is on his back, swing ball from left to right, then from head to toe.

3. Striking activities: repeat the above activities but using striking motions.

DIRECTIONAL COMMANDS

1. The following are some examples of patterns in which children may move in order to enhance directional awareness. The number of possibilities is limitless. Use your imagination:

    a. Run forward 10 steps and walk backward five steps.
    b. Put your feet together and jump to one side.

c. Hop forward three times one one foot, then backward three times on the other foot.
d. Move sideways across the room.
e. Have the child move close to you and then move far away.
f. Move from the front of room to the rear of room, going over one object and under another object.
g. Stand near the desk.
h. Stand far away from the pencil sharpener.
i. Point to the wall nearest you and walk to that wall.
j. Place the closest chair between the desk and the wall.
k. One child sits and another stands. Have the standing child move in front of, to the side of (etc.) the sitting child.

OVER, UNDER, AND AROUND

1. Long jumping rope

   a. Two people hold a jump rope and place the rope on the floor. The child runs and jumps over it. The rope is raised slightly for each succeeding jump. Game ends when the child hits the rope.
   b. Go under a high rope which is then lowered slightly each try.
   c. Walk over instead of running and jumping.

2. Place several objects around the gym such as jump ropes, walking boards, mats, chairs, tires, ladder, or any large equipment. Children follow the leader and imitate as he moves around the obstacles.

   a. Could be played in the classroom as leader moves around room.
   b. Place objects on the floor and permit each child to go around the objects in his or her own direction and name the direction in which he went.
   c. Give verbal commands for the direction of each obstacle.
   d. Blindfold the children. Have them work with a "seeing" partner who gives directional commands (no tactile clues) on how to get to the object.

DIRECTIONAL WALKING-BOARD ACTIVITIES

1. Walk forward.
2. Walk backward—discourage looking back
3. Walk sideways—slide one foot over, then bring the other one to meet it.
4. Turn on the board:

   a. Walk forward, turn, and walk sideways.
   b. Walk forward, turn, and return, walking forward.

   c. Walk backward, turn, and return walking backward.

   d. Vary combinations.

5. Step over and under objects placed on the board.

6. Walk across the board carrying heavy objects.

DIRECTIONAL, UNILATERAL, BILATERAL, AND CROSS-LATERAL ACTIVITIES

1. Bilateral Movements:

   a. Lie flat on the floor on your back with your arms at your sides and your feet together.

     i. Move feet apart as far as you can, keeping the knees stiff.

     ii. Move the arms along the floor until the hands come together above the head, keeping elbows stiff.

     iii. Move the arms and legs at the same time.

2. Unilateral and cross-lateral movements:

   a. Lie flat on the floor on your back with your arms at your sides and your feet together.

     i. Move the right leg only to an extended position and return it.

     ii. Repeat the above with the left leg only, right arm only, and left arm only.

     iii. Move the right leg and right arm together.

     iv. Move the left arm and leg together.

     v. Move the right arm and the left together.

     vi. Move the left arm and the right leg.

DIRECTIONAL THROWING ACTIVITIES

1. Use beanbag and a wastebasket:

   a. Set a basket in front of the child and have him throw at it.

   b. Vary the basket's orientation to the right or left and throw at it.

2. Use ball to roll at a bowling pin.

   a. Vary the location of the bowling pin or the child.
   b. Vary the distance of the roll.

3. From a prone position, or a supine position, have the child throw a beanbag:

   a. Upward
   b. Forward
   c. Backward
   d. To each side.

DIRECTIONAL CHALKBOARD ACTIVITIES

1. Dot-to-dot. Teacher makes two dots, child connects, teacher makes a third dot and child connects, and so on. (Do not cross child's midline here.)
2. Dot-to-dot, but cross child's midline.
3. Draw double circles and change directions after completion and/or in the middle of drawing.
4. Draw "lazy-eight" figures. With one hand, then the other, one direction, then reverse.
5. Draw vertical lines, up–down, down–up.
6. Draw horizontal lines, left–right, right–left.
7. Draw horizontal lines and vertical lines simultaneously.
8. Draw a square, then alter size, direction, and starting point.

DIRECTIONAL LADDER ACTIVITIES

1. *Walking:* Looking straight ahead, the child walks the length of the ladder.

   a. Walk forward in the spaces.
   b. Walk backward in the spaces.
   c. Walk sideways in the spaces. Walking sideways may be done by:

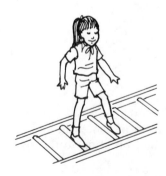

      i. Leading with the left foot
      ii. Leading with the right foot
      iii. Continually crossing the lead foot in front
      iv. Continually crossing the lead foot in back
    d. Walk the rungs (forward, backward, sideward).

2. *Crawling:* The ladder is turned on its side, and to secure it, the teacher sits on the top side. The children crawl in and out of the spaces.

    a. Crawl forward.
    b. Crawl backward.
    c. Do not touch the rungs if possible.

TWIST-BOARD ACTIVITIES

1. The child places his feet about shoulder width apart on the board and bends his knees slightly. He may twist by:

    a. Moving both of his arms to one side and then to the other side.
    b. Swinging one arm forward and up, and swinging the other arm backward and down.

2. The child puts his left arm behind his back and uses his right arm to simulate a one-arm breast stroke. This will cause the child to turn completely around.
3. Repeat step (2), and change arm positions (right arm behind back, left arm moving).
4. While twisting, the child:

    a. Crosses his arm in front of his chest.
    b. Extends his arms (hands clasped):
      i. In front of his body
      ii. Behind his body
      iii. Over his head

DIRECTIONAL CREEPING AND WALKING ACTIVITIES

1. Creeping

    a. Creep in a homolateral pattern (left hand with left knee, right hand with right knee) while looking at target placed at eye level.
    b. Creep in a cross-lateral pattern (left hand with left knee, right hand with right knee) looking first eye-leved target, then at the forward hand.
    c. Creep in a homolateral pattern while looking at the hand that goes out in front.
    d. Creep forward, backward, and to the side using the above patterns.

2. Walking:

    a. Walk in a homolateral pattern (left hand points to left toes while right arm is stretched behind the child, then right hand points to right toes).
    b. Cross-lateral walking.
    c. Mid-air change—begin with the left arm forward and the left foot forward, with the weight evenly distributed on both feet. Right arm should be straight out in back. On command "change" each child jumps up in the air, reversing the position of arms and legs. The eyes should fixate on a target at all times and the child should land on the take-off spot.
    d. Mid-air change—cross-lateral movement (left arm and right leg forward).

DIRECTIONAL BALL ACTIVITIES

1. Use one hand, then repeat the skills with the other hand:

    a. Tap a swinging ball.
    b. Bounce and catch a ball with one hand.
    c. Dribble a ball with one hand.
    d. Bounce and catch with alternating hands.
    e. Throw in various directions.
    f. Catch from different directions.

2. Use one foot, then repeat the skills with the other foot.

    a. Kick a ball with alternate feet, using the toe.
    b. Kick a ball with alternate feet, using the instep.
    c. Trap a ball with one foot, then the other.
    d. Trap a ball with one knee, then the other.

ACTIVITY IDEAS FOR ENHANCING TEMPORAL AWARENESS

Temporal awareness involves the development of a time structure within the body. Eye–hand coordination and eye–foot coordination refer to the child's ability to coordinate movements and are the end result of a fully established time structure within the child. This "clock mechanism" helps children to better coordinate the movements of their bodies with the various sensory systems.

Specific Objectives

Through temporal awareness movement activities children will learn:

1. Synchrony, which is the ability to get the body parts to work together smoothly.
2. Rhythm, which is the process of performing many synchronous acts in a harmonious pattern or succession.
3. Sequence, which is the proper order of actions required to perform a skill.
4. Eye–hand coordination and eye–foot corrdination, which are the end result of synchrony, rhythm, and sequence being efficiently integrated.

Movement Experiences

BALL ACTIVITIES

1. Stationary ball:

   a. Contact it with an open hand.
   b. Contact it with an implement.
   c. Kick at it.
   d. Contact it with various body parts.

2. Swinging ball:

   a. Contact it with an open hand as a fist.
   b. Alternate left and right hands.
   c. Contact it with various body parts.
   d. Contact it with various implements moving from shorter to longer levers (spoon, table tennis, paddle, tennis racket, baseball bat).

    e. Catch the swinging ball with both hands.
    f. Catch the swinging ball with one hand.
    g. Visually track the ball as it swings, without moving the head.
    h. Visually track the ball and point at it as it swings.

RHYTHMIC TRAINING

1. On the signal have each child find his own "personal space." Have them make a low, balanced shape, keeping one hand free to tap on the floor along with the beat of the drum. When the drum changes beat and pattern, the children must do the same.
2. Remaining balanced, have the children tap with a foot, elbow, and heel. Have a body part move in the air, following the drum. Use different tempos in each position. Keep the tempo even. Don't accelerate or decelerate.

MY BEAT

This activity, called "My Beat," enables the children to make and follow their own tempo and sequence.

1. Each child makes his or her own accompaniment and sets his own beat. They can make noises with their mouths or slap a hand against their bodies. Once they have established even beats, have them explore their personal space (the area around them) whild moving to the beat.
2. Have each child explore around the room while moving to the beat. Let them move to a different tempo.

FREE FLOW

1. Ask the children to perform a relaxed, smooth swinging motion with their bodies. The motion can take them anywhere around the play area. (Stress spatial awareness to them to avoid collisions.) Have them perform a controlled swing so that it can be stopped on command. Make sure that when they stop a movement they are in complete balance and control.
2. Introduce physical obstacles that the children must successfully negotiate so as to improve body control and movement.

MOVING-TARGET TOSS

1. Have the children line up facing the target. Use an inflatable toy punching clown that will right itself after being pushed down. Use a barrel, waste basket, or pot and attempt to toss an object at it while it is moving from a reclining position to its normal upright position.

2. Suspend a hoop from a rope. Start it swinging in a pendular motion. Have children throw beanbags through the swinging hoop.
3. Roll a hoop or tire along the floor. Toss objects through it.

BALLOON-VOLLEYING ACTIVITIES
Keep a balloon up in the air:
    a. Use a volleying motion.
    b. Hit it underhand.
    c. Hit it above the head.
    d. Use it below the waist.
    e. Use various body parts to hit the balls.
    f. Weight the balloon slightly and repeat the above activities.

MISCELLANEOUS LARGE-MOTOR TEMPORAL ACTIVITIES

1. Move in different ways to a beat.
2. Jump rope to a beat.
3. Bounce a ball to a beat.
4. Pass a ball rhythmically.
5. Partners make their own beat and move to it.
6. Perform movements in sequence.
7. Accelerate and decelerate movement.
8. Create and absorb force.
9. Perform tossing and catching activities.
10. Perform kicking and trapping activities.
11. Perform dodging activities.

MISCELLANEOUS FINE-MOTOR TEMPORAL ACTIVITIES

1. Bead stringing
2. Jacks
3. Pick-up sticks
4. Lacing and sewing cards
5. Clay modeling
6. Cutting
7. Coloring and pasting
8. Finger painting
9. Nuts and bolts
10. Sewing
11. Weaving
12. Zipping, snapping, and buttoning
13. Carpentry activities
14. Puppets

15. Chalkboard activities
16. Tracing
17. Pouring skills

SUGGESTED READINGS

Canonico, Alan. *Sequential Skill Development in Early Perceptual Motor Learnings*, West Virginia Department of Education, Charleston, West Virginia 25305.

Chaney, Clara M. and Newell C. Kephart, *Motoric Aids to Perceptual Training*, Columbus, Ohio: Charles E. Merrill, 1968.

Cratty, Bryant J. and Sister Margaret Mary Martin, *Perceptual–Motor Efficiency in Children,* Philadelphia: Lea and Febiger, 1969.

Frostig, Marianne, *Move, Grow, Learn: Teacher's Guide*, Chicago: Follett Educational Corporation, 1969.

Gilliom, Bonnie C. *Basic Movement Education for Children*, Reading, Mass.: Addison–Wesley, 1970.

Ingles, David. *Perceptual Motor Stations For Grades K-6*, Pamphlet distributed by the West Virginia Department of Education, Charleston, West Virginia 25305.

Leaver, John; Bill McKinney, Eliane Poe, and Judy Verhoeke, *Manual of* Perceptual–Motor Activities: *A Guide for Elementary Physical Educators and Classroom Teachers*, Johnstown, Pa.: Mafex Associates, Inc., 1969.

Mourougis, Ann, Donna Wemple, James Wheeler, Linda Williams, and Susan Zurcher, *Body Management Activities: A Guide to Perceptual–Motor Training*, Cedar Rapids, Iowa: Nissen Company and MWZ Assoc., 1970.

SUGGESTED RECORDS

Brazelton, Ambrose. *Clap, Snap and Tap*, Kimbo Records, Deal, New Jersey, Box 246, EA48.

Cratty, Bryant J. *Physical Development for Children*, Kimbo Records, Deal, New Jersey, Box 246, EA-PD.

Hissan, Harold. *Coordination Skills*, Kimbo Records, Deal , New Jersey, Box 246, KEA6050.

Palmer, Hap. *Getting to Know Myself*, Educational Activities, Freeport, New York, Box 392.

Riccione, Georgiana. *Developmental Motor Skills for Self-Awareness*, Kimbo Records, Deal, New Jersey, Box 246, KIM9075.

Chapter 10

Movement Experiences for Enhancing Visual, Tactile, and Auditory Abilities

CONTENTS

Introduction
  General Objectives
Activity Ideas for Enhancing Visual Perception
  Depth Proception
    Specific Objectives
    Movement Experiences
  Form Perception
    Specific Objectives
    Movement Experiences
  Figure-Ground Perception
    Specific Objectives
    Movement Experiences
Activity Ideas for Enhancing Auditory Perception
  Listening Skills
    Specific Objectives
    Movement Experiences
  Auditory Discrimination
    Specific Objectives
    Movement Experiences
  Auditory-Memory
    Specific Objectives
    Movement Experiences
Activity Ideas for Enhancing Tactile Perception
  Tactile Discrimination and Matching
    Specific Objectives
    Movement Experiences

Tactile Memory
  Specific Objectives
  Movement Experiences
Suggested Readings
Suggested Records

I did not reach
yet I was touched,
Now there is feeling
where I was numb.
Unknown

INTRODUCTION

The development of one's perceptual abilities begins at birth and is discussed in detail in Chapter 4. Movement is one of the primary modes by which children develop and refine their perceptual world, and it may be used effectively by the classroom teacher and motor development specialist as a means of enhancing these abilities. The movement activities contained in this chapter may be described as "motor–perceptual" rather than "perceptual–motor," as in the previous chapter, although the differences are subtle and of no significant consequence when actually dealing with children. The activities contained in this chapter are motor activities designed to enhance the functioning of specific perceptual modalities, whereas the activities in the preceeding chapters are movement activities designed to enhance *both* perceptual *and* motor abilities.

In this chapter we will examine the contribution of movement experiences to the development of visual perception, auditory peception, and tactile perception. The olfactory and gustatory modalities have not been included because of their limited role in the education of children.

GENERAL OBJECTIVES

The general objectives of the movement experiences contained in the following pages are:

1. To enhance visual perceptual abilities involving depth perception, perception of form, and figure–ground perception.
2. To enhance auditory perceptual abilities involving listening, auditory discrimination, and auditory memory skills.
3. To enhance tactile perceptual abilities involving tactile discrimination and matching and tactile memory.

ACTIVITY IDEAS FOR ENHANCING VISUAL PERCEPTION

The visual apparatus is complete and functional at birth. Visual abilities develop rapidly during the early years of life and are crucial to effective functioning in a world that is visually oriented. The process of both maturation and experience contributes to the development of highly sophisticated visual perceptual abilities. It has been estimated that up to 80 percent of all information we take in and utilize comes from the visual modality. As a result it becomes abundantly clear that the development and refinement of accurate visual perception is extremely important. The following pages contain a variety of movement experiences that have been found helpful in developing three aspects of visual perception crucial to effective functioning in school and the world, namely depth perception, form perception, and figure–ground perception.

Depth Perception

Depth perception is the ability to judge relative distances in three-dimensional space. Teachers working with depth-perception activities need to consciously plan many and varied spatial and dimensional cues to serve as reference points for judgment of distance.

Specific Objectives

1. To enhance the ability to accurately judge distances and depth.
2. To increase the ability to utilize external clues in determining depth distance and size.
3. To enhance the ability to move efficiently in three-dimensional space.
4. To enhance fundamental movement abilities.

Movement Experiences

BOWLING   When rolling ball toward an object, line the lane moving toward the target with Indian clubs or markers of some type.

TARGETS   A box within which balls land in various lengths and depths can be used for a target for throwing, striking, and kicking a

The videotape machine is an excellent aid to visual perceptual development.

light ball. Target throwing with all types of objects and at various distances is helpful.

HOOPS Hula hoops arranged in three-dimensional formations, plywood boxes with shapes cut out of the sides, pipes, and logs are good for tactile realization of depth.

JUMPING Jumping from heights, over objects, and from one object to another develops perception of depth and distance. Use jumping from various heights on an angled balance beam or steps to the floor.

BALANCE BEAM Place a balance beam diagonally toward the wall. Have the children find the point where they can reach and touch the wall while walking on the beam. Tape several points onto the balance beam. Show the children one piece of tape; remove it and have the children walk and stop where they think the tape was.

BOXES Place boxes of various heights in the center of a room. Attach objects at various heights to the wall. Instruct the children to select the box that will best assist them in retrieving the object they want.

Form Perception

Form perception or the ability to recognize shapes, forms, and symbols is necessary for academic success. Young children may be able to identify shapes correctly, but because of distortions of their visual memory, are often unable to reproduce them. Perception of shape constancy becomes crucial to children's ability to recognize shapes. They must learn that two-and three-dimensional forms belong to certain categories of shapes, regardless of size, color, texture, mode of representation, or the angle seen by the perceiver. Recognition of similarities and differences is the first step in identifying shapes and forms. Object discrimination is the second.

Three-and 4-year olds rely on shape or form rather than color for identification of objects. At 5 years of age, color is generally a more important tool than form for identification of an object. At age 6–7 years, color and form are both important.

Specific Objectives

1. To recognize and reproduce basic shapes.
2. To perceive differences in shapes and pieces of a puzzle.
3. To match similar symbols.
4. To recognize and reproduce basic forms and to use them in generalized situations (e.g., to be able to see that a square and a trinagle can form a house).
5. To be able to draw forms that exist in the environment and that can be seen in isolation of one another.

Movement Experiences

SHAPE WALKING Walk simple geometric shapes placed on the floor.

1. Have the children walk a rope that is placed in various geometric shapes. Walking barefoot will enhance the tactile clues.
2. Walk a masking tape line and "feel" the shape with your toes.
3. Present a simple geometric shape to the children. Permit them to visually monitor it while they attempt to walk out the shape on the floor. They should strive to arrive back at the starting point when they complete the shape.
4. Repeat the above activity but do not permit visual monitoring of the displayed form.
5. Name a shape and have the children walk it out, returning to the starting point when they have completed the shapes.

TRACING Trace around geometric shapes with the fingers.

1. Use three-dimensional shapes.
2. Use templates.
3. Trace shapes drawn on a sheet of paper.
4. Reproduce the shapes by tracing over them.
5. Have the children complete incomplete geometric shapes drawn for them.

MAKING THINGS Make a variety of things utilizing various ahapes.

1. Make a collage of geometrical shape.
2. Use various-shaped blocks to build a familiar object.

3. Draw a picture of a person composed entirely of different geometrics shapes.

4. Make shapes using toothpicks, straws or tongue depressors.

BODY SHAPES Have the children use their bodies to make a variety of shapes.

1. Have the children form various shapes, letters, and numerals with their bodies.

2. Have the children from part of a shape with their bodies. Ask another to help complete the shape he thinks the others are forming.

SHAPE TAG Play tag using selected shapes as free places.

STEPPING SHAPES Spread various shapes on the floor around the room. Have the children step only on certain shapes. Make and play a game of twister using shapes as the focal point.

MATCHING SHAPES Play matching games using various shapes and sizes. Sort objects according to shape.

BEANBAG TOSS Throw beanbags on targets with different-shaped holes cut out. Points are scored for throwing through the various shapes.

SHADOW PANTOMIME Hang a sheet with a light in front of it in a closet with the door open. Have child imitate physical activities while the others guess what they think is being done.

Figure–Ground Perception

Visual figure–ground perception is the ability to select a limited number of stimuli from a mass. These particular stimuli (auditory, tactile, olfactory, kinesthetic, visual, and/or gustatory) form the figure. The others form a dim field. This figure is the center of attention. When the attention shifts, the former figure fades into the background. We can only perceive something in its relation to its field.

In teaching children who have not fully developed their figure–ground perception, attempt to limit the number of stimuli in the background and progress by adding gradually. For example, practice dribbling the "red" ball *not* on the red-and-black tiled floor, but on a posterboard (white or light solid color) or sheet to simplify contrasting the figure of attention and the background. Do not place the children in a milieu of posters, streamers, and other attention-grabbers.[1]

Specific Objectives

1. To be able to focus attention on the object of regard.
2. To be able to move efficiently through the visual field.
3. To be able to locate objects located in field of vision.
4. To improve eye-hand and eye-foot coordination.

Movement Experiences

DISCRIMINATION Discriminate between various objects in a room. Find objects that are difficult to locate.

SORTING Sort accorting to size, shape, color, texture, number, thickness, and length.

ATTENTION Practice shifting attention by selecting designated objects from a box or bag.

LADDER MAZE Place a ladder on a floor of a solid design, on one with a diagonal design, and on one with various other designs. Have the children step between the rungs without touching them.

---

[1] Gallahue, David L. "The Relationship Between Perceptual and Motor Abilities," *Research Quarterly*, December 1968.

TARGET TOSS   Use targets to focus attention. Throw beanbags at selected parts of the target. For example, you may use a large chosen target and throw at various body parts.

EGG-SHELL WALK   Place a path of egg-shell halves on the floor. Cross that path with other paths of various materials, such as rope, tape, and paper. Have the children step only on the egg shells.

ROPE WALK   Walk on a rope winding through a myriad of objects.

PADDLE BALANCE   Have the children balance a ball on a paddle or board.

ROPE MAZE   Form a maze on the floor of rope paths. Have identical clues at each end of the same rope. Send the children to find the match of the clue they are given.

CANDYLAND   Play a life-sized version of "Candyland" (by Parker Brothers), where the children spin for colors and take their places on the appropriate color on the "board."

TETHERBALL   "Tetherball" is a good game for developing one's ability to concentrate on one figure through a field (first grade onward).

FIND HIDDEN OBJECTS   Use *Highlights* magazine for pictures with concealed objects that the children can find.

FINGER FIXATION   Have the children hold their right and left forefingers about a foot apart and a foot from their eyes. They then look quickly from one finger to the other. They must be sure to "land" each time. If they have difficulty they can be helped by having another person move their own finger in the same way the eyes are to move.

PENCIL–WALL FIXATION   The children hold a pencil erect about 10–12 inches in front of their nose. They then look from pencil to numbers on a claendar (or picture on the wall) and back again for several "round trips." They must move their eyes quickly and fixate on each object.

PAPER-PUNCH PICTURE   Punch holes in a picture until the children are no longer able to obtain meaning from the pictures. Pictures of many objects are harder to perceive than pictures of only one subject.

ACTIVITY IDEAS FOR ENHANCING AUDITORY PERCEPTION

The development of auditory perceptual abilities has not received the attention by authors and practioners as has the visual modality. Auditory perception, however, is nonetheless important, particularly with young children. Their inability to read makes their formal education primarily one of: (1) listening to auditory clues, (2) discriminating between sounds, and (3) applying meaning to them.

Auditory perception is enhanced when children attend to verbal direction, translate music into movement, and interpret the "feel" of various sounds through movement. The use of musical instruments aids in developing the auditory abilities. The following pages contain numerous activities for developing and reinforcing listening skills, auditory discrimination, and auditory–memory abilities.

Listening Skills

It is important for children to hear and remember what is said, but it is also crucial that they first *listen* to what is being said. Learning to listen is basic to auditory perception. Many children have been conditioned to "tune out" certain auditory clues. Take, for example, the child engrossed in a television program who somehow manages not to hear the pleas of mother or father to come to dinner. We are all familiar with children who "never listen." Learning to listen to auditory clues can be developed through a variety of activities. Games that involve an awareness and identification of sound sources enhance listening abilities. Activities that require the following simple directions are also helpful, as well as activities that require a motoric response to a verbal command.

Specific Objectives

1. To develop an awareness of sound sources.
2. To be able to identify the various familiar sounds.
3. To develop the ability to listen to auditory clues in the immediate environment.

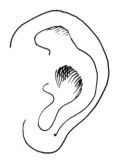

4. To respond appropriately to auditory commands.
5. To be able to respond efficiently, through movement, to auditory clues.
6. To enhance the ability to discriminate between various auditory clues.

Movement Experiences

TRADITIONAL GAMES Many traditional games that children have played down through the years involve a considerable amount of listening skills:

1. Simon Says
2. Mother May I
3. Red Rover (p. 187)
4. Red Light (p. 183)

HOT AND COLD Hide an object somewhere in the room while "it" is not looking. "It" attempts to find the object by moving around the room and listening to the loudness or softness of the classes clapping. As he approaches the object the clapping becomes louder. As he moves away from it the clapping becomes softer.

CLAP CLAP The class is spread out around the room. One child is told to clap her hands twice when "it" says "clap clap." "It" points to the person who she thought did the clapping.

POEMS Read a poem to the class requesting them to fill in the rhyming words.

MUSIC Listen to music that has a variety of fast and slow sections. Request that they move about the room in time to the music. If space does not permit active movement, simply have the children raise their hands when they hear the fast part or the slow part.

BOUNCE BOUNCE Have a small group of children sit down with their backs toward you. Drop a utility ball from waist height and let it bounce. Children should count the number of bounces that the ball makes.

ACTIVE ANIMALS Use a variety of rhythm instruments to depict the sounds of moving animals while telling a story containing the names of several animals. Whenever the animals name is mentioned the child with the corresponding instrument makes its sound. For example:

1. Drum for a lumbering elephant
2. Sandpaper blocks for a slithering snake
3. Triangle for birds
4. Xylophone–for caterpillar
5. Rhythmic sticks for galloping horses

HANDS One child is blindfolded and must guess what another child is doing with her hands. She may, for example, be clapping, snapping, rubbing, scratching the desk, or tapping the chalkboard.

ECHO The teacher claps out a simple rhythmic pattern and the children repeat it. Progress from simple to more complex clapping patterns.

MOVEMENT CLAPPING The teacher claps out a rhythmic pattern using slow or fast beats, even or uneven beats, and the children respond by moving around the room to the appropriate beat.

LISTENING WALK The children and teacher take a walk around the neighborhood for the purpose of listening to and identifying different sounds. Sounds may be categorized as:

1. Human sounds (walking, talking, etc.)
2. Animal sounds (running and cries of cats, dogs, birds, etc.)
3. Machinery sounds (noise of cars, buses, power mowers, trucks, etc.)
4. Nature sounds (wind, rustling of trees, leaves, etc.)

IT IS I Play this game when the children know one another fairly well. One child sits in a chair with his back to the class. Another child comes up behind the seated child and knocks three times on the back of the chair. The seated child asks, "who is knocking at my door?" and the other child replies, "it is I." The seated child tries to guess who is knocking by identifying the child's voice. The teacher sets the number of guesses permitted.

TAPE-RECORDER SOUNDS Use a tape recorder to record many familiar and easily distinguished sounds, such as a car horn, paper tearing, breathing, crying, clock ticking, sneezing and so forth. Make a list of the sounds in their proper order so that you know what they are. Have the children try to identify the sounds.

VOICE RECORDING Record several children's voices on the tape recorder and have them attempt to identify their classmates' voices and their own.

FREEZE AND MELT The teacher or a student says word "freeze" while the class is moving about the room. They immediately stop what they are doing and cease all movement (of the body and the mouth). When the word "melt" is called out they resume moving around the room. This is an effective activity for the teacher to introduce first as a game and to later incorporate in the classroom as a means of getting the immediate attention of the class.

MARCHING Performing a variety of marching activities in which the children must respond to verbal commands is excellent for helping older children learn to listen. Marching is also helpful in developing directional awareness.

Auditory Discrimination

Auditory discrimination is similar to visual figure–ground perception. It is the ability to detect one specific tonal quality and frequency within a whole complexity of sound stimuli. Individuals tend to initate movement toward the direction from which the sound cue emerges (directional awareness). Auditory rhythm is an aspect of discrimination and is the ability to identify a regulated series of sounds interspersed by regulated moments of silence in repeated patterns.

The following is a list of general teaching hints for children experiencing difficulty in auditory discrimination.

1. Speak slowly, distinctly, and on the child's level.
2. Speak in natural volume. Extra volume can confuse the child's ability to discriminate what you say.
3. Speak so that the child can see your lips (for severe disabilities).
4. Maintain eye–to–eye contact.
5. Deliver brief, simple directions.
6. Control the environment.
7. Use situations with verbal responses, physical responses, and both responses.
8. Avoid repeating directions whenever possible.
9. Use a blindfold for emphasis on developing auditory sensations.

Specific Objectives

1. To be able to respond to sounds or verbal commands.
2. To be able to react independently to verbal commands without visually monitoring others.
3. To be able to listen to a command and then carry it out without verbal repetition.
4. To enhance fundamental rhythmic abilities.
5. To be able to distinguish between similar sounds.
6. To be able to distinguish between dissimilar sounds.

Movement Experiences

CLOSE YOUR EYES Ask the children to close their eyes as you clap your hands several times. Ask the children to "clap just as I did." Vary this procedure by clapping in different rhythms.

1. You may also use two drums, having children imitate drum beats.
2. Repeat the activity with stamping, clapping, and snapping fingers.
3. Begin with even beats and progress to syncopated rhythm.

TAPE RECORDER Using a tape recorder, encourage children to say their names, imitate animals, and sing songs. The tape recorder may teach sounds not easily found in the child's environment. Encourage children to discuss and name the various sounds.

MUSICAL INSTRUMENTS Select several rhythm-producing instruments such as a drum, a triangle, a sand block, or a wooden block. Children watch as you make a sound on each. Ask the children to close their eyes and listen carefully. Strike a sound on one of the instruments such as a drum, and have the children open their eyes and tell you which instrument you played. Next have the children close their eyes as the teacher plays two instruments. Have the children tell you which instrument was played first, and which one was played last.

WHAT DOES IT SOUND LIKE? Using familiar noises have the children differentiate between loud and soft, fast and slow, first and last, high and low.

WHAT IS IT? Place a number of objects on a table. Tap these objects in order to familiarize the children with the sound produced. Have the children put their heads down. Tap an object and ask, "what is it?" After the children have become familiar with the objects, tap several of them and ask which you tapped first, second, and so on.

WHERE IS THE BELL? Seat the children in a circle. Have one child leave the room. Give one of the children in the room a bell small enough to hide in his hand. Ask the child who left the room to come back in. When the child has returned, have all of the children stand and shake their fists above their heads. You may use more than one bell when the children become accustomed to the game.

KEEP OFF   A stretched canvas piece is needed to be strung taut in a rectangular frame, about 3½ feet off the floor. The child is beneath. The teacher tosses a beanbag onto the canvas. By the sound of its landing, the child can hear where to bump it to hit it off the canvas.

WALL TARGETS   Throwing blindfolded, the children listen to hear their beanbag hit a target made out of a resounding material.

BOUNCE OFF   Various textures and materials are situated as targets around the gym. They are used as rebound targets for the children throwing balls to hear the difference in sounds the bounces make.

MATCH THE CANS   Take 10 cans. Fill five with five different materials and duplicate these with the last five cans. Mix up the order and ask the child to match the cans by sound.

Auditory Memory

Auditory memory is the ability to retain auditory clues. Since much of the child's world involves the auditory modality, a great deal of information must be stored and retained. The following activities are designed to encourage retention of auditory clues.

Specific Objectives

1. To enhance the ability to remember auditory clues.
2. To enhance the ability to readily remember directions.
3. To develop listening skills.
4. To enhance comprehension of what is heard.
5. To increase the ability to move efficiently to a series of auditory clues.

Movement Experiences

A TRIP TO THE ZOO Begin a story about a trip to the zoo and all the animals that you will see. Give each child the name of an animal to imitate. When you name that animal in the story the child with the name of that animal acts out his or her interpretation.

Perform the same activity, having the children repeat the actions of the animal mentioned along with those that preceded it.

STORY TELLING Tell a familiar story (such as *Green Eggs and Ham, Cat in the Hat,* or *Jack in the Beanstalk*), having the children supply the repetitive phrases at the proper place in the story.

ACTION RHYMES Sing a familiar "action" rhyme such as *Head, Shoulders, Knees and Toes.* Omit a word from the song such as "head" and have the children touch that body part instead of naming it.

INSTRUMENT PLAYING Using the same idea as above play a simple pattern of notes on an xylophone several times. After the pattern is well known, omit a note and have the children fill it in.

SILLY HAT Using an old hat (a beanbag will do), give the children a series of silly things to do. Start with two directions and gradually increase the numbers and complexity of the instructions.

HORSE RACE Using children as the "horses," conduct a horse race. Put a number on each child. Begin the race using only two or three "horses." Have them race (gallop) to a designated point and declare a winner indicating the number of the "horse" and its place (e.g., "number three came in first, and number eight came in second").

Have the remainder of the group tell you the order of the finish, using the horse numbers only. Increase the number of horses to four or more after practice with having the children recall the first three, four, or five "horses" to cross the finish line.

THE WINNER IS. . . .   Repeat the above activity but declaring the ribbon winners. For example, "the horse that came in first wins the blue ribbon. Which number was it? The horse that came in second wins the red ribbon. Which number was it?" and so forth. You may then want to continue with "what color ribbon did number four win?" and so forth.

LOST AND FOUND   Pretend that several children in class lost an article of clothing. Have the children recall the names of those missing something.

ACTIVITY IDEAS FOR ENHANCING TACTILE PERCEPTION

The development of the sense of touch serves as a means of enhancing children's knowledge of the world about them. It is the modality by which they come into actual physical contact with their world. As with the visual and auditory channels, the tactile modality is developed through experience with objects in the environment. Tactile discrimination is the first and most basic aspect of tactile perception and involves the development of an awareness of the "feel" of things. Tactile memory, involves the ability to associate tactile impressions with known objects.

The tactile modality is often neglected in the education of young children, and is assumed to develop "naturally." It has been the experience of the author, however, that touch plays an important role in developing a more accurate sense of body-awareness. Frostig[2] incorporates numerous tactile experiences in body image–development activities.

[2] Frostig, Marianne. *Movement Education Theory and Practice,* Chicago: Follett Educational Corporation, 1970, pp. 52–53.

Cutting a variety of different textured materials enhances tactile perception as well as fine motor coordination.

Children should learn to direct their tactile movements in such activities as climbing a ladder, crawling through a tunnel, tracing a maze blindfolded, or walking on a slippery surface.

Tactile Discrimination and Matching

Tactile discrimination is the earliest form of tactile development and involves developing an awareness of things through touch. Young children developing their tactile discrimination abilities are also in the process of developing a corresponding vocabulary of words such as hard, soft, spongy, rough, smooth, bumpy, coarse, slick, and sticky. The ability to distinguish form through tactile clues also begins to develop. Differentiating between circles, squares, and triangles as well as large and small objects develops, along with the ability to sort and match objects tactilely.

Specific Objectives

1. To develop an awareness of tactile sensations.
2. To be able to discriminate between tactile clues
3. To be able to sort objects according to tactile characteristics
4. To be able to match objects according to feel.

Movement Experiences

COLLECTIONS   Make collections of several types of objects and describe how they "feel."

1. Cloth (nylon, cotton, velvet, fur, burlap, dotted swiss, leather, wool, corduroy, etc.)
2. Balls (ping-pong, rubber, cork, styrofoam, steel, fringe balls, beach balls, golf balls, bowling balls, etc.)

3. Seeds (to pine cones, black walnuts, chestnuts, buckeyes, acorns, cocoanuts, sumas, beans, pods, etc.)
4. Minerals (shale, sandstone, gypsum, granite, marble, limestone, etc.)
5. Sandpaper (assorted grades of sandpaper ranging from coarse to very fine)
6. Food wrap (aluminum foil, waxed paper, plastic wrap, butcher paper, cellophane, brown baper bags, etc.)
7. Household staples (salt, sugar, flour, pepper corns, rice, macaroni, "Cheerios," etc.)
8. Kitchen items (blunt scissors, butter spreader, various-sized spoons, fork, spatula, rubber scraper, cookie cutter, etc.)
9. Miscellaneous (plastic, metal, aluminum, steel, glass, tin, etc.)

TEXTURED PAINTINGS   Make textured paintings using glue to secure such things as rice, sawdust, tissue paper, small stones, seeds and pods, popcorn, and sand.

COLLAGES   Make collages using a wide variety of textures.

CREATIVE MOVEMENT   Discriminate between various textures through movement. Have the children feel a texture such as silk and interpret it by moving the way it feels. Use a variety of textures that exhibit characteristics such as:

1. Bumpy
2. Smooth
3. Coarse
4. Prickily

MYSTERY BAG   Place familiar but similar objects in a sack such as a toy car, boats, and trucks. Have a child reach in the bag, without looking, and describe how one object feels to the class. Children guess what object is being held.

Repeat the above activity but have the child reaching in to guess what the object is after describing it to the class.

TAG AN OBJECT   Place several different objects on the floor (use as many different objects as there are children). Blindfold each child (four to eight at a time works well) and whisper the name of the object they are to locate. On the signal "go," send them around the area trying to locate their object. They may remove their blindfold when they think they have located the proper object.

Repeat the same activity using several geometric shapes.

GEOMETRIC SHAPES Blindfold a child. Hand the child one geometric shape at a time and have him tell all about it and name the shape.

SHAPE TRACE Using your finger trace a geometric shape on the child's back. The child then tells about the shape and names it if possible.

HEAVY AND LIGHT Sort a variety of objects into two categories of heavy and light. The same may be done with rough–smooth, soft–hard.

SANDPAPER SORT Using different grades of sandpaper sort them according to texture blindfolded.

Repeat the above activity but sort according to size, shape, texture. Perform first while visually monitoring the blindfold.

TOUCH TAG Play a game of tag in which you tell the children to touch something "soft", "hard," "smooth," "wide," "sharp," and so forth. The last child touching that type of object sits in the "mush pot" for one turn (avoid excluding children in games of this nature).

SEARCH Place several different objects in a large cloth bag. Have the children reach in without looking and find, by touch, the correct object described such as:

1. "Find something you eat with"
2. "Find something you wear"
3. "Find something you write with"

Tactile Memory

Tactile memory activities are similar to discrimination and matching activities but involve a greater degree of sophistication. Memory activities require the child to discriminate nonvisually from familiar and unfamiliar objects and to apply verbal lables to these tactile clues.

Specific Objectives

1. To remember what objects feel like.
2. To be able to identify tactilely unfamiliar objects by touch.
3. To be able to identify tactilely familiar objects.

Movement Experiences

WHERE IS IT?   Using a textured drawing of a familiar figure (kitten, donkey, Santa Claus), have the children locate its various body parts while blindfolded.

GUESS WHO?   Have the children form a circle. "It" is blindfolded, turned around twice, and placed in the center of the circle. He then steps forward until he touches another child and attempts to determine who it is. He feels that child's clothing, hair, face, and so forth in an effort to determine who it is. Three guesses are permitted, then a new child is "it."

PUT IN ORDER   Scatter several objects on the floor. Blindfold the children and tell them the type of object they must locate. Begin with three types. Have them locate the objects and place them in order. For example, tell them to find something round, then something hard, then something smooth.

MEMORY BALL   Secure several different types of ball from the gymnasium (football, basketball, baseball, softball, soccerball, volleyball, kick ball, tennis ball, and wiffle ball). Place the balls on the floor and have the children, blindfolded, locate and name the various balls and tell what they are used for.

SANDPAPER NUMBERS AND LETTERS Blindfold the children and have them distinguish between various numbers and letters by touch. Older children can solve simple addition or subtraction problems using the numbers or spelling words.

SUGGESTED READINGS

Chaney, Clara M. and Newell C. Kephart, *Motoric Aids to Perceptual Training,* Columbus, Ohio: Charles E. Merrill, 1968.

Early, George H. *Perceptual Training in the Curriculum,* Columbus, Ohio: Charles E. Merrill, 1969.

Frostig, Marianne. *Movement Education: Theory and Practice,* Chicago: Follett, 1970.

Getman, G. N. and E. Kane, *The Physiology of Readiness,* Minneapolis: Program to Accelerate School Success, 1964.

Harvat, Robert. *Physical Education for Children with Perceptual–Motor Learning Disabilities,* Columbus, Ohio: Charles E. Merrill, 1971.

Kidd, Aline H., and Jeanne L. Rivoire, *Perceptual Development in Children,* New York: Internal Universities Press, 1966.

Knight, Melanie. *Activities for Early Development of Perceptive Skills.* University City, Missouri: School District of University City, 1958.

Witten, Betty Van. *Perceptual Training Activities Handbook,* New York: Teachers College Press, 1967.

SUGGESTED RECORDS

Finger Games, Bridges, 310 W. Jefferson, Dallas, Texas 75208, HYP506.

Kaplan, Dorthy. *Perceptual Development Through Paper Folding,* Bridges, 310 W. Jefferson, Dallas, Texas 75208, LP9010.

Lummi Stick Fun, Kimbo Records, Deal, New Jersey, Box 246, KIM2000.

Riccione, Georgiana. *Fun Activities for Fine Motor Skills,* Kimbo Records, Deal, New Jersey, Box 246, KIM9076.

Chapter 11

Movement Experiences for Enhancing Academic Abilities

CONTENTS

Introduction
General Objectives
Activity Ideas for Enhancing Science Abilities
    Specific Objectives
    Movement Experiences
Activity Ideas for Enhancing Language Arts Abilities
    Specific Objectives
    Movement Experiences
Activity Ideas for Enhancing Mathematic Abilities
    Specific Objectives
    Movement Experiences
Activity Ideas for Enhancing Social Studies Abilities
    Specific Objectives
    Movement Experiences
Suggested Readings
Suggested Records

I hear and I forget,
I see and I remember,
I do and I understand.
Anonymous

INTRODUCTION

In the area of cognitive development, movement can serve as an effective reinforcer of academic concepts and contribute to academic readiness for schoolwork. For preschool and primary-grade children, movement is a primary means by which they explore and discover the world about them. It is incumbent upon us to see that children are permitted and encouraged to explore their ever-expanding world. This does not mean that they should be permitted "total" freedom without any restrictions. It does mean, however, that their environment should be one that is conducive to exploration. It should be nonthreatening, nonhostile, and responsive to their natural curiosity and inquisitiveness.

Since moving is central to children's total growth and development, it should be recognized that while children are indeed learning to move for *movement's* sake, they are also learning through movement for *learning's* sake. In a developmental perspective there is a reciprocal relationship between moving and learning. Because of the need for movement children learn about their environment and because of their need to learn they move about in their environment. Without the medium of movement children lose one of the basic modalities through which they learn. The information-gathering avenues that movement offers for the learning and reinforcing fundamental perceptual–motor and academic concepts is central to the lives of many children. Although not a *necessary* condition for perceptual and cognitive development to occur, gross motor movement has been shown to be a *sufficient* and often very effective condition.

In many instances, movement may serve to enhance the learning activity and make it more relevant to the child as a whole. The learner grasps many fundamental concepts more readily if a greater number of sensory modalities are involved. Through total involvement of the sensory apparatus the learning of academic concepts can be facilitated. Movement permits children to experiment with the concept personally through their own actions. It also promotes overlearning because a greater number of senses are involved. By facilitating a more complete and balanced involvement of the senses, movement serves as an effective vehicle for stimulating academic readiness.

Children's learning, when viewed from a developmental perspective, progresses from the concrete to the abstract. In early learning when the senses apprehend by concrete means, movement serves the function of providing contact with concrete phenomena. For example, the manipulation of concrete objects paves the way for later abstract comprehension of size, shape, and volume. Also, locomotion involving directional awareness develops from the child's own internal awareness of left and right and progresses to an external concept of left and right in relation to other objects and people.

This process proceeds from the concrete "me" to an abstract "other," and movement plays a key role in this transition.

In Chapter 4 the role of movement in the cognitive development of children was discussed in detail. Chapters 9 and 10 dealt with movement experiences for enhancing a variety of perceptual–motor and perceptual abilities respectively. This chapter is designed to provide a variety of movement experiences appropriate for reinforcing specific academic understandings in science, mathematics, language arts, and social studies. Examples of 10–12 activities are presented in each of the above academic areas. For more comprehensive coverage in each of these areas the reader is referred to the work of Cratty,[1,2] Humphrey,[3] and Gallahue, Werner, and Luedke.[4]

ACTIVITY IDEAS FOR ENHANCING SCIENCE ABILITIES

Many basic science concepts can be illustrated effectively through movement. Movement is a natural means of helping children understand basic principles in physics involving, levers, and Newton Laws of Motion. A variety of other science concepts can also be effeciently dealt with through the medium of movement. The following is only a representative sampling of the vast number of science concepts that may be explored through movement.

[1] Cratty, Bryant J. *Intelligence in Action,* Englewood Cliffs, N. J.: Prentice–Hall, 1973.

[2] *Active Learning: Games to Enhance Academic Abilities,* Englewood Cliffs, N. J.: Prentice–Hall, 1971.

[3] Humphrey, James. *Child Learning through Elementary School Physical Education,* Dubuque, Iowa: W. C. Brown, 1974.

[4] Gallahue, David L., Peter H. Werner, and George C. Luedke, *A Conceptual Approach to Moving and Learning,* New York: Wiley, 1975.

Specific Objectives

Practice in science games such as the examples that follow will aid in reinforcing the development of:

1. Skills in the observation of nature.
2. An awareness of plants and animals in their world.
3. An awareness and understanding of climatic and seasonal changes.
4. The ability to apply fundamental mechanical principles to one's own movement.
5. Curiosity and investigative abilities into the properties and function of objects.

Movement Experiences

LEVERAGE

Desired outcomes

1. To experience the principle of leverage through the use of a teeter–totter.
2. To shift one's own weight, then that of other objects back and forth from the center point.
3. To experience the principle of leverage by moving the fulcrum off center, then trying to balance.
4. To enhance static-balance abilities.
5. To enhance vocabulary development through the use of adjectives such as heavy–light or verbs such as add–subtract.

Equipment

Use a board with a movable support under it, two light objects of equal weight, and two heavy objects of equal weight.

Procedures

Ask the children to balance the "teeter–totter," using the various objects. Have them find a partner and balance their own weight. Ask them to discover who weighs more. Weigh objects in the room by this method, using adjectives such as heavy and light. Move the center support and find out what happens.

Variations

Use weights to introduce addition and subtraction.

MACHINES

Desired outcomes

1. To encourage investigation of how objects are put together and how they function.
2. To enhance children's desire to explore and discover mechanical objects in their environment.
3. To allow opportunities to manipulate familiar objects without the fear of breaking them.
4. To enhance fine motor manipulative abilities.

Equipment

Have different workable objects available such as meatgrinder, ballpoint pen, flashlight, padlock, tennis racket, and an old camera.

Procedures

Permit the children to experiment with the objects by taking them apart and reassembling them. Then have them imitate the function of their particular object while others guess what it is.

Variations

Give each child one object. Have a race to see who can take apart and-/or put back together the object the quickest. Change objects. Which object is the easiest and which the hardest to take apart? Why? Since it is usually more difficult to put an object back together, do not be too stringent on this phase of the activity. It's more important that the children discover how to take the object apart and explore its working parts.

LEAF STUDY

Desired outcomes

1. To sharpen the children's observation of nature, specifically that there are different kinds of leaves with different shapes.
2. To enhance the children's perception of shapes.
3. Awareness of shape in relation to size may be enhanced (that is, the leaves may be different sizes but still the same shape.)
4. To enhance fundamental locomotor abilities through running.

Equipment

A variety of leaves and lotto cards with corresponding leaf shapes drawn on them.

Procedures

Divide the group into teams. Place the lotto-leaf cards within running distance for preschoolers. Pass out a leaf to each child. Each child runs in turn and places his or her leaf on the same-shaped leaf of the lotto card. The first team finished wins.

Variations:

This lotto activity may be used in any subject area to show one-to-one correspondence. It may also be used for classes of objects or people, colors, animals, jobs people do, and so forth.

A walk in the woods can serve as an excellent learning experience.

SEASONS

Desired outcomes	1. To recognize signs of the four seasons.
	2. To imitate actions indicative of summer, fall, winter, or spring.
	3. To enhance creative expression through movement.
Equipment	None needed.
Procedures	Develop a story play such as: In autumn, the leaves turn red or brown or yellow on the trees and drop off to cover the ground. The days get shorter.

ANIMAL IDENTIFICATION

Desired outcomes

1. To become knowledgeable about animals.
2. To be able to imitate a variety of animal movements.
3. To stimulate imagination and creative expression through movement.

Equipment

None needed.

Procedures

Children take an imaginary trip to the zoo. Before going, discuss what animals they would see at a zoo and types of habitat the various animals live in. While walking around the gym or classroom imitate the animals when going by their cages.

Variations

Half of the class visits the zoo while the other half pretends they are animals in their cages (each child being a different animal), then children can switch roles. The trip can be to the farm, jungle, circus, and so on.

SIMILARITIES AND DIFFERENCES

Movement skills

Jumping, running, and hopping forward and backward on one then both feet.

Desired outcomes

1. To enhance the ability to determine logical consistency and inconsistency within movement tasks.
2. To enhance the ability to differentiate between similar and dissimilar things.
3. To enhance fundamental running, jumping, and hopping abilities.

Equipment

Hoops, balls, ropes, wands, mats, gym floor, or large grassy area.

Procedures

Teacher executes a group of two to six movements (depending on the visual memory skills of the children) such as a jump forward, hop backward, jump sideways, three successive 2-foot jumps forward, and four successive 2-foot jumps backward.

The children then determine which of the series or movements "does not belong" with the rest. In the group above, one might say that all are forward and backward movements except one, or perhaps all are 2-foot jumps except one.

Another series of movements, perhaps more or less than above, may then be executed by a child or, after planning, by one of the group of children. Observers again must determine which of several does not belong.

Variations

The children may first plan a movement series on paper prior to executing it. More than one movement may be found to be different within a series. The length of a series of movements may be shortened or lengthened, from two to six, as the children are found to be more or less capable of discovering differences.

ANIMALS WITH HORNS

Desired outcomes

1. To enhance the ability to identify animals that have horns and those who do not.

2. To enhance fundamental hopping and running abilities.

Equipment

None needed.

Procedures

Children stand in a circle. Teacher says, "deers, horns up!" If that animal does have horns the children will hop or run in place. Then the teacher might say, "pigs, horns up!" This time, since the animal does not have horns, children squat down. After the game, teacher shows pictures of animals showing whether they have horns or not. Discussion is generated on why some animals have horns and others do not. What do animals use horns for? What would some animals look like if they didn't have horns?

Variations

Instead of the teacher reciting the names of animals, she may show a picture and the children must identify the characteristic movement of that animal.

SHADOWS

Desired outcomes

1. To be able to demonstrate knowledge of shadows by showing how to get away from "it."
2. To enhance fundamental running abilities.

Equipment needed

None.

Procedures

This activity must be played in a sunny area with a few objects that cast shadows. One person is "it." If "it" can step on or get into the shadow of another player, that player becomes "it." A player can keep from being tagged by getting into the shadow by moving in such a way that "it" finds it difficult to step on his shadow.

Variations

Observe the other objects from shadows. When are the shadows the longest and biggest? When are they the smallest?

PARTS OF A PLANT

Desired outcomes

To be able to identify the different parts of a plant and their positions.

Equipment

Large cut-outs of flowers, tape.

Procedures

Several relay teams are needed. Large parts of a plant with tape on the back are needed. When the teacher says "go" to the first runner, he runs to the pieces, picks one up and sticks it to the wall or floor. The second runner picks up another part and puts it in the correct place. The first team finished with all parts in the correct places wins.

Variations

Use a dismembered cardboard skeleton and have the children put the body parts in the correct places.

INERTIA

Desired outcomes

1. To develop an awareness of physical principles governing the absorption of energy and giving impetus to objects.
2. To enhance understanding of the meaning of "to start" and "to stop."
3. To stimulate divergent think-

ing through the application of principles to many situations.

4. To enhance fundamental stability and locomotor abilities.

Equipment

None needed.

Procedures

Ask what things on the playground start and stop (e.g., children, balls, ropes, swings), what else in life starts and stops. (cars, trains, schools, etc.), and ask children to experiment. "How many ways can we start ourselves?" Emphasize push-off. The harder the push-off, the faster the start. "Now, how do we stop? Watch each other. How can we stop most quickly? Stop with the body high— then low."

Variations

Experiment starting and stopping with a ball. (Use the feet, arms, and body.) Discuss the mechanical principles that start and stop our bodies and other objects.

ABSORPTION OF FORCE

Desired outcomes

1. To know that moving objects slow down before they stop.
2. To enhance fundamental running abilities.

Equipment

A perpendicular line is made 50 feet from the starting line with measurements of 1-foot intervals drawn beyond the line.

Procedures

The teacher says "go" and one of the children starts running. The teacher says "stop" when the children reach the 50-foot line. The intervals past this line show how many feet it took to stop after hearing the signal.

Variations

Using lines on the gym or classroom floor, each child has a partner who gives the signals. Then they see how far it took the runner to stop.

ROTARY MOTION

Desired outcomes

1. To be aware of how the earth spins.
2. To enhance fundamental jumping abilities.

Equipment

None needed.

Procedures

The children stand with their feet close together and their arms at their sides. They jump into the air and with the use of the arms attempt to turn around making quarter, half, three-quarter and full turns to their original position.

Variations

Members of the class are stationed in positions of where the planets are relative to each other and the sun.

ACTIVITY IDEAS FOR ENHANCING LANGUAGE ARTS ABILITIES

The movement games found in this section are designed particularly for preschool–primary grade children. They may serve as a means of reinforcing the development of communication skills as well as memory and reading abilities. Practice in movement games involving skills in the language arts is particularly helpful to children because it puts the learning of various concepts (such as letter recognition, letter sounds, and spelling) into a nontraditional medium. All too often children learn the alphabet through a characteristic sing-song rhythm, or learn to recognize letters or words only in a specific context on a page. The activities that follow provide another sensory modality through which these concepts may be *internalized* rather than merely *memorized* in an isolated situation. They are merely a sampling of the numerous movement possibilities. They may be modified and expanded in a variety of ways.

Specific Objectives

Practice in language arts games such as the ones that follow will aid in reinforcing the development of:

1. Communication skills
2. Auditory memory abilities
3. Letter identification
4. Language expression
5. Language comprehension
6. Reading abilities
7. . Spelling abilities

Movement Experiences

FOLLOWING DIRECTIONS

Desired outcomes

1. To enhance listening to and remembering oral directions.
2. To enhance ability to sequence actions in following directions.
3. To enhance fundamental locomotor manipulative and stability abilities.

Equipment: None needed

Procedures: The teacher is the leader and lists a series of actions the children are to perform. The children may not move until the directions are finished. They then perform the actions in sequence.

Variations:

May be used as a relay game. The first child completing the actions wins a point for his or her team. To increase the difficulty, actions can involve more complicated tasks or a greater number of tasks in the sequence.

DESCRIBING OBJECTS

Desired outcomes

1. To enhance oral communication skills by giving practice in the use of adjectives to describe objects.
2. To utilize the haptic modalities in "visualizing" an object by combining the tactile and kinesthetic senses.

Equipment

Sack filled with assorted familiar objects, for example; toothbrush, candle, mirror, spoon, and pencil.

Procedures

May be an individual, partner, or group activity. The child puts his hand into the bag and feels one object. He then describes it by how it feels and what it does. He does *not* recite the name of the object; the other children guess what the object is. When someone guesses the object, it is taken out for all to see.

Variations

May be adapted for a pantomine activity if the children act out what the objects can do.

Classes of similar objects may also be used to increase the difficulty (e.g. foods, utensils).

VERBAL DIRECTION DISCRIMINATION

Desired outcomes	1. To enhance left–right discrimination in hand and foot use.
	2. To practice moving oneself into positions described by words such as in, on, under, between, beside, and beneath.
	3. To enhance use of words to describe one's own actions.
Equipment	None needed
Procedures	Leader gives commands such as "place your left hand under the chair," or "put your right foot beside the wall."
Variations	May be varied as a "Mother May I" game. Watch for the child who consistently mimics other children. It may appear that he does have a grasp of the concept, but to be certain you may have to test this child individually or give extra practice by himself.

LETTER SHAPES

Desired outcomes	1. To recognize letter shapes and categorize them according to line composition.
	2. To develop an awareness of left, right, open and closed letters; vertical and horizontal lines.
Equipment	Chalkboard, movable cards with upper and lower case letters.
Procedures	Children are asked to classify uppercase letters according to "shape."

(E.g., circle letters OCS, slant line, and straight Y V W A K N M X Z, curved and straight lines B D G J P Q R U, and horizontal lines E F H L T.) The children may be asked to position their bodies in the proper positions for each one, or to jump into a playground maze containing letters of each type or to run and collect letters of each type from a pile of movable letters.

Variations

Make letters using hands, limbs, or the entire body. Walk through the letters in a sandbox or over a rope formed into the shape of various letters.

BIG LETTERS, SMALL LETTERS

Desired outcomes

1. To enhance discrimination of letter shapes seen in various forms.
2. To enhance foot-eye coordination.
3. To enhance jumping, running, and fundamental manipulative abilities.

Equipment

Upper- and lower-case letters (some movable, some on cards, some on fixed grids) and a blackboard.

Procedures

Written letters presented on cards may be found in a pile of upper-case letters, as children see who can run to the pile and pick up appropriate letters first. Children may be asked to spell out a word seen in lower case by jumping onto upper-case equivalents.

Variations

Children should be able to match capital and small letters when presented to them in any situation.

COLORS AND COLOR WORDS

Desired outcomes

1. To be able to associate colors with the words that represent them.
2. To reinforce following directions.
3. To enhance fundamental locomotor abilities.

Equipment

Cardboard or paper colors, string.

Procedures

Children are in a circle formation. Every other child steps to the inside of the circle and faces the person that was to his right. Each child in the center circle is given a different color on cardboard to hang around his neck. Each child in the outside circle is given a color word to hang around his or her neck. An uneven number is needed and that child is in the center. Any type of music may be played or sung by the teacher. When the music stops, the children must match themselves with the proper color or word. At this time the center child tries to steal a place in the circle. If successful, another child who did not correctly match his color or word must take the center position. The children on the inside move clockwise. The children on the outside move counterclockwise. "X" in the middle gets to name the type of locomotor movement used in running, hopping, and so on.

Variations

Numbers and letters may be used, as well as any other word associations.

DO WHAT I SAY

Desired outcomes

1. To enhance communication skills
2. To enhance language comprehension.
3. To enhance the ability to express and communicate orally, clearly and concisely.
4. To be able to follow directions and sequence movements.

Equipment

Balls, chairs, tables, hoops, and ropes, laid out as an obstacle course in a straight line.

Procedures

The teacher or a directing child describes the sequence of what the performing children should do. The observing children attempt to determine whether the directions have been carried out correctly.

Variations

A chain of children can be formed, the first child making up directions and whispering them to a second child, who may whisper them to the person next to him and then to a third. The last person in line performs the action sequence whispered to him. The other children determine if that is the correct interpretation of the original message.

ACTING OUT WORDS

Desired outcomes

1. To read and act out the meanings of words (verbs).
2. To enhance a variety of fundamental movement abilities.

Equipment

Flash cards containing action words.

Procedures

Each child has a partner who shows a card. The partner must act out the verb, such as run, climb, or strike. The observing child checks him and if he is correct, he becomes the "teacher," and the partner must do the acting.

Variations

Use as a relay in which each child runs to the pile of cards, picks one up, acts it out, puts the card in a discard pile, runs back, and tags the next runner.

"Cracking the code" in reading is essential to success in school.

STORY RELAY
Desired outcomes

1. To be able to write down a word to help make a sentence.
2. To recognize sentences.
3. To enhance fundamental running abilities.

Equipment	Chalk and blackboard.
Procedures	Two or more relay teams are formed. The first runner goes to the board and writes a word to begin the sentence. He tags the second runner, who writes another word. This continues until all members write a word to make one or more coherent sentences.
Variations	Each child must write a whole sentence to make up a small story.

SAME OR OPPOSITE

Desired outcomes	1. To identify a pair of words as having the same meanings, opposite meanings, or neither.
	2. To reinforce auditory memory abilities.
Equipment	None needed.
Procedures	The teacher recites a pair of words. The children must clap once if they are the same, clap once and stomp feet once if opposites, or clap once, stomp once, and clap twice if they are neither.
Variations	Use different signals for the various pairs. Have students think up pairs of words and give them. Teacher can give one word and clap once so that the child called on must give back a word with a similar meaning.

RELAY SPELLING

Desired outcomes	1. To put letters together to spell a given word.
	2. To enhance fundamental running abilities.

Equipment

Chalkboard, chalk, or two sets of alphabet letters.

Procedures

At least two teams are needed. The letters are scattered on the floor in a designated place for each team. The teacher writes a word or words on the board. First runner on each team runs to their alphabet area to get the first letter and places it down in the correct spot. Then he runs and tags the second runner, who gets the second letter. The first team to complete the word or list of words wins.

Variations

Instead of writing words on the board, the teacher gives them orally. Each child runs up and gets his letter and the team stands in a line spelling out the word.

READ AND FOLLOW DIRECTIONS

Desired outcomes

1. To be able to carry out directions in the order in which they are given.
2. To enhance gross and fine motor abilities.

Equipment

Card with simple directions written on it and corresponding equipment.

Procedures

The child is given a card on which a list of several directions is written. He is given time to read it carefully. Then, after giving back the card, he must go through the set of directions exactly as they were written.

Variations

Increase the number of directions given and increase the complexity of each direction. Give the directions orally instead of letting him read them. For example say, "clap your hands once," "touch your head," "run in place ten times," "touch your toes," and "say your name."

ACTIVITY IDEAS FOR ENHANCING MATHEMATIC ABILITIES

There are a wide variety of movement activities available that will contribute to children's understanding of basic concepts in mathematics. Almost all movement activities involve some form of grouping and/or counting. The innovative and creative teacher will take advantage of the numerous "teachable moments" for reinforcing mathematic comprehension through movement.

The medium of movement appears to be particularly effective in the area of mathematics because it permits children to deal with such abstract concepts of counting, addition, subtraction, and measuring in concrete terms. Children are actually able to see the results of their numerical manipulations and thus gain first-hand knowledge of fundamental mathematic operations.

The activity ideas that follow are but a mere sampling of the almost limitless possibilities. They may be expanded upon and modified in a wide variety of ways.

$$
\begin{array}{ccc}
4 & 5 & 6 \\
+3 & -2 & -3 \\
\hline
\end{array}
$$

$$
\begin{array}{ccc}
7 & 2 & 4 \\
+1 & +3 & -2 \\
\hline
\end{array}
$$

Specific Objectives

Practice in mathematic games such as the ones that follow will aid in reinforcing the development of:

1. Shape and size discrimination
2. Number-identification abilities

3. The ability to order numbers
4. Concepts of greater and less than
5. Adding and subtracting abilities
6. Concepts of volume and length

Movement Experiences

MEASURING VOLUME

Desired outcomes

1. To enhance ability to make elementary measurements of volume through everyday activities.
2. To help prepare for addition, subtraction, and fraction concepts through concrete experiences.
3. To enhance scientific concepts of characterizing solids and liquids through observing their properties.
4. To enhance fine motor manipulation by using various utensils.

Equipment

Containers of varying sizes. Have different utensils available such as spoons, ladles, and measuring cups. Have assorted solids and liquids for measuring materials such as sand, beans, rice, pebbles, water, and juice.

Procedures

Let the children explore the pouring action by using any materials desired. Give a problem such as "which spoon will empty the rice bowl the fastest?" or "how many little cups equal one big cup?" Let them discover the answer.

Variations

Demonstrate a specific concept first. For example, show ½ by using 1-cup and a 2-cup measuring cups. Let the children experiment with different containers to show two times and four times.

MEASURING LENGTHS
Desired outcomes

1. To practice fundamental measurement of lengths through use of familiar objects.
2. To provide concrete experiences in preparing to measure with feet and yards.
3. To use adjectives such as long–short (descriptive), longer–shorter (comparative), and longest–shortest (superlative).
4. To enhance fundamental movement abilities involving lifting and carrying.

Equipment

Boards arranged in step fashion in graduated lengths up to 1 yard.

Procedures

Ask the child to choose one board. Have paper strips cut to the length of each board and ask each child to put their board on the strip that is the same length as their board. Mix up the boards so they are not in step fashion and repeat. Compare each board to the ruler and yardstick using phrases "longer than" or "shorter than."

Variations

Use a meter stick-as the basis of measurement. Measure familiar objects with the ruler or yardstick. Measure each child's height.

SHAPE, SIZE AND COLOR DISCRIMINATION
Desired outcomes

1. To help the child gain perception of shape, size, and color through gross motor activity.

2. To demonstrate class inclusion and exclusion concepts.
3. To demonstrate the use of more than one adjective simultaneously to describe an object.

Equipment

Paper cut-outs differing in shape, size, and color.

Procedures

Let each child choose one cut-out. Then give different directions such as "all the green circles, clap your hands," "all the big green circles, clap your hands," and "all the circles, clap your hands."

Variations

Creative dramatics may be incorporated. Give directions such as "all the red objects, form a circle." Show how your color makes you feel. To increase the difficulty level, add more different colors, shapes, or sizes.

MONEY TWISTER

Desired outcomes

1. To be able to identify the values of money.
2. To enhance static-balance abilities.
3. To enhance spatial and directional awareness.

Equipment

Have an oilcloth made up similar to the "twister" game. Instead of different colored circles, use coins or numbers painted on the circles. As the teacher calls out "left foot on penny," the four children standing on the edges put their left feet on the penny symbol. This continues until all combinations have been used. Can the child identify the symbols for the Roman numerals? Can the child identify left from right?

Variations

Roman numerals or Arabic numbers may be substituted for coins. Addition and subtraction problems may also be explored.

NUMBER SEQUENCES

Desired outcomes

1. To enhance the ability to put numbers in their correct order.
2. To enhance fundamental running abilities.

Equipment

Two or more relay teams and two or more number cards.

Procedures

First runner runs to the card pile, finds the first number in the counting series, brings it back, and puts it in the designated place. The second runner is tagged and runs to find the second number. The first team to have the entire counting sequence finished wins.

Variations

Have various sequences: 1–10, 30–40, count by 10s to 100, count by 2s, 3s, 5s, 100s. Instead of placing numbers in a certain area, the runners run back to the team and hold the number in front of them, so that when they are all through, they all hold up a number in the sequence.

JUMP AND MEASURE

Desired outcomes

1. To enhance number comparisons.

2. To demonstrate the concepts of shorter or longer.
3. To develop the concept of greater than or less than and-/or long jumping abilities.
4. To enhance vertical jumping abilities/and or long jumping abilities.

Equipment

Tape marked off in inches and feet.

Procedures

Using tape, place a vertical line on the wall. The children take three turns to see how high they can jump. They write their three tries down and then make comparisons by using "greater than" and "less than" signs. They then decide which is the highest jump and the shortest jump.

Variations

Using the same procedures as above, jump for distance. If the room has tiled floors, the tiles can be used instead of inches and feet.

BEANBAG ADDITION AND SUBTRACTION

Desired outcomes

1. To enhance ability to solve beginning addition and subtraction problems.
2. To enhance fundamental throwing abilities.

Equipment

A set of beanbags that are made to look like numbers. Numbers painted or taped on regular beanbags will do nicely. Hoops are also needed.

Procedures

The child throws several beanbags into a hoop on the floor. The teacher says "plus" or "minus." The child then tries to add the total or subtract it from a given number.

Variations

To develop facility for understanding directions, the teacher can tell children to throw the beanbag over a child, under a chair, through a hoop, to the left or to the person on the right. Then the children together can add up their beanbags.

ADDITION RELAY

Desired outcomes

1. To be able to give two numbers that add up to a given number.
2. To enhance throwing abilities.

Equipment

A numbered grid is drawn on the blackboard or made with tape on the floor.

Procedures

The children form teams. The first person throws the beanbag at numbers. If he hits 8, he must say two numbers that will make 8. If he does, he gets 1 point for his side. The other team does the same thing with their number grid. The first team finished is the winner if its score is the highest.

Variations

For later in the year, use larger numbers on the grid, such as 13, 14, or 15. This makes for good practice with mathematical facts.

ODD AND EVEN

Desired outcomes

1. To enhance ability to identify odd and even numbers and their sequence.
2. To enhance fundamental throwing and catching abilities.

Equipment

Ball.

Procedures

Children stand in a circle. The first child says either an odd or even number. He throws the ball to another child, who must give the next odd number after 1. If the first child has said 2, the second child has to give the next even number after 2. The second child throws to a third child, who must give the next even number in the sequence.

Variations

The first child says any number and throws the ball to anyone in the circle. That child must tell whether that number was odd or even. Then he says a number and throws to someone else, who continues the process.

MATH HOPSCOTCH
Desired outcomes

1. To enhance ability to add or subtract according to the sign.
2. To enhance fundamental throwing and jumping abilities.

Equipment

Make a hopscotch diagram on the floor, using tape for the outlines. Put numbers in each area. Use a beanbag that has a plus on one side and a minus on the other.

Procedures

Child throws the beanbag on a number. If it lands on the plus side, he adds that number to the next number that he throws. If it lands on a minus, he subtracts the two numbers.

Variations

Have several relay teams. See who can get through the fastest with the correct answers. Besides throwing the beanbag, the child must jump to the numbers and recite the problem as he is jumping.

SKIP COUNTING

Desired outcomes

1. To enhance ability to skip count.
2. To enhance fundamental catching abilities.

Equipment

Beanbag.

Procedures

As the children pass the beanbag down their line, they count off by 2s. They keep going until they reach a predetermined number, or they get through their line. For example, the first team to reach 50 wins.

Variations

Use other skip counting such as by 4s, or 5s.

ACTIVITY IDEAS FOR ENHANCING SOCIAL STUDIES ABILITIES

When we view the societal understandings expected of preschool and primary-grade children it becomes readily apparent that a great number of these competencies may be developed or reinforced through the use of movement activities. Young children's natural love for creative expression and their fertile imaginations makes creative drama a natural avenue by which they may come to know more about themselves, their families, communities, and world. The use of story plays and mimetic activities, as well as role playing and other forms of creative expression, serves as an excellent means for enhancing social studies abilities. The following activities are designed to stimulate the creative and innovative teacher's imagination. The possibilities are considerably greater than presented here. Therefore these activities should be viewed as stimulators, or "teasers," for the modification and expansion of social studies abilities.

SPECIFIC OBJECTIVES

Practice in social studies games such as the ones that follow will aid in reinforcing the development of:

1. An awareness and desire for self-care.
2. Recognition of the variety of one's daily activities.
3. Recognition of the many tasks that parents perform.

4. Making the transition from the home into the community.
5. Knowledge of the functions of various community helpers.
6. The ability to observe and obey traffic signals.
7. The ability to understand and follow directions.

MOVEMENT EXPERIENCES:

IT IS I

Desired outcomes

This role-playing activity may involve locomotion, manipulation, and stability activities in order to:

1. Increase the child's awareness of his own self-care duties.
2. Develop a desire for performing these skills independently.
3. Enable the child to more closely observe activities of others in his environment.
4. Enhance creative expression through pantomime and role playing.

Equipment

None needed.

Procedures

The leader whispers to a child an action which he or she is to perform for the others to guess. The list might include, "you are brushing your teeth . . . combing your hair, buttoning your shirt, and answering the telephone."

Variations

To exemplify the jobs people do, a child acts out one profession. The list might include dentist, firefighter, police officer, barber and others.

IT EATS, PLAYS, AND WORKS

Desired outcomes

1. To allow the child to experience that his and others' everyday activities have different aspects.
2. To enhance creative expression through role-playing activities.

Equipment

Cards with pictures of objects from three realms of daily life; eating (spoon, cup, napkin, salt-shaker, etc.), working (hammer, axe, shovel, etc.), and playing (ball, bat, balloon, top, jumprope, etc.).

Procedures

Pass out the cards randomly and ask the children to do what their object does. Now tell them that each object either eats, works, or plays. Ask them to get together with other objects that ". . . work like your object works" or ". . . play like your objects plays," and so on. The first group to find all of its members wins.

Variations

For beginning readers, write the words on the cards in addition to or instead of the picture clue. To simplify the activity, have the children act out their object separately and have the group guess. The first to guess correctly is the next to act out an object.

SHOPPING BASKET

Desired outcomes

1. To prepare the child for the transition from the immediate home environment to the larger community.
2. To illustrate that memory is essential in daily living.
3. To enhance auditory memory abilities.

Equipment

Shelves with assorted objects commonly found in a grocery store.

Procedures

Teacher or another child may act as leader. The leader says, "I have a shopping list and it says that I should bring (bar of soap, eggs, loaf of bread, etc.)." The leader says., "I have a shopping list and it says that I should bring (bar of soap, eggs, loaf of bread, etc.)." The leader names two or three objects on the shelf. The shopper is to go to the "store" and bring back the correct items in his basket.

Variations

As a team game, attach money values to items. The team gets paid in points for the cost of the item. If an item is forgotten or the wrong item is brought, the value of the item is subtracted from the team's score.

COMMUNITY HELPERS

Desired outcomes

1. To enhance ability to act out the movement pattern of the various community helpers.
2. To enhance creative play skills.

Equipment

Pictures of community helpers.

Procedures

Using pictures of various community helpers, the class discusses how people in our community help us and what kinds of movement they do in their jobs. Then the children take turns acting out a community helper while the rest try to guess.

MAP OF THE COMMUNITY

Desired outcomes

1. To enhance the ability to follow directions and read a map in order to get from one location to another.
2. To develop an awareness of the directions north, south, east, and west.
3. To enhance listening skills.
4. To enhance fundamental locomotor abilities.

Equipment

A map layout of the community sketched on large newsprint or drop cloth and taped on classroom or gym floor (or even drawn in chalk on the playground). Size should be approximately 8 feet by 10 feet.

Procedures

Children may be grouped in pairs and take turns giving complete directions to get from one location to another. The other child must walk the route without asking for further help (if possible). Then the children exchange roles.

Variations

Start with simple directions to one location, then proceed to more difficult directions involving two or three steps on the way to the destination.

MULBERRY BUSH

Desired outcomes

1. To be able to demonstrate the different activities of parents.

2. To enhance auditory rhythmic abilities.
3. To enhance skipping abilities.

Equipment

None needed.

Procedures

Players form a circle and join hands. They sing "here we go round the mulberry bush." Go through the verses, "Monday, wash the clothes, Tuesday, iron; Wednesday, scrub the floor; Thursday, mend clothes; Friday, sweep; Saturday, bake bread; and Sunday, go to church." Then talk about why and how we do these things. Do you always do them on certain days? Do we bake bread anymore? Why not? What things do we do? What other things does your mother or your father do?

Variations

Make up verses for what children and fathers do on different days of the week.

TRAFFIC SIGNS
Desired outcomes

1. To enhance ability to understand, observe, and obey traffic signals and signs.
2. To enhance fundamental locomotor abilities.

Equipment

Red, yellow, and green flash cards, cardboard steering wheel.

Procedures

Each child drives her or his own "automobile" and uses a steering wheel made out of cardboard. The teacher has flash cards—yellow, green, and red. The children drive around—running, hopping, skipping, and follow the traffic signals as they are raised.

Variations

To make it more difficult, several children also serve as traffic signals. Different traffic signs are place around the room: (e.g., "no left turn"). A specified path is followed. The children can be divided into relay teams and must negotiate the path according to the signs.

EQUATOR

Desired outcome

1. To enhance ability to give hints using the word equator so that another child can find the object.
2. To develop the concept that places near the equator have hotter summers and warmer winters.

Equipment

None needed.

Procedures

The children scatter themselves throughout the area. The teacher places an object on one of the players. The object does not have to be concealed, but small enough so that it can be seen. All of the players except "it" know where it is. "It" tries to locate the object and is given clues by the other children. The players call out "equator" in different tones—soft to mean farther away and loud to mean very close. When "it" finds the object, he calls out the person's name who has it and all of the players run to a previously designated safe place before being tagged by "it."

Variations

Discussion can be generated after the game about what types of housing and clothing would be needed in countries near the equator. What other things would be different about living near the equator? Can the children give a hint using "equator" so that another child can find the object?

SUGGESTED READINGS

Cook, Myra B. and Joseph H. Christiansen, *The Come Alive Classroom,* West Nyack, N. Y.: Parker Publishing Co., 1967.

Cratty, Bryant. *Active Learning: Games to Enhance Academic Abilities,* Englewood Cliffs, N. J.: Prentice–Hall, 1971.

Cratty, Bryant J. *Intelligence in Action,* Englewood Cliffs, N. J.: Prentice–Hall, 1973.

Crescimbeni, Joseph. *Arithmetic Enrichment Activities for Elementary School Children,* West Nyack, N. Y.: Parker Publishing Co., 1965.

Gallahue, David L., Peter H. Werner, and George C. Luedke, *A Conceptual Approach to Moving and Learning,* New York: Wiley, 1975.

Henderson, G., *Let's Play Games in Mathematics—Kindergarten Volume,* Skokie, Ill.: National Textbook Co., 1974.

Humphrey, James. *Child Learning Through Elementary School Physical Education,* Dubuque, Iowa: W. C. Brown, 1974.

Platts, Mary. *SPICS, Suggested Activities to Motivate the Teaching of Primary Language Arts,* Stevensville, Mich., Educational Service, Inc. 1973.

SUGGESTED RECORDS

Palmer, Hap. *Learning Basic Skills Through Movement,* Vols. I and II, Educational Activities, Freeport, New York, Box 392, AR514 and AR522.

Palmer, Hap. *Learning Basic Skills Through Movement—Building Vocabulary,* Educational Activities, Freeport, New York, Box 392, AR521.

Palmer, Hap. *Learning Basic Skills Through Movement—Health and Safety,* Educational Activities, Freeport, New York, Box 392, AR526.

Palmer, Hap. *Math Readiness—Addition and Subtraction,* Educational Activities, Freeport, New York, Box 392, AR541.

Palmer, Hap. *Math Readiness—Vocabulary and Concepts,* Educational Activities, Freeport, New York, Box 392, AR540.

Palmer, Hap. *Singing Multiplication Tables,* Bridges, 310 W. Jefferson, Dallas, Texas 75208, 45-101.

Wilson, Robert, et al. *Teaching Reading Through Creative Movement,* Bridges, 310 W. Jefferson, Dallas, Texas 75208, LP5070.

Chapter 12

Children's Play, Toys, and Play Spaces

CONTENTS

Introduction
Play
  Why Children Play
  Developmental Aspects of Play
Toys
  War Toys
  Toy Safety
  Choosing Toys
  Toy Libraries
Play Spaces
  Indoor Play Spaces
    The Indoor Movement Center
  Outdoor Play Spaces
    The Outdoor Movement Center
Conclusion
Suggested Readings

The Great Man is He Who Does
Not Lose His Child's Heart.
Mencius

INTRODUCTION

For children, play is essentially a learning medium but for too many years it has often been viewed as a frivolous pastime. It seems unnecessary among knowledgeable people to assert that play is valid as a learning medium as well as for its own inherent values, especially with the attention that the writings of Piaget,[1] Erikson,[2] and others have commended in recent years with these implications for developing cognitive and affective structures through play. Frank, however, has noted that "within recent years there has been a strong movement to restrict the play of children, young and older, to adult-imposed patterns in order to promote formal learning, especially preparation for school."[3] We must, therefore, reassert the validity and the necessity for play in child development.

The greatest values of play in education are that it is interesting to children, holds their attention, arouses their enthusiasm, and is fun. As a result a primary distinction between the terms "work" and "play" is that play is engaged in simply for its own sake. Play does, however, through proper guidance, have numerous residual benefits that make it a desirable medium through which a myriad of psychomotor, cognitive, and affective competencies may be developed. Play is an effective learning medium because of the importance placed on it by children and its potential influence on all aspects of behavior. It is time that the validity of children's play be recognized. In order to do this we must pay more than lip service to its values. We must become sensitive to the play of children, and in doing so must become familiar with the types of toys and play spaces that are conducive to children's optimal growth. This chapter is focused on three important aspects of children's lives, namely play, toys and play spaces.

PLAY

The meaning of the word "play" is elusive and has various connotations to many people. Ellis,[4] in the excellent book *Why People Play*, explores in detail the questions as to what play is and why people play. Play is usually considered to be pleasant and voluntary. With reference to children, the definition of play offered by Galambos is perhaps the most appropriate for our discussion of motor development. Galambos considers play to be "direct,

---

[1] Piaget, Jean. *Play, Dreams and Imitation in Childhood,* London: Heinman, 1957.

[2] Erikson, Erik. "Toys and Reason," in *Childhood and Society,* New York: Norton, 1963.

[3] Frank, Lawrence K. "Play is Valid," *Childhood Education,* March 1968, pp. 433–440.

[4] Ellis, M. J. *Why People Play,* Englewood Cliffs, N. J.: Prentice–Hall, 1973

spontaneous activity by which children engage with people and things around them. It is imaginative, usually active; youngsters perform it with all their senses and use their hands or their whole bodies."[5]

The following is a discussion of why children play and the developmental aspects of play. It should be read carefully in order to gain greater insight into the child's world of play.

Why Children Play

To children, play is serious business and it is this seriousness of purpose that gives it its educational value. Play is the way in which children explore and experiment with the world around them as they build up relations with that world, others, and themselves. Children in play are discovering how to come to terms with their world, to cope with the tasks of life, to master new skills, and to gain confidence in themselves as worthwhile individuals. Play provides a medium through which young children can learn through trial and error. It provides a means through which they can experience an endless number of real-life situations in miniature form with a minimum of risks, penalties, and pain for mistakes. It is an excellent way in which to learn how to cope with the "real" world.

Play provides an avenue through which children gradually learn the difference between *mine* and *yours.* It permits children to first discover themselves and then to reach out to others in their rapidly expanding world. Through play children learn basic patterns of living. Their imagination and love for creative drama enable them to assume various roles, feelings, attitudes, and emotions.

Play is also necessary for the mental health of children. Young children engage in play wholeheartedly, discarding all self-consciousness and restraint. They reveal their true nature through play and often provide the parent and teacher with subtle indicators of their emotional well-being. Immature children that have had limited play experiences often need to be taught how to play in a meaningful and constructive manner. These children exhibit their lack of ability to play through their wandering, constant boredom and pleas that "there is nothing to do." Aggressive behavior is often exhibited through destructive play and is typified by children that always manage to break their toys or inevitably end up in a wrestling match with their peers. Children that are emotionally disturbed often prefer to play with things rather than interact with other children and are demanding of

[5] Galambos, Jeanette W. *Organizing Free Play,* Office of Child Development, Department of Health, Education and Welfare, February 1970, p. 61.

Play is for everyone.

adult attention and approval of their play. Young children that are well adjusted find it easy to slip into and out of various roles in dramatic play.

Play helps meet children's emotional need to belong and to have status within a group and a feeling of personal worth. As a result they will generally play at things in which they do well (much the same as adults) and have experienced a reasonable degree of success.

Through active play children learn to move for movement's sake as well as for learning's sake. Directed play experiences can serve as an effective means by which they may develop and refine a variety of fundamental movement abilities in the areas of locomotion, manipulation, and stability. It also serves as a facilitator for enhancing physical fitness and motor abilities. The natural drive by most children to be active needs to be continually nurtured by both parents and teachers. We are in danger of reducing the vigorous play world of children to little more than 30 minutes of activity a day. Two 15-minute periods a day for recess is a far cry from the 3–4 hours of vigorous play per day recommended by most experts in the field. We need only to look at the daily schedule of many children to see that we are indeed in danger of developing a nation of youth lacking in physical abilities and vigor. A full day of school followed by 2–3 hours of television and homework does not leave much time for vigorous play. This coupled with a host of environmental problems such as a lack of space for vigorous play, poor facilities and equipment, and a lack of encouragement from parents and teachers lead to many hours of sedentary play. This is not meant to imply that the relatively inactive forms of play are of little or no value. It simply means that we should strive for a better balance between quiet and vigorous play in order that the optimum development of children be encouraged in all areas of behavior.

Developmental Aspects of Play

When viewing the play behavior of children it is readily apparent that there is a predictable sequence of emergence of developmental aspects. The play of the infant and toddler is considerably different from that of the primary-grade child. Increased complexity of the neuromuscular apparatus plus higher-order cognitive functioning and increased affective competencies make for characteristic forms of play at various ages. However, when observing play one runs the risk of interpreting it within the context of one's own interests and understandings and failing to see it in its complete form. As a result a narrow view of play is often developed. For example, a teacher primarily interested in the motor development of children may view play from the perspective of gross motor activities, games, and sport. Teachers

Play is adventure.

interested primarily in cognitive development often view play from the quiet activity aspect of problem solving and experimentation with new equipment, materials, and ideas. Persons primarily concerned with the affective domain often view play from the functions that it serves as a socializing agent, without regard to either its active or its quiet forms. Play in actuality incorporates all aspects of development, whether psychomotor, cognitive, or affective. We must, therefore, view play in light of its total contribution to the growth and development of children.

Play during the first year of life does not look much different from normal daily activity. The infant is constantly involved in using all of his or her senses and, when awake, appears to be in almost constant motion. The play of infants is centered around their own bodies, the bodies of others, and concrete objects. It involves the exploration and repetition of perceptual cues and is purposeful. Through play the infant comes to grips with his or her world and develops a host of cognitive, affective, and psychomotor competencies. For example, the ever-popular game of peekaboo is enjoyed by all infants and may be viewed from a cognitive standpoint as a learning activity in which the child learns, through experience, the complex ideas of permanence, consistency, and reliability of objects, and that objects can reappear once they have disappeared. Peekaboo also has implications for affective development in that it provides a medium for the infant to learn to trust the world, to shape it, and to make things happen. From a psychomotor standpoint it provides practice in controlling the musculature of the hands and proper sequencing of events in time.

The play of infants involves coming into contact with shapes, textures, colors, and sounds. A great deal of time is spent in looking, listening, grasping, sucking, teething, and exploring. In short, the play of infants is a sensorimotor experience that involves the broadening use of all of the senses in order to come to better know and to function better in the immediate world.

The toddler rapidly expands beyond the play of infancy. It is a time of reaching out into the world through ceaseless, joyful movement in an effort to order the world. The play of toddlers is primarily egocentric, that is, it is confined to the individual and does not involve interaction in a constructive manner. Toddlers use their newly acquired mobility to explore space. They spend a great deal of time trying out their movement potentialities. They crawl, climb, scoot, walk, run, roll and jump. They attempt to order their world by classifying objects and searching for patterns. They enjoy play with small manageable toys, lining them up, stacking them, and exploring them with their mouths. They play at classifying objects according to size, shape, color, and function. Toddlers also spend a great deal of time testing the limits of their world through imagination, imitation, and dramatic play. The imitative play world of toddlers enables them to make sense of experience through dramatizing it in action. Toddlers enjoy loading and unloading objects of various sizes into containers and by doing so are developing concepts of volume and permanence. Stroking different-textured objects is a favorite quiet play activity of toddlers and they often have a favorite cuddly toy or blanket. This may be viewed as an attempt by the child to find warmth and security at a time when many demands for more mature behavior are being made, such as with developing the self-help skills of feeding and toiletry.

The play of the preschooler is an elaboration of the earlier forms of play and also involves new aspects. Children at this age enjoy using and "mastering" a wide variety of materials. They thoroughly enjoy working with paints, sand, clay, water, and blocks. The use of these materials begins by being purely exploratory and then becomes more systematic, organized, and takes on concrete form. The imitative play of the toddler gives way during these years to highly involved sociodramatic play, with a more mature grasp of what is real and what is fantasy. They enjoy acting out social situations, dressing as grown-ups, and travel play with cars, fire engines, and airplanes. Preschool-age children enjoy active play. They love to run and jump, throw, and catch and need little encouragement for active movement. They enjoy building things and progress from blocks to more advanced forms of construction.

Primary-grade children enjoy many of the same activities as preschoolers, but exhibit increasing ability to work with others in small groups. They are more interested in active games and table games with rules and regulations. They enjoy art and making designs in two-and three-dimensional form. Primary-grade children enjoy drawing, painting, and molding as an expression of their creativity. Their imagination, however, is often less vivid than preschoolers and care must be taken by adults to nurture it. Primary grade children enjoy discovery play, problem solving, and generally like vigorous movement activities.

There is considerable overlap between the play of toddlers, preschoolers, and primary-grade children. Older children will often retreat to earlier forms of play in order to reestablish their security and self-confidence. Younger children likewise will often attempt older more sophisticated forms of play behavior of an older brother or sister, only to find that they do not possess the necessary gross or fine motor coordinations, nor the cognitive or affective capacity for successfully engaging in that form of play. We return to the principle of *readiness* as the primary determinant of what, when, and how children play. We should view each child as an individual and structure play situations that are appropriate for that particular person.

Play is thrilling.

TOYS

One of the most visible differences between today's modern schools and traditional classrooms is the number of objects made available for the purpose of helping children learn. Traditionally schools have transmitted facts and concepts in an abstract way, by means of words, in an atmosphere removed from the everyday environment. In an effort to see that every child receives a socially useful and personally satisfying education, it has become apparent that this is not the only way for children to learn. For many it is not the best way, and for some, no way at all. Educators are discovering that many children can learn better through activities that look suspiciously like play. Activities that involve toys, games, and puzzles, manufactured and self-made; tools and materials; expressive media; models and replicas from the physical and social environment, concrete items that children can touch, handle, manipulate, and interact with are all being utilized with increasing frequency as an effective learning medium. In such ways they lay a solid foundation for abstract learning. This new emphasis is disturbing to many parents and some educators. "Why," they say, "the children are only playing.

They can do that at home!" Such persons should be led to understand the many specific learning purposes for such "play" activities.

Toys and expressive media are often useful as tolls for the various types of diagnosis that teachers make about the developmental stage, educational needs, and emotional health of their students. It is important, for example, for teachers to discover the maturational level of children entering the preschool or primary grades. Observation of their skills in using materials and their interaction with the materials and other children is revealing and valid to the knowledgeable observer. Toys such as building blocks are a good example. They give children power to construct and manipulate their world within their own frame of reference. Their building may be free in form and unstructured, or realistic and elaborated. In watching such activities, as well as in talking with children, the teacher receives clues to many of their perceptual, cognitive, and emotional needs.

The therapeutic value of letting children express themselves in activities like finger painting, clay modeling, pounding, playing with dolls and other people figures, and role playing with the help of costumes or puppets, has been commonly accepted. They are useful in determining whether the child's need to relieve his or her anxieties and to express his concerns is temporary or results from a more deep-seated problem involving motor or perceptual difficulties or expressing hostilities, fears, or other symptoms of psychological and social maladjustment.

Another use of tangible objects in the educational process, which teachers can apply with most children, is developmental. To determine whether a child's lack of readiness for academic work is due to age or to lack of stimuli in the home environment, object-oriented (toys) activities are a valuable aid. They encourage the desired learning in the cognitive psychomotor, or affective area, or in a combination of these.

On the cognitive level, immature children must be encouraged to furnish their mind with the concrete experiences that are the necessary foundation for the increasing complexity and level of abstraction of their thoughts. Being deprived of these opportunities at home or at school may make it impossible for them to develop to their full potential for abstract thinking. Remediation by furnishing an environment rich in stimuli can do much to overcome the original deprivation. But the child's way of thinking may have been so affected that he or she will respond most easily to ideas demonstrated in a concrete way. An effective teaching strategy for such children is to give them solid, manipulable objectives designed to demonstrate the desired concepts. Word games, cut-out letters, puzzles, and Cuisenaire rods are examples. Older children do better when ideas are presented with examples from their own experience. Such a presentation does not handicap the learning of children who are able to handle abstracts; it simply helps reinforce the concepts for them.

The development of psychomotor skills is dependent in large part on the availability of objects for children to interact with. They need things that can be folded, bent, nailed, glued, cut, sewed, stretched, bounced, poured, twisted, punched, tied, blown into, and crushed; surfaces that can be painted, carved, attached to, and washed; items to look at, listen to, sniff, taste, fondle and stroke; and objects to climb, swing on, sit on, stamp on, jump over, and crawl through.

The ways that toys contribute to learning in the affective area are also many and varied. Games and toys help children learn to discriminate between and interrelate with their environment and with other people. The skills they develop as they interact give them a feeling of being able to cope, and of being in control of themselves and their surroundings. Becoming familiar with objects from the outside world, such as toy trucks, buildings, and household equipment, helps broaden their concepts in realistic terms. Trying out other roles, through dolls, puppets, and toy or real objects similar to those adults use or wear, also helps children explore and discover their own identity, and provides a safe way to try out more mature or different real-life roles.

Toys are big business, according to the toy manufacturers of America, there are approximately 150,000 diverse toys on the market with about 5000 new toys being introduced each year. Parents buy toys for a variety of reasons, ranging from tradition to providing toys that they never had. Some people buy toys and use them as bribes or rewards, hence toys are often used as a substitute for love and attention, to ease guilt, or to mold the child in the parents' image. For whatever purpose they are purchased, toys occupy many hours of the child's play and should be carefully selected.

Table 12.1 presents a list of appropriate types of gross and fine motor toys for children from infancy through the primary grades. It must be remembered that play materials must be safe, durable, and interesting to children.

War Toys

When reviewing Table 12.1 it should be noted that there are no war toys (guns, etc.) listed. It is my feeling that the use of toy guns is not a form of play to be encouraged by adults. The purchase of commercially manufactured toy guns is discouraged because of their realism. One need only to visit a local toy store to see guns that smoke, "bang," look like machine guns, shotguns, and even the M14 rifle used in Viet Nam. The use of guns purchased from the toy store serves no useful purpose. Many will argue this, claiming that toy guns provide children with an avenue to work out their aggressions, and that they will outgrow their need for violent expression. It does seem ludicrous, however, that in a society which claims to abhor

TABLE 12.1 APPROPRIATE PLAY MATERIALS FOR YOUNG CHILDREN

INFANTS (0–1 years)

1. Teething ring	6. Mirror
2. Rattles	7. Shapes
3. Hedgehog	8. Crawligator
4. Textured ball	9. Crib mobile
5. Ball rattle	10. Buttons on a cord

TODDLERS (1–2 years)

1. First blocks	9. Washable doll
2. Nesting boxes	10. Bells and music box
3. Peg board	11. Squeeky toys
4. Stacking toys	12. Push and pull toys
5. Snap toys	13. Sand toys
6. Cuddly toys	14. Sturdy picture books
7. Step stool	15. Simple inlay puzzles (3–6 pieces)
8. Soft throwing toys	

PRESCHOOLERS (3–5 years)

1. Picture books	13. Climbing equipment
2. Dress-up clothes	14. Balancing equipment
3. Shape, size, and texture toys	15. Striking toys
4. Miniature toys	16. Beanbags
5. Cardboard boxes	17. Woodworking equipment
6. Blocks	18. Wading pool
7. Dolls and puppets	19. Record player and records
8. Furniture	20. Musical instruments
9. Puzzles (8–20 pieces)	21. Blunt scissors, paste, and paper
10. Painting and coloring materials	22. Modeling clay
	23. Simple story books
11. Pots and pans	24. Floating bath toys
12. Large balls	

PRIMARY GRADES (6–7 years)

1. Large and small balls	10. Playing cards
2. Climbing rope or ladder	11. Building toys
3. Climbing frame	12. Story books
4. Balance beam	13. Chalkboard
5. Tumbling mat	14. Science toys
6. Jump rope	15. Globe
7. Bicycle	16. Dolls and puppets
8. Tinker toys	17. Playhouse
9. Flash cards	18. Water toys
10. Playing cards	19. Workbench and tools

killing and violence, that we go to such great lengths to ensure realism in the toy guns made for children. If children truly outgrow their need for violent expression, why then are the television channels and movie theaters filled with realistic scenes of violence and killing?

Children have a right and need to express themselves through fantasy play. Such things as "cops and robbers," "war," and "cowboys and Indians" are forms of fantasy play that have been engaged in by children for generations. Children have a right to work out their aggressions and they should be permitted to do so but in a manner that does not encourage or promote *realism*. Perhaps the use of a fantasy gun (such as a stick or the index finger) in this form of fantasy play would reduce the realism created by a commercially purchased toy gun.

Guns themselves are not an evil. It is the way that we condone and use them in our society. Whether in real life or play, shooting someone is not a form of behavior to be viewed as the norm for society, even though it takes place during war and is an aspect of law enforcement. The use of toy guns should be discouraged among children.

Toy Safety

The Child Protection and Toy Safety Act was passed by the United States Congress in 1969. This law prohibits the sale of toys that may prove harmful to children. Any toy that presents an electrical, thermal, or mechanical hazard, or that may endanger the safety of children through sharp or protruding edges, fragmentation, explosion, strangulation, asphyxiation, electrical shock, or fire is not to be sold. The Bureau of Product Safety, a division of the Food and Drug Administration, prevents such products from entering the market and is responsible for recalling unsafe toys from the market.

Toy manufacturers have the responsibility to design toys in such a way that the materials used and the methods of construction make the toy as childproof as possible. That is, the toy should require a minimum of education of the user to make it safe. Ideally, no imaginable use or abuse of the toy by a child should make it unsafe.

The following is a listing of examples of toys that have been deemed unsafe by the Food and Drug Administration:

1. Sharp or protruding objects:

    a. *Dolls of pliable plastic*—The doll can be bent to position in several directions. By doing so, however, sharp wires, serving as joints, protrude from the ends of the doll's hands and feet. This could puncture a child seriously.

b. *Large ring darts*—The darts are one foot long and weigh about ½ pound. The child could easily lose an eye or receive puncture wounds on the body.

2. Fragmentation:

Clackers—Fairly recently "clackers" were introduced to the toy market. This created great fun for children of all ages. However, these are quite dangerous because the clackers may chip or fragment from being struck together. These flying pieces could cause serious eye injury.

3. Explosive toys:

Wasp cap gun—Potential cause of deafness to children. Noise reaching decibels of 130 are safe. At a distance of 2 feet, the noise produced by the gun was 150 decibels. A child who fires shots in succession indoors could be exposing himself and others to a continuous sound level roughly 15 times louder than that considered dangerous for continuous sound.

4. Strangulation:

Crib mobiles—Stuffed animal characters are often suspended from the side of the infant's crib and over the crib. When one of the figures is pulled, the plastic bracket that supports the mobile often breaks near its base, sending the entire assembly into the crib. The strings could cause strangulation and the broken bars could cause serious injury.

5. Asphyxiation:

Fringed balloon squeakers—The balloon is blown up and let go. As the air escapes from the balloon, it makes a loud noise because of a metal noisemaker lodged in the mouthpiece of the balloon. If the child does not take the balloon out of his mouth and allows the air to escape into his mouth, the noisemaker, caused by the air pressure, acts as a missile and may shoot down the child's mouth. This could become lodged in the throat, causing asphyziation.

6. Burns caused by electrical toys:

Ovens—A toy stove was recently introduced on the market. The stove reached temperatures of 200° F on the sides of the oven. On top it reached 300° F, and the inside of the oven rose to an unbelieveable level of 660° F. Most kitchen ranges rise to temperatures under 180° F on the non-cooking surfaces. A child could easily receive serious burns from such a toy.

7. Toxicity:

Rhythm band set—One such set includes toy musical instruments, one of which is a pair of maracas. The maracas may come apart, and they contain pellets made of metallic lead. Lead is poisonous mainly in the form of lead salts. The chance of inhaling the tiny pellets into the lungs also makes them a serious hazard to children.

8. Flammability:

Foam balls—A popular brand foam ball was tested against the Flammability Standard set by the 1969 Child Protection and Toy Safety Act. Under the specified conditions, the ball not only ignited within the time limits specified for contact with a candle flame, but it smoked profusely while it burned and shed drops of burning substances.

When a toy is determined to be unsafe for children's usage, it can be banned, according to the decision by the Division of Children's Hazards. When a toy is banned it means that the item cannot be sold in interstate commerce. It is also considered illegal to sell banned items that are already on the store shelves.

Choosing Toys

Even though the Food and Drug Administration does attempt to prevent the sale and use of toys determined to be unsafe, much of the burden of protecting children from the dangers of toys still rests with parents and teachers. A good deal of caution needs to be exercised in the purchase of toys. The following are among the most important questions to ask yourself when buying a toy for a child.

1. Is it safe?
2. Is it appropriate to the developmental level of the child?
3. Is it durable?
4. Is it fun (for the child)?
5. Will it stimulate the child's imagination?

A good toy is one that does not do all of the playing for the child or "have all the fun." Many top companies list the approximate age range of interest in the toy and its potential benefits on the box or package. This information should be read carefully but used only as a general guide for purchasing the right toy for that particular child. A great deal of money is spent on the purchase of toys and we should be careful to get the most for our money.

All too often a youngster will open an expensive new toy and proceed to play with the box rather than the toy. If the toy does not stimulate the interest or imagination of the child, no amount of encouragement will get him or her to play with it. Answering the five questions outlined above will do much to ensure the purchase of toys that children will play with, learn from, and enjoy.

The following is a partial list of safety recommendations to take into consideration when selecting toys for children.

1. Toys should fit the child's age and physical skill.
2. For children under 3 years of age, avoid toys with small or easily removable parts (loose nuts, bolts, removable eyes, projections, needles, nails, etc.).
3. Look for toys that do not shatter or break easily.
4. Wait until a child is at least 8 years old before giving him or her chemistry sets, bow and arrows, and sharp-edged toys which might come into contact with the hands, clothes, or other parts of the body and cause bruises, cuts, punctures, or fractures.
5. Only electrical toys with the Underwriters Laboratory (U.L.) seal should be purchased. This seal means that the toy is required to have a safety device that prevents the child from putting his hands in the heated area when the toy is hot. Cooking, melting, and molding toys should be used by older children and only under adult supervision.
6. All toys should be sturdy and durable.
7. Look for areas where the fingers can become pinched in slots, holes, on the underside of the wheels, and in wind-up mechanisms.
8. Darts, archery sets, or spring-loaded guns with rubber suction cups that can be removed may cause punctures. Avoid such toys.
9. Avoid crib or playpen toys that are suspended on strings.
10. Avoid purchasing helmets or play eyeglasses that can shatter. These could result in serious head and eye injuries.

Toy Libraries

On the assumption that parents can provide significant educational experiences for their preschool children, a toy-lending library program has been developed for parents whose incomes are too high for their children to be eligible for Head Start programs but too low to provide tuition to private nursery schools. It is one of 15 nonprofit organizations authorized by Congress to start and test new educational programs. The four objectives of the program are:

1. To help parents facilitate the development of a healthy self-concept in their children.

2. To help parents promote their children's intellectual development, using toys and learning situations that are designed to teach specific skills, concepts, or problem-solving abilities.
3. To help parents stimulate their children's intellectual abilities by improving interaction between parent and child.
4. To help parents participate in the decision-making process that affects the education of their children.[7]

Parents attend night classes once a week for 10 weeks at a toy-lending library. At each meeting they are shown films on preschool education and are taught how to use such toys as "feely bags" to teach shape recognition, sound cylinders for auditory discrimination, flannel boards for relative position, rods for length comparison, and stacking toys for size, color, and pattern discrimination. Equipped with printed instructions about how to play with a given toy and what to expect from the child, the parents then take the toy out of the library for a week and return a week later to report on its success. There are two general instructions given the parents. First, the child, not the parent, may change the rules of the game; secondly, the game should be ended when the child seems to lose interest in the toy. Many parents have been impressed at how much they could teach their children and how much their children could learn through toys.

PLAY SPACES

The play environment that is provided for children should be one that is conducive to all aspects of their development. It should be safe, attractive, and provide for a wide variety of stimulating and interesting activities. All too often, however, the indoor and the outdoor play space is one that for a variety of reasons limits or discourages gross motor activities. As a result there has, over the past several years, been a tremendous emphasis on the cognitive and affective aspects of the toys, games, and play equipment found in the indoor and outdoor play space. If we subscribe to the notion the balanced development of children in the psychomotor as well as the cognitive and affective areas of behavior is important, we must then see to it that children's play environments also stimulate gross motor activity. Children have a basic need to be active. Through the proper design of play environments, as well as the use of appropriate methods of teacher interaction, this need for activity will be successfully channeled to promote children's learning to move, and hence learning through movement.

[7] Nimicht, G. P. and E. Brown, "Toy Library," *Young Children,* December 1972, p. 114.

Inner tubes tied together make excellent tunnels.

Indoor Play Spaces

Historically the indoor play space found in most nursery schools has been one of children's "interest centers." The environment has been designed around a variety of areas that are geared to the children's needs, abilities, and interests. The following is a list of the various interest centers typically found in nursery schools. It should be noted that inclusion of any or all of these areas into the indoor play space is dependent primarily on budgetary considerations and the availability of space.

1. *Block area*—the block area requires plenty of space and should be carpeted, if possible, to reduce the noise factor.
2. *Housekeeping area*—this interest center should be equipped with a toy sink, stove, refrigerator, table, and chairs. Dolls, doll beds, and dress-up clothing are also found in this area. The housekeeping area provides for considerable dramatization and role playing.
3. *Book area*—to be effective, this should be in a quiet part of the room. Books may be kept on shelves and/or a table. If possible, the area should be carpeted in order that children may sit comfortably on the floor if they so desire.
4. *Creativity area*—easels with paint and paper should be available for those children who want to paint.
5. *Science area*—this should be where materials can be easily displayed and seen by the children. Room to spread out leaves, stones, shells, and other "collector's" items should be provided in this area. Magnets, magnifying glasses, terrarium, and aquarium might also be added. Space should also be provided for pets brought into the room.
6. *Water–sand area*—ideally, a table with built-in sections for sand and water is the best kind of equipment for this activity. Also included should be shovels, small buckets, things that float, things that sink, funnels, straws, and soap.
7. *Music area*—the music area is a must in any program. A record player, records, cassette tape recorder, a variety of musical instruments, and a piano will make this an ideal area.
8. *Carpentry area*—the carpentry area should include a workbench with an attached vise. An assortment of tools, nails, and wood should be available.
9. *Nesting area*—in this area the children should have an opportunity to "escape" from the hustle-bustle of the classroom. Nesting cubes, an old refrigerator carton, or collapsible tunnel make an ideal nesting area.
10. *Movement center*—A movement center is an essential part of the

indoor play space for preschool children and is discussed in detail in the following section.

The Indoor Movement Center

Contrary to popular belief, an indoor movement center requires little space. The author has developed several movement centers in nursery schools in an area no larger than 8 feet by 10 feet. The key to success in developing an indoor movement center is to first establish the specific objectives that you want the children to achieve through participation in this activity area. Then, taking the space limitations and safety factors into consideration, carefully design and construct the movement center around the objectives. For example, you may have as one of your primary objectives "to provide the children with opportunities to enhance their movement abilities in a variety of fundamental stability, locomotor, and manipulative abilities." Therefore the movement center should contain equipment that will encourage practice in a variety of stability, locomotor, and manipulative activities. The following is a partial list of equipment, which may be purchased commercially or made by hand, that is appropriate for use in an indoor movement center.*

1. Stability

    a. Balance beam
    b. Balance board
    c. Bounding board
    d. Newspaper mats
    e. Coffee-can stilts
    f. Ladder
    g. Inner tubes

2. Locomotion

    a. Collapsible tunnel
    b. Carpet squares
    c. Ankle jump
    d. Cubes
    e. Portable climbing equipment
    f. Climbing rope

---

* Please refer to *Developmental Play Equipment for Home and School,* Wiley, 1975, for instruction on how to build numerous pieces of indoor and outdoor play equipment.

3. Manipulation

   a. Beanbags
   b. Hoops
   c. Yarn balls
   d. Automobile tires
   e. Targets
   f. Suspended balls

The indoor movement center should also include a variety of perceptual–motor stimuli. Play equipment consisting of various textures, colors, and geometric shapes is encouraged. The use of mirrors, for children to observe their movements, and portable equipment that may be used both indoors and outdoors is also recommended.

Outdoor Play Spaces

The opportunity for active movement in the outdoor play space should go well beyond the traditional recess period characterized by mass confusion, boredom, and fighting. The outdoor play area should first of all be designed for children in such a way that it stimulates their interest, imagination, and large muscle development. As simple as this sounds, one need only look at the majority of outdoor play spaces at the nursery-school and elementary-school levels to see that they are *not* designed for children. All too often the outdoor play space is constructed with its primary objectives being to amuse children and require minimum upkeep rather than encouraging their motor development. As a result a typical outdoor play space, unfortunately, often consists of acres of blacktop and galvanized swing sets, teeter-totters, and slides.

"Outdoor equipment and structures should be selected to invite creative expression and imaginative interpretation by the children," according to Haase.[8] The outdoor equipment should be abstract or neutral in its sculptural form in order to stimulate the child's imagination. It should stimulate a variety of locomotor, manipulative, and stability activities. Although individualistic in nature, outdoor play materials and equipment should encourage social contact. They should also stimulate imagination and cognitive processes through media that invite physical exploration and enjoyment.

---

[8] Haase, Ronald. *Designing the Child Development Center,* U. S. Office of Education, Project Head Start: Washington, D. C.: U. S. Government Printing Office, 1968, p. 10.

In planning an outdoor play space the following questions must be answered:

1. Is it safe?
2. Is it of *real* interest to children?
3. Is it developmentally appropriate?
4. Is it practical?
5. Is it economically feasible?
6. Can it be easily supervised?
7. Can it be maintained with a minimum of maintenance?
8. Can it be made available to the general public?

The outdoor play area should provide children with a variety of large and small muscle activities. It should contain a wide selection of equipment that promotes its use in a manner that is creative, challenging, and developmentally appropriate. The outdoor area should provide:

1. Large muscle activities to enhance all areas of children's motor development:

   a. Locomotion
   b. Manipulation
   c. Stability

2. Experiences with various media:

   a. Art
   b. Woodwork
   c. Dirt
   d. Sand
   e. Water

3. Places for seclusion and quiet activities:

   a. Tunnels
   b. Nesting cubes

4. Opportunities to observe nature:

   a. Animals
   b. Gardens
   c. Trees and shrubs

5. Opportunities to dramatize real-life experiences:

   a. Playhouse
   b. Junk car
   c. Boat

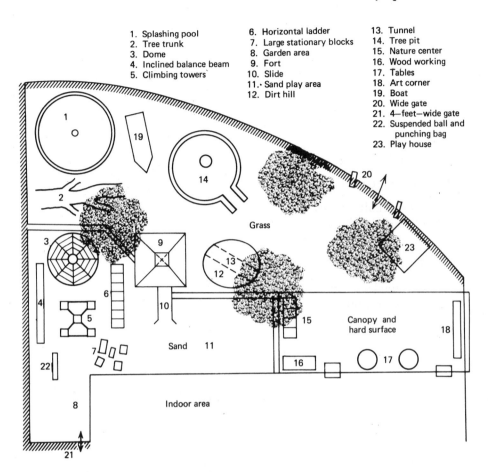

1. Splashing pool
2. Tree trunk
3. Dome
4. Inclined balance beam
5. Climbing towers
6. Horizontal ladder
7. Large stationary blocks
8. Garden area
9. Fort
10. Slide
11. Sand play area
12. Dirt hill
13. Tunnel
14. Tree pit
15. Nature center
16. Wood working
17. Tables
18. Art corner
19. Boat
20. Wide gate
21. 4—feet—wide gate
22. Suspended ball and punching bag
23. Play house

Figure 12.1 Design for an outdoor play space.

The Outdoor Movement Center

The outdoor movement center is easily incorporated into the total outdoor play space. There should be ample space for children to move freely. Ideally there will be a large grassy area and hillside for running, jumping, sliding, rolling, and climbing. There will also be a hard surface area for riding wheel toys and activities with balls. Trees should be an integral part of the movement center, not only to provide shade but to encourage climbing. A variety of equipment that encourages gross motor activities should also be located in the outdoor play space. This equipment may be used in addition to or in conjunction with the equipment found in the indoor movement center. Climbing, striking, and balancing equipment should be an integral part of the outdoor area. The following is a partial list of suggested types of equipment designed to encourage the development of these abilities.

1.   Climbing equipment:

   a.   Teepee tower
   b.   Cargo net climber
   c.   Climbing frames
   d.   Barrel pyramid
   e.   Climbing towers

2.   Striking equipment:

   a.   Tetherball frames
   b.   Striking frames
   c.   Rebound nets

3.   Balancing equipment:

   a.   Inclined balance beams
   b.   Bouncing buddy
   c.   Telephone poles
   d.   Barrels
   e.   Spools

CONCLUSION

The rapidly expanding world of young children is one in which play, toys, and play spaces are in central focus for their learning to move and learning through movement. As a result it is important to have a clear understanding of what constitutes play, why children play, and the developmental aspects of play. The toys that we provide for children to play with and their play environment are important to their total balanced development.

The selection of children's toys should be a matter for considerable thought and careful attention by parents and teacher. A variety of questions should be answered prior to the purchase of any toy, whether it be for active or quiet play, large or small in size, inexpensive or expensive.

The indoor and outdoor play environment for children should be carefully designed. It should be conducive to gross motor development as well as social interaction and cognitive growth.

Play, toys, and play spaces are important to children. This fact alone should be ample reason to see to it that the learning experiences within children's environments responds to their interests, needs, and developmental capabilities.

SUGGESTED READINGS

Ellis, M. J. *Why People Play,* Englewood Cliffs, N. J.: Prentice–Hall, 1973.

Erikson, Erik. *Childhood and Society,* New York: Norton, 1963.

Galambos, Jeanette, W. *Organizing Free Play,* Office of Child Development, Department of Health, Education and Welfare, February 1970.

Guides for Selection of Indoor and Outdoor Equipment and Materials (Experimental Pre-Kindergarten Programs), Albany, New York: The State Education Department, Bureau of Child Development and Parent Education, 1966.

Herron, R. E. and Brian, Sutton–Smith. *Child's Play,* New York: Wiley, 1971.

Jameson, Kenneth and Pat Kidd. *Pre-School Play,* New York: Van Nostrand–Reinhold, 1974.

Markun, Patricia Maloney (ed.). *Play: Children's Business,* Washington, D. C., Association for Childhood Education International, 1974.

"Protecting Your Child From Dangerous Toys," *McCall's,* December 1972.

Stone, G. J. *Play and Play Grounds,* Washington, D. C.: National Association for the Education of Young Children, 1970.

Sunderlin, Sylvia, and Nan, Gray (eds.), *Bits and Pieces: Imaginative Uses for Children's Learning,* Washington, D. C.: Association for Childhood Education International, 1967.

Chapter 13

Education of Young Children

CONTENTS

Introduction
The Motor Development Dilemma
Programs for Preschoolers
   Day Care Centers
   Head Start Programs
   Nursery Schools
   Parent Cooperatives
   Home Day Care
   Kindergarten
Moving to Learn
The Quality Preschool Program
The Teacher of Young Children
The Parent Helper
Organizing the School Day
Conclusion
Suggested Readings

No Printed Word,
No Spoken Plea
Can Teach Young Minds
What Men Should Be,
Not All the Books on
All the Shelves,
But What the Teachers
Are Themselves.
Anonymous

INTRODUCTION

Traditionally, the education of young children has been assumed almost entirely by the family. The quantity and quality of learning experiences engaged in by children have been left to the discretion of parents. Little consideration has been given, until recently, to education outside of the home for the vast majority of preschool age children. Many have scoffed at the Soviet practice of education by the State for children beginning at the age of 2 years rather than our more conservative and "acceptable" practice of beginning formal education at around age 5 or 6. This early education of children was often looked upon as something that could not and would not be tolerated in our society. We looked at the education of young children as being the sole responsibility of the home, except in extreme cases. In recent years, however, there have been three major developments that have resulted in a dramatic reassessment of this position: (1) the marked change in the social structure of our society, (2) the rapidly changing economic structure of our society, and (3) the increased professional interest in the contribution of early learning to later development. A closer look at each of these factors will help us to more fully appreciate their significance.

Our North American society is currently experiencing tremendous changes in the role of women in society. Heretofore, a woman's place was literally viewed as being in the home. Women have been considered as the "weaker sex," discriminated against, and discouraged and abused with respect to their opportunities in the working world. The woman's liberation movement, along with a growing awareness of the validity of equality for *all*, is making for dramatic social change. Many women are no longer satisfied with keeping a home and devoting a good portion of their life to the important but often frustrating task of raising children. Instead, they are returning to school, seeking full-or-part time employment, or searching for other expressions of fulfillment outside the home.

Our rapidly changing economic structure during the past few years has often made it extremely difficult for families to "survive" without two incomes. The present inflationary spiral has significantly reduced the amount of spendable income for many. The reduction of spendable income is coupled with the fact that many families find it "necessary" to have all of the luxuries and so-called necessities so skillfully advertised by the media. These factors have played an important role in the tremendous increase in the number of children enrolled in some form of day-care or nursery-school program.

The dramatic growth of interest in the contribution of early experiences to the later development of young children is the third factor that has led to increased interest in early childhood education. Jean Piaget[1] was among

[1] Piaget, Jean. *The Origins of Intelligence in Children*, New York: International Universities Press, 1952.

the first to stress the importance of early experience on future development. His stress on the importance of perceptual–motor experiences as a facilitator of cognitive development as well as physical development has been a prime factor in stimulating this interest. The "late start" by the United States into the Space Age brought about by the "Sputnik Era" of the 1950's stimulated many to begin viewing the potential of the early years as important determiners of later behavior. The 1960 White House Conference on Children and Youth[2] was a first national look into the education of young children. The Conference stressed that nursery schools, day-care centers, and kindergartens be open to *all* children from all walks of life under the qualified direction of a person trained in early childhood education.

Nursery schools, day-care centers, and other organizations are now concerned with the care and education of a large number of our nation's young children for all or part of their day, and the number is increasing daily. The responsibility of programs for preschoolers for the psychomotor, cognitive, and affective development of children has been a topic of considerable debate during recent years. As a result we have witnessed a rapid increase in the types as well as the number of programs available.

THE MOTOR DEVELOPMENT DILEMMA

Movement is of central importance to young children and their optimal development. Contributions to the psychomotor development of children is certainly a worthy goal of any early-childhood educational program. Enhancing children's ability to move efficiently and effectively, with control and with joy should be as important to the teacher of young children as is their affective and cognitive development. Realization that the balanced motor development of children also has implications for both these areas should amplify the importance of gross motor development. The fact is, however, that the vast majority of early childhood educators are: (1) poorly informed as to why motor development is important, (2) poorly informed as to what forms of physical activity to include in their programs, and (3) inadequately prepared as how to go about such a task. As a result the movement education of children is often taken for granted or dealt with solely through loosely supervised free play. Although free-play activities can and should play a part in the nursery-school experience, it is not enough to assume that the purchase of expensive pieces of indoor and outdoor play equipment will effectively aid in the development and refinement of the children's movement abilities. Too often children are turned loose on vari-

---

[2] Conference Proceedings, Washington, D. C.: The Golden Anniversary White House Conference on Children and Youth, Inc., 1960.

The education of young children has traditionally been the responsibility of the home.

ous forms of apparatus and expected magically to develop efficient forms of movement behavior on their own. Only through wise guidance, thoughful interaction and careful planning can we assure the proper development of children's movement abilities.

The following is a discussion of five types of programs available for young children. The extent to which movement plays a role in each of these programs depends on individual teachers, their expertise, and their commitment to the *total* development of children.

PROGRAMS FOR PRESCHOOLERS

The number and types of program available for preschool children has increased tremendously during the past 10 years. Data from the 1970 census survey clearly indicate that the number of children under 5 years of age is on the increase, even though the general population under 14 is predicted to drop by 1980. That is, there were 55,000,000 children under 14 years of age in the United States, according to the 1970 census report. A total of 18,013,000 were under 5. By 1980 these figures have been predicted to be 52,736,000 children under 14, but 19,881,000 under 5 years of age.[3] Also the number of working mothers with children under 6 has increased significantly from 12.8 to 30.4 percent between 1948 and 1969 (over 50 percent of the mothers with children between ages 6 and 17 years were gainfully employed by 1970).[4]

The rise in the number of preschool-age children, coupled with the high percentage of working mothers, makes it abundantly clear that millions of children are cared for by persons other than the parents, relatives, or baby-sitters.

Over 8.7 percent of the total population in the United States is made up of children under 5 years of age.[5] The need for their care, supervision, and education is apparent, and many communities are rising to the occasion to meet this need.

During the past several years a variety of preschool programs have emerged. Each of these programs represent a particular philosophical outlook and attempt to provide for the particular developmental needs of young children. The brief review of the major types of programs in existence throughout North America today is designed to provide the reader with a broader prospective of the nature and scope of programs for preschoolers. Although each program differs in its purposes and content, all have a place in our society and can make a positive contribution to the development of young children.

Day-Care Centers

The day-care center or day nursery, as it was previously termed, has come into wide use in recent years. Day-care centers are established primarily to serve the needs of working mothers. Upon their inception they were often places where children could be safely "stored" for the day with general assurance that their basic physical needs would be met. Little was done beyond serving their needs for basic physical care and ensuring that they were returend home in more or less the same condition in which they came. Today, however, several day-care centers are broadening their scope and

---

[3] *Profiles,* White House Conference on Children, Washington, D. C., Superintendent of Documents, U. S. Government Printing Office, 1970, p. 85.

[4] *Ibid.,* p. 140.

[5] *Ibid.,* p. 85.

beginning to hire trained professionals who are developing sound programs that deal with the affective and cognitive growth of children.

The tremendous increase in demand for full-day care of children has caused many educators to reevaluate the role of the day-care center and attempt to upgrade its quality. The National Committee for Day Care of Children has established goals of good day care as:

> Good day care provides educational experiences and guidance, health services, and makes available social services as needed by the child and his family. It safe guards children and helps parents to maintain the values of enriched family life.[6]

The typical day-care center is open on weekdays from 7.00 in the morning until 6.00 in the evening. There are no set hours of attendance for the children, but rather they come and go based on their parent's schedule. A great number of children require full-day care. Most of these children are of working parents, one-parent families, broken homes, or low-income families.

The cost of quality day care is high and generally ranges within $35–60 per week per child for full-day care in a licensed day nursery. The cost is high because of the number of hours involved per week, the high demand for the low supply of quality centers, and the limited number of trained professionals. Many communities and county governments, as well as church-affiliated organizations, have seen fit to aid in the support of the many children in day-care centers from low-income families. Communities far-sighted enough to help share the burdens of the disadvantaged home by making quality day care available are aiding society greatly. Their early concern for good care may help alleviate later delinquency, emotional problems, and frustrations, and do much to help children develop into happy, healthy, contributing members of society. The day-care center is in an unique position to have a tremendous positive effect on the lives of children and will pay dividends in the future.

The continued upgrading of day-care programs through the hiring of trained professionals and meeting State certification requirements is an important community matter. Day-care centers need to concern themsevles more with the development of children and must cease to view their purpose as simply a "storage place" for children. The opportunities are great and so are the responsibilities. The early years are too important to be left to chance and quality day care can go a long way toward ensuring for our society a large segment of the care and nuturing it requires.

---

[6] *Newsletter*, National Committee for Day Care of Children, Vol. 5, No. 4, Spring 1965.

Head Start Child Development Programs

These programs are a relatively recent phenomenon in our American society. They were established as a result of the Economic Opportunity Act of 1964, which authorized the establishment and program for economically deprived preschool-age children.[7] Head Start Child Development Programs were designed to help prepare children for public school as a part of the Federal Government's war against poverty.

The 1960's have become known to many as the decade of the disadvantaged. Head Start programs were one means by which the Federal Government made vast attempts at breaking the poverty cycle and alleviating cultural deprivation. Cultural depriviation has been defined as "individuals or a group of people who lack social amenities and cultural graces associated with middle-class society."[8]

Head Start is an all-inclusive program designed to meet the physical, mental, and emotional needs of young children in an effort to prepare them for *success* in school. The program involves medical and dental services, social and psychological services, and nutritional care. Parents and local community volunteers are encouraged to take an active role whenever possible performing many of the nonprofessional duties.

The program itself stresses development of language skills, personal health, self-concept, curiousity, and self-discipline. Head Start programs broaden the range of children's experiences and help them learn how to cope successfully with their environment. They attempt to help children overcome some of the deficiencies of their environment by providing early enrichment experiences in order to help them more effectively meet the demands of school.

Children are selected on the basis of a minimum income, where the family lives (rural or urban), and the number of children in the family. The vast majority of children come from poverty-level homes.

In a good Head Start program, classes are kept small. Children receive individual help and the school is well staffed. Parents and community volunteers share in the decision making. Home and school are closely correlated in the program in an effort to help the home as well as the individual child better share in the responsibilities and benefits of our society.

The Head Start program has had a tremendous impact on early childhood education: (1) national attention has been focused on preschool education, especially that of culturally disadvantaged children, (2) the philosophy of

[7] Brieland, D. "Cultural and Social Change," *Young Children,* 20 (4), 223–229, 1965.
[8] Leeper, Sarah, et al. Good Schools for Young Children, New York MacMillan, 1974, p. 86.

early education of the young has undergone radical changes, (3) facilities and materials for young children have been vastly expanded, and (4) it has been documented that young children learn faster and earlier than previously thought to be true. Head Start has truly had a lasting impact on our society. Despite the claims by some that "you can't make a silk purse out of a sow's ear," Head Start has clearly shown that you can certainly make a fine "pigskin purse." It is through the early enrichment of countless young lives that the poverty cycle can be broken and the culturally disadvantaged can become valued, contributing members of society.

Nursery Schools

The nursery school is not to be confused with the day-care center. Unlike the day-care center, nursery schools are established primarily to enhance the cognitive and affective development of children. They operate for only a portion of the school day. The children generally attend for 2–3 hours daily or every other day for the same period of time. The nursery school is the first in the series of units that make up elementary education. Public nursery schools generally begin at age 4 years. When operated privately, they often include children 2–4 years of age.

The nursery school is an educational experience that has been the primary form of preschool education for over 50 years. At their inception nursery schools were primarily conducted as laboratory schools by colleges and universities. They were used extensively as training and testing grounds for teachers and materials. The early laboratory schools served a valuable purpose in enhancing our insight into the nature and characteristics of preschool children. Many laboratory schools continue to serve as valuable information-gathering and research centers.

Today nursery schools are conducted on both public and private bases throughout North America, the premise being that early experiences offered in the proper setting by trained professionals will have a positive effect on children's development. Today's nursery school serves the needs of 2–4 year-old children by providing them with experiences based on what is known about their developmental needs. It shares with parents the responsibility for promoting meaningful learning during a period when growth is rapid and significant.

The typical nursery school is an active one in which the open classroom concept is extensively employed. The children generally work in small groups at various interest centers such as the doll corner, carpentry corner, block area, and reading and puzzle corner. The teacher acts as a stimulator or motivator for involvement, encouraging experimentation and exploration of new ideas and ways of doing things.

Nursery-school programs vary greatly but may be classified into two general types. The first type is what is sometimes termed the *traditional nursery school.* The traditional nursery school places emphasis on the development of affective competencies. The learning of social skills such as sharing, taking turns, working constructively with others, and accepting simple responsibilities are all important aspects of the traditional program. Formal means of instruction are frowned upon, and informal play experiences are the primary mode of instruction. The teacher establishes an environment conducive to learning and social interaction. Play experiences are utilized as a means of socialization skills. Less emphasis is placed on the *formal* development of cognitive abilities, although considerable cognitive development often occurs as a by product of a good program.

The *modern nursery school* is the second type of nursery school program. Unlike the traditional nursery school, greater emphasis is placed on the development of cognitive abilities. A more complete balance between affective and cognitive development is sought. Sometimes teachers in the modern nursery school view psychomotor development as an integral part of their program.

The program in the modern nursery school utilizes a portion of the day for directed activities and the remainder for relatively free activities. The concepts that children learn in the directed aspect of the program are reinforced during play by the teacher directing the child's attention to factors in the environment that may otherwise be missed or minimized.

Parent Cooperatives

The parent cooperative has become a popular form of preschool education in recent years. The cooperative is formed by parents and often completely staffed by them. Parents are regularly required to participate in the program and to plan and supervise its activities. The parent cooperative enables children to attend a preschool program for a minimum cost. The quality of cooperatives varies greatly depending on the parents commitment to the program, their ability to work constructively with groups of children, and the number of people involved.

Some cooperatives are able to hire a qualified professional to provide leadership, guidance, and training. Programs that are fortunate enough to enlist the aid of a trained professional often blossom into excellent programs. On the other hand, a great many parent cooperatives flounder for lack of leadership. Problems often arise in scheduling, planning, staffing, and providing continuity when the duties are rotated between parents.

Home Day Care

The number of home-care facilities has increased rapidly during the past few years. Home-care programs are those in which a mother will generally care for from three to 10 children in her home. Several States require licensing of home-care facilities, but the quality of such programs runs from excellent to terrible. The home-care program often is nearly one of baby-sitting for a group of children for either half or full days.

The licensing requirements of many States for home care are quite rigid. These regulations have been established in order to help, as much as possible, ensure a safe and hygienic environment for the children.

Kindergarten

Kindergartens have been in existence for over 1 century. The first public kindergarten was established in St. Louis in 1873. Many kindergarents operate on a private basis. The first private one was established in Watertown, Wisconsin in 1855. The number of children attending both public and private kindergartens has been steadily increasing for the past 20 years. Many States include kindergarten programs as a portion of the total public-school program. In States that do not have public kindergartens, several licensed, and privately operated church-related kindergarten programs exist.

Kindergarten is that part of the school program that enrolls 5-year-old children for one year prior to entering the first grade. Kindergartens are generally half-day programs designed to help prepare children for the first grade. They are operated by licensed teachers and one or two assistants. The program is generally individualized in order to meet each child's needs within a group setting as much as possible. The atmosphere of the kindergarten is one of little pressure in which exploration and investigation experiences are encouraged. The purpose of such a program is to help children learn to enquire and wonder, learn self-direction, self-selection, and the discovery of meaning. The kindergarten program helps children form the basis for life-long habits of disciplined, joyful learning.

The objectives of the kindergarten may be stated as:

1. To recognize the value and dignity of all people.
2. To emphasize the importance of self-worth and realization of one's goals.
3. To develop an appreciation of different social, cultural, or ethnic groups.
4. To promote emotional stability in a world of rapid change, opportunities, and responsibilities.

5. To encourage independent thinking and to foster creativity within each individual.
6. To provide experiences geared to the needs and ability levels of each child.
7. To foster positive attitudes toward learning and school.
8. To develop basic readiness skills necessary for success in school.
9. To encourage the development and refinement of fundamental movement abilities.
10. To enlarge the concept of reliable citizenship, at both individual and group levels.

The kindergarten is an exciting first step into the world of learning for most children. It is an integral part of the elementary school that makes available the type of experience best suited to the immediate needs of children. It provides an atomsphere in which children develop new skills and ideas, increase their fund of information, and gain a better understanding of their neighborhood and community. It is a place where they learn to plan and think through simple tasks. They learn to share and do their part in taking responsibility for themselves and their work. Kindergarten is a happy place filled with eager faces, bright smiles, and active bodies. It helps to prepare children for the challenges forthcoming in the elementary school.

MOVING TO LEARN

The directed play experiences of young children can serve as a primary vehicle by which they learn about themselves and their environment. Play and work are not opposites, as is often thought. For children, play is their way of exploring and experimenting while they gain information about themselves and their world. Through directed play experiences that have been carefully structured and preplanned (but avoid teacher domination), children learn how to come to grips with their world, to cope with life's tasks, to master fundamental movements, and to gain confidence in themselves as individuals, moving effectively and efficiently through space. These early years serve as a time when children are intently involved in the process of *learning to move* and *moving to learn*. Although it is not possible to separate these two processes, it is important that the differences implied by the terms be understood.

Learning to move involves the continuous development of children's fundamental movement abilities. Preschoolers have passed through the period of infancy and are no longer immobilized by the confines of their crib or playpen. They can now move through their environment (locomotion), impart force to objects (manipulation), and maintain their equilibrium in re-

TABLE 13.1 TYPES OF PRESCHOOL PROGRAM

PROGRAM	AGES	DESCRIPTION
Day-care center	8 weeks–6 years	Usually a full-day program between 7 a.m. and 6 p.m. Programs vary greatly in quality and trained leadership.
Head Start Child Delopment Programs	4–6	Federally supported compensatory program designed to provide enrichment experiences for culturally deprived children: half-day sessions, medical and dental programs, and hot meals. Trained staff volunteer and parent help.
Nursery school	2–5	Generally privately supported but some publicly supported programs. Half-day session "traditional" and "modern" approach. Trained staff, volunteers, and aids.
Parent cooperative	2–5	Formed by parents. Program developed and staffed by parents. Cost is minimal and quality varies greatly.
Home care	2–6	Private facilities often need to be licensed. Babysitting service for groups of 3–10 children. Half or full day.
Kindergarten	5–6	Public and privately supported. Certified teachers staff the program. Geared to preparing children for the first grade.

sponse to the force of gravity (stability). The development of effective patterns of movement permits them to move about freely and in control of their bodies. Children involved in learning to move are constantly exploring, experimenting, practicing, and making a variety of spontaneous decisions based on their perceptions of the moment and past experiences. They are involved in a continuous process of sorting out their many daily experiences in order to gain increased knowledge about their body and its potential for movement.

While involved in learning to move, young children are simultaneously involved in moving to learn, a process that involves utilizing movement as a means to an end rather than as an end in itself. Children involved in moving to learn use their bodies to gain increased knowledge about themselves and their world. Their basic inability to conceptualize at a sophisticated level makes it difficult for them to learn through formal means of education. As a result, movement becomes one of the primary agents by which they grasp fundamental cognitive and affective concepts of direction, space, time, peer relations, and self-assurance. Movement serves as a medium by which they can increase their fund of knowledge in all aspects of their behavior and is not limited to the physical self.

The balanced motor development of children can and must become a concern of the teacher of young children. The important contributions of movement to learning to move and learning through movement should be carefully studied by all. Table 13.1 presents a schematic representation of the different types of preschool programs and the obligation of these programs to the development of the total child. The extent to which any program incorporates meaningful movement depends on the specific program, its educational goals, and the expertise of the teacher.

THE QUALITY PRESCHOOL PROGRAM

Due to the ever-increasing number and types of program for preschoolers, it becomes continually more difficult to distinguish between quality programs and those which are poor. Caution should be taken not to consider all preschool programs as the same, with little real differences existing between them. On the countrary, the differences between programs is often striking. The name of the program, whether it incorporates the term "nursery school," "day-care center," "play school," or "parent cooperative," is only one indicator of the type of program available. Careful attention should be given to the program itself in order to determine if it will suit the child's needs and your own personal needs best. The importance of this point cannot be overemphasized. Careful attention must be paid to determining the type of preschool experience best suited to each individual child. Careful attention must also be paid to distinguishing good programs from poor ones. No program, no matter what its intentions, is any better than the individuals who implement it. The following guidelines, however, may serve as a questionnaire that will provide indications of a good program. A checklist of important considerations is included along with each question.

1. *Is a safe and healthful environment maintained?*

    a. Approved fire protection?
    b. Adequate evacuation procedures?

Young children are moving to learn while they are learning to move.

    c. Proper heating facilities?
    d. Liability insurance?
    e. Proper lighting?
    f. Good ventilation?
    g. Clean room and lavatories?
    h. Adequate restroom facilities?
    i. Freedom from obvious dangers?

2. *Is there plenty of indoor and outdoor space available?* (Minimum of 35 square feet per child indoors and 75 square feet of space outdoors.)

    a. Adequate space for active outdoor play?
    b. Adequate space for quiet outdoor play?
    c. Adequate indoor space?
    d. Isolation area in case of illness?
    e. Freedom from outdoor hazards (cars)?
    f. General feeling of "room to move?"

3. *Is the child's health protected and promoted?*

    a. Medical examinations prior to entering?
    b. Physician on call?
    c. Trained first-aid personnel always available?
    d. Adequate first-aid supplies?
    e. First-aid supplies properly stored?
    f. Close observation of child's daily health?
    g. Attempt to prevent spread of communicable disease?

4. *Is the program adequately staffed?*

    a. Licensed teachers?
    b. Trained assistants?
    c. At least one assistant per teacher?
    d. Limit of 15–20 to a group?
    e. Provisions for participating parents?
    f. Plan for substitutes in case of absence?

5. *Is there an adequate amount of appropriate play equipment and other materials to be made available to each child?*

    a. Adequate large muscle equipment?
    b. Adequate fine motor equipment?
    c. Equipment to enhance locomotor ability?
    d. Equipment to enhance manipulative ability?
    e. Equipment to enhance stability abilities?

   f. Equipment to enhance creativity abilities?
   g. Musical instruments?
   h. Plenty of good books, puzzles, and pictures?

6. *Is cognitive development adequately stimulated?*

   a. Creativity encouraged?
   b. Opportunities for problem solving?
   c. Provisions made for developmental differences?
   d. Field trips and out-of-class experiences?
   e. Variety enough for everyone?
   f. Opportunities to "show" and "tell?"
   g. Active exploration and experimentation?

7. *Is affective development adequately stimulated?*

   a. Provide for sharing experiences?
   b. Encourage considering others' feelings?
   c. Respect rights of others?
   d. Help child feel at ease?
   e. Encourage group participation?
   f. Encourage child to stand up for his rights?
   g. Self-esteem promoted?
   h. Reasonable expectations promoted?
   i. Success-oriented experiences provided?
   j. Individual differences respected?

8. *Is psychomotor development adequately stimulated?*

   a. Opportunity for vigorous activity?
   b. Planned motor-development program?
   c. Adequate indoor area for active play?
   d. Adequate outdoor area for active play?
   e. Variety of indoor and outdoor equipment?
   f. Play equipment that interests children?
   g. Directed play experiences?
   h. Free-play experiences?
   i. Commitment to motor development?

9. *Does the school include the parents and consider their thoughts, ideas, and needs?*

   a. Parents encouraged to observe?
   b. Parents encouraged to make suggestions?
   c. Parents encouraged to talk to teacher about their child?
   d. Parents invited to participate?

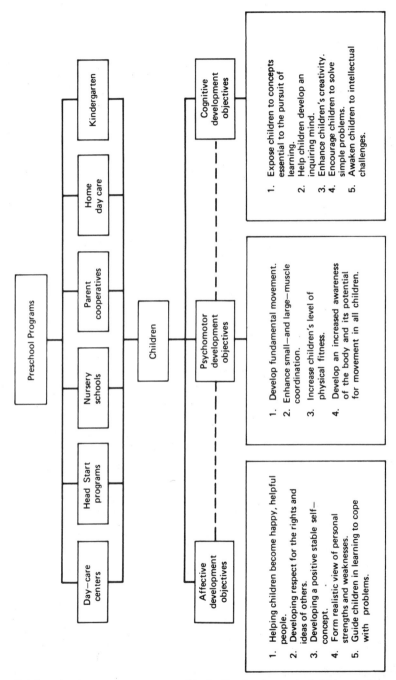

Figure 13.2 Preschool programs are responsible for the development of children in the affective, psychomotor, and cognitive domains of behavior. The extent to which they develop these areas depends on the type of program offered and the individual expertise of the teacher.

    e. Regular conferences scheduled?

    f. Teachers willing to discuss situations affecting the child?

10. *Does the school keep accurate records on the child's progress, and are these records used to help both the parents and the teacher more effectively work with the child?*

    a. Records contain physical examinations?

    b. Record of height and weight?

    c. Record of special health needs?

    d. Record of specific medications routinely given?

    e. Record of specific precautions?

    f. Indication of specific developmental difficulties?

    g. Needs and interests recorded?

    h. Special achievements and abilities recorded?

    i. All records handled in a confidential and professional manner?

THE TEACHER OF YOUNG CHILDREN

In the final analysis, the quality of any preschool program (or any other educational endeavor) is only as good as the persons implementing it. Although this statementnonetheless true. The individual teacher and assistants responsible for the care and education of children are the key factor to a program's success and the positive growth and development of children. The teacher is influenced by two primary factors, namely *professional training* and *personal life experiences* brought to the job. The combination of these two factors on the job are what makes each teacher a unique individual with a particular set of talents and limitations.

The training that the teacher brings to the school includes what has been learned about the growth and development of children, mastery of teaching approaches, knowledge of techniques, curriculum planning, and daily procedures. Knowledge of how to deal with a variety of situations, ranging from how to mitigate a fight to how to organize groups, is learned.

The personal life experiences of individuals also have a tremendous affect on how they perform as teachers. One's values, attitudes, and background play an important role in how one behaves as a teacher. The combination of training and life experiences is what causes each teacher to be unique.

The teacher of young children should possess many desirable traits and characteristics. The teacher should objectively analyze the motives for personally being in education. Being personally well adjusted, having a real love for children, and sincere interest in their development are among the most important. These motives should not be based on sentimentality, or the

The effective teacher of young children has a genuine love for children.

need for personal affection, but rather on the premise of wanting to help maximize the potential of the early years for later development. Teachers of young children must be able to impart a feeling of sincere warmth to children. They must be genuinely interested in *all* children but avoid "over-mothering." Effective teachers have the ability to be firm yet gentle and consistent yet flexible according to individual needs. They possess knowledge and understanding of the growth and development of children as well as child psychology, nutrition, curriculum planning, and parent education. Teachers are often responsible for the cognitive, affective, and psychomotor development of children. It is their responsibility to see that they are adequately trained in each area, make effective plans, and execute a program that promotes the balanced development of children in all areas.

Teachers of young children must possess the ability to work effectively with parents and community personnel as well as groups of children. They must be able to provide direction and guidance in the optimal education of the young. They will be called upon to plan curriculum, counsel parents, supervise volunteer help, and lend guidance to the community.

Teachers of young children must be able to help children express themselves as individuals; good teachers encourage experimentation, exploration and creativity. They are creative and imaginative themselves, for they often have to improvise or "make do" with the equipment and materials available. They should be able to guide children in the wholesome expression of their feelings, hostilities, and fears and help them recognize their abilities as well as their limitations.

In short, teachers of young children are expected to be masters of all that goes on in the preschool program. "Impossible," you say? Impossible, maybe, but it is the true teacher, concerned for the development of children, who constantly tries to achieve the "impossible." The tremendous responsibilities, challenges, and rewards offered through the effective teaching of children makes it necessary to strive to develop one's potential to the highest degree.

THE PARENT HELPER

Parents play an important role in many preschool programs. They are used by many day-care centers, nursery schools, and virtually all parent cooperatives. The reasons for utilizing parents are many and varied. The primary reasons, however, are: (1) it helps to reduce costs considerably, (2) provides a smaller child/teacher ratio, (3) frees the school staff to work with a greater number of children, and (4) provides parents with greater insight into the program.

Parent helpers generally participate on a rotating basis, with specific days of participation scheduled well in advance. The typical parent will assist in the program from four to eight times during the school year. One of the difficulties often encountered by the parent helper is knowing what to do and how to go about doing it. Unlike in the home, the cooperating parent is now faced with 15–20 children, each with varying backgrounds, needs, and interests. The teacher may wish to provide a list of hints for the participating parents and delineate specific procedures to be followed. The following is a compilation of a variety of helpful hints for the participating parent:

1. Be calm and deliberate in manner of speech and movements to avoid exciting or overstimulating the children.
2. Say "do" instead of "don't." Positive redirecting of children's interest is better than restraint. (e.g., instead of saying "don't run," say "walk.")
3. Observe children at play. Offer assistance only when children are unable to do so for themselves.
4. Guide children to the correct social approach. Help them to say "thank you", "please give me a turn when you are finished," "I'm sorry," and "I forgive you."

5. Praise children for their good actions, such as "it is fun to help or share with others" and "that is a friendly thing to do."
6. Do not let one child make another feel inferior or unworthy.
7. Do not crush children's ideas, but add something to them to make them fit into the pattern.
8. Give children a choice. Nothing is gained when there is a clash of wills.
9. Explain the behavior of one child to the other. For example, if Johnny shows his affection for Mike by pushing too hard, say to Mike, "Johnny likes you." This isn't the same as excusing behavior, just helping each child understand what is behind another's action. On the other hand, explain to Johnny the correct way of doing something.
10. On any creative work, encourage children to work out their own ideas.
11. Avoid doing creative handwork (such as drawing) in front of the children. It will discourage them because it will always be better than their best.
12. Creative work (such as free-hand crayon drawings), no matter how imperfect from an adult standpoint, is a more effective teaching method than the use of prepared materials (such as outline figures to be colored).
13. Instead of saying "what is it?" when talking about children's creative work, say "would you like to tell me about it?" or "show me what it does."
14. Do not laugh at the children (any more than you would at an adult) but be happy around them and laugh with them.
15. Be interested in what they are interested in and be sensitive to their moods.
16. Use short sentences and simple words, but do not talk "down" to them.
17. Talk slowly and in a quiet manner and voice.
18. Let them do *everything* they can do even though it takes longer. Do not do anything they can do for themselves.
19. Remember that children learn by doing.
20. Greet each child (by name, if possible) and let them know you are glad he or she came.
21. Give them every opportunity possible to "live" what you want them to learn (taking turns, being friendly, sharing, etc.).
22. "Come and see" is an invitation that must *not* be declined when given by young children. Their appreciation of beauty will grow as you respond to their eagerness to share it.
23. Remember that you are working with *children*, so therefore the body of information and materials are secondary, even though important.

CONCLUSION

Parents, teachers, psychologists, and pediatricians are becoming increasingly aware of the critical need for young children to move about freely in order that they may grow and develop to their maximum potential. The literature on child growth and development is replete with information indicating that the child's experiential background in movement plays an important role in his total growth and development.

Teachers of young children should be concerned with developing a variety of fundamental movement abilities involving locomotion, manipulation, and stability. This may be accomplished by structuring the environment and providing opportunities for the performance of the fundamental movements with a judicious degree of teacher direction and interaction. For individuals untrained in this area of education, it may be difficult initially to structure movement experiences and provide the proper degree of guidance, but with practice and study, successful experiences will be forthcoming.

Teachers of the young need to develop a keen awareness of the importance of directed movement experiences in the lives of children and to become knowledgeable as to how to implement successful programs in this area. It is time that the so-called frivolous play experiences of children be viewed in light of their potential educational value. Psychomotor development must be put into proper perspective in the education of young children for it truly plays an integral part in their total growth and development.

SUGGESTED READINGS

Association for Childhood Education International, *Bits and Pieces: Imaginative Uses for Children's Learning*, Washington D. C., 1967.

Hess, Robert D. and Doreen J. Croft, *Teachers of Young Children*, Boston Houghton–Mifflin, 1972.

Leeper, Sarah, Ruth Dales, Dora Skipper and Ralph Witherspoon, *Good Schools for Young Children*, New York: MacMillan, 1974.

Margolin, Edythe. *Sociocultural Elements in Early Childhood Education*, New York: Macmillan, 1974.

Milgram, Joel I. and Dorthy June Sciarra, *Childhood Revisited*, New York: MacMillan, 1974.

Moore, Shirley and Sally Kilmer, *Contemporary Preschool Education: A Program for Young Children*, New York: Wiley, 1973.

Read, Katherine *The Nursery School: A Human Relationships Laboratory*, Philadelphia, W. B. Saunders, 1971.

Torrance, E. Paul *Creativity*, Belmont, California: Fearon Publishers, 1969.

Author Index

AAHPER, 105, 115
Annarino, Anthony A., 20
Arbuckle, Wanda, 256
Astrand, Per-Olaf, 69, 72
Ayres, Jean, 105

Ball, Eleanor, 256
Barlow, David, 58-60
Barrett, Kate, 175
Barsch, Ray, 90
Bayley, Nancy, 56
Bender, Laura, 106
Bendick, Jeanne, 105
Bernard, J., 87
Berry, K. E., 106
Bilbrough, A., 175
Boorman, Joyce, 256
Brazelton, Ambrose, 288
Brieland, D., 385
Brookover, W. B., 114
Brown, E., 369
Brown, Roscoe, 105

Caplan, Frank, 48
Carmichael, L., 85, 88
Chaney, Clara, 288, 313
Cheffers, John, 20

Chever, R., 106
Christiansen, Joseph, 352
Clark, Harrison, 71
Clifford, C., 114
Collingswood, Thomas, 116
Combs, Arthur, 125
Cononico, Alan, 288
Congar, J. J., 48
Congdon, Paul, 256
Cook, Myra, 352
Cooper, John, 58
Corbin, Charles, 69, 71, 73, 78, 176
Cornwell, George, 256
Cratty, Bryant J., 10, 12, 13, 68, 79, 82, 101,
    105, 112, 115, 123, 126, 288, 317, 352
Crescimbeni, Joseph, 352
Croft, Doreen, 400
Curry, Nancy, 126

Dales, Ruth, 400
Dauer, Victor, 20, 213
Delacato, Carl, 101
De Santis, Gabriel, 213
Doll, Edna, 106, 256
Drorvatyky, John N., 79

Early, George, 313

Eckert, Helen, 79
Ellis, M. J., 354, 377
Engen, T., 88
Engstrom, Glen, 20, 76, 79
Erikson, Erik, 24-25, 29-32, 110, 354, 377
Erikson, E. L., 114
Espenschade, Anna, 79
Evans, Douglas, 176

Fantz, R. L., 86
Felker, Donald, 126
Fendeck, Ruth, 176
Fiorentino, Mary, 58, 59
Flinchum, Betty, 79
Frank, Lawrence, 354
Fredelle, Maynard, 126
Fretz, B. R., 116
Freud, Sigmund, 24
Frost, Reuben, 123, 126
Frostig, Marianne, 10, 101, 106, 288, 313

Galambos, Jeanette, 366, 377
Gallahue, David L., 4, 12, 64, 79, 126, 213,
   317, 352
Gardner, E. D., 60
Gerhardt, Lydia, 105
Gesell, Arnold, 57
Getman, G. N., 10, 101, 313
Gilliom, Bonnie, 288
Ginott, Haim, 126
Glassow, Ruth, 58
Godfrey, Barbara B., 79
Gordon, Ira J., 126
Gray, Nan, 377
Gray, V., 60

Haase, Ronald, 373
Hackett, Layne, 176
Hallenbeck, Gertrude, 176
Harvat, Robert, 313
Harrow, Anita, 20
Havighurst, Robert, 26
Henderson, G., 352
Henry, Franklin, 9
Herman, Michael, 256
Herron, R. E., 377
Hershey, Gerald, 48
Hess, Robert, 400
Hilgard, J. R., 57
Hissan, Harold, 288
Hockey, Robert, 9

Holt, John, 126
Horne, D., 106
Humphrey, James, 10, 12, 101, 317, 352
Hupprich, Florence, 73

Ingler, David, 288

Jameson, Kenneth, 377
Janeak, William, 256
Jeason, Robert, 176
Johnson, Julian, 116
Johnson, W. R., 116
Joiser, L. M., 114
Jones, P., 175
Joyce, Mary, 256

Kane, E., 10, 313
Kagan, J., 48
Kaplan, Dorthy, 313
Karpovitch, Peter, 69
Katz, J., 106
Kay, H., 88
Keogh, Jack, 48, 75
Kephart, Newell, 10, 79, 90, 101, 105, 106,
   313
Kidd, Aline, 313
Kidd, Pat, 377
Kilmer, Sally, 400
Kirk, Samuel, 106
Klenging, James, 79
Knight, Melanie, 313
Kraus, Hans, 68

Laban, Rudolph, 130
Latchaw, Marjorie, 20, 176
Leaver, John et. al., 288
Lecky, P., 114
Lee, Karol, 176
Leeper, Sarah, 385, 400
Leventhal, Alice, 88
Lincoln-Oseretsky, 75-76
Lipsett, L. P., 88
Lowry, George, 43
Luedke, George C., 4, 12, 64, 101, 131, 317,
   352
Lugo, James O., 48

McCandless, Boyd R., 48, 83, 86
McGraw, Myrtle, 57
MacKenzie, Marlin M., 20
Maier, H., 48

Margolin, Edythe, 400
Markum, Patricia, 377
Marten, Mary, 58
Mathews, Donald K., 8
Maynard, F., 111
Meadors, William J., 213
Melograno, Vincent, 79
Metheny, Eleanor, 20
Milgram, Joel, 400
Miller, Arthur G., 20
Moore, Shirley, 400
Mourouglis, Ann et. al., 288
Munen, Paul H., 48
Murray, Ruth, 256

Nelson, Mary, 256
Nimicht, G. P., 369
North, Marion, 20, 176

O'Rahilly, R., 60
Oxendine, Joseph, 79

Palmer, Hap, 256, 352, 288
Pearce, Marcia, 257
Platts, Mary, 352
Piaget, Jean, 26-27, 32-36, 82, 102, 354
Pratt, K. C., 85
Prudden, Bonnie, 79

Rarick, Lawrence, 48
Read, Donald G., 116
Read, Katherine, 400
Riccione, M., 288, 313
Rini, Lisa, 105
Rivoire, Jeanne L., 313
Roach, Edward, 106
Rogers, Donald, 9
Rowne, Betty, 213
Russell, Joan, 256

Schurr, Evelyn, 20
Sciarra, Dorothy, 400
Segerseth, Peter, 73
Seidel, Beverly, 20
Semel, E., 106
Seyler, Anita, 256
Sherman, M., 85

Shirley, M. M., 56
Sinclair, Caroline B., 79
Skipper, Dora, 400
Sloan, W., 75
Smart, Millie S., 48
Smart, Russell C., 48
Smith, Hope, 82
Smith, Lester V., 213
Snygg, Donald, 125
Sobberg, Patricia, 85
Sontag, L. W., 87
Spears, W. C., 86
Stanley, Shelia, 176, 256
Stone, G. J., 377
Stuff, John, 116, 126
Sundberg, Ingelman, 48
Sunderlin, Sylvia, 377
Sutton-Smith, Brian, 377
Sweeney, Robert T., 20

Torrance, Paul, 400
Tuddenham, R. S., 12

Valett, Robert, 106
Vannier, Maryhelen, 20

Wagner, Guy, 213
Wallace, Richard N., 116, 126
Wattenberg, W., 114
Wellman, B. L., 56
Wepman, J., 106
Werner, Peter H., 4, 12, 64, 101, 105, 131, 317, 352
Whitcomb, Virginia, 20
Wickstrom, Ralph L., 79
Willett, Leonard, 116
Williams, Harriet G., 105
Wilson, Robert, 352
Winters, Shirley J., 256
Witten, Betty Van, 313
Wunderlick, Ray, 105
Wylie, Ruth, 126

Yamamoto, Kaoru, 110, 117, 172

Zeitlin, Patty, 257
Zubek, J. P., 85

Subject Index

Academic ability, 315-352
  language arts abilities, 327-337
  mathematics abilities, 337-345
  and movement, 316-317
  science abilities, 317-327
  social studies abilities, 345-352
Academic concepts, 12-14
Accent, 218
Acceptance, 124
Acuity, visual, 86
Adaptation, 23
Adventure, 120-121
Affective development:
  definition, 14
  peer relations, 17-18
  play, 17-18
  self-concept, 14-17, 107-126
Aggressive behavior, 355
Agility, 76
Animal walks, 151-154
Appropriate activities, 119-120
Auditory discrimination:
  discussion of, 302-303
  objectives of, 303
  movement experiences, 303-305
    close your eyes, 303
    tape recorder, 304
    musical instruments, 304

    what does it sound like, 304
    what is it?, 304
    where is the bell?, 304
    keep off, 305
    wall targets, 305
    bounce off, 305
    match the cans, 305
Auditory memory:
  discussion of, 305
  objectives of, 306
  movement experiences, 306
    a trip to the zoo, 306
    story telling, 306
    action rhymes, 306
    instrument playing, 306
    silly hat, 306
    horse race, 306
    the winner is, 307
    lost and found, 307
Auditory perception:
  discussion of, 88, 299
  listening skills, 299-302
  auditory discrimination, 302-305
  auditory memory, 305-307
Auditory rhythm, see Rhythms, auditory
Autonomy, 30, 38-39
Axiel movements, 68

Balance, 78, 131-150
  beam, 144-146, 294
  blocks, 139
  boards, 137-139
  dynamic, 68
  ropes, 141
  static, 68
Balloons, 174
Barrels, 140
Beanbags, 143, 172-173
Beat, 218
Belonging, 357
Benches, 144-146
Bending, 132-134
Body awareness:
  definition of, 91-92
  activity ideas, 92-94
  discussion of, 261
  objectives of, 261
  movement experiences, 261-271
    locating the large body parts, 261
    locating the small body parts, 267
    move and listen, 263
    partner practice, 263
    body-part differentiation, 264
    where can you bend?, 266
    paired parts, 266
    rhymes, 267-269
    finger plays, 269-270
    put together people, 270
    mirror activities, 271
    miscellaneous, 271
Bounding board, 149
Boxes, 163-164
Bureau of Product Safety, 365

Catching, 66, 167-168
Centers, interest, 371-372
Cephalocaudal, 51
Challenge, 123
Challengers, 117
Characteristics of children:
  preschool, 37-42
    psychomotor, 39-40
    cognitive, 40
    affective, 41-42
    implications, 41-42
  primary grade, 42-46
    psychomotor, 43-44
    cognitive, 45
    affective, 45

implications, 45-46
Child development models, 28-36
Children, characteristics of, *see* Characteristics
    of children
  immature, 355
Coffee can stilts, 139-140
Cognitive development, 81-106
  definition, 9-11
  perceptual-motor concepts, 11-12
  academic concepts, 12-14, 316-352
Color, 86
Combination approach, 130
Competition, 116, 119-120
Concrete operations, 36
Cooperatives, parent, 387, 390
Coordination, 76
Creative drama, 355
Creative rhythms, 218-227
Creativity, 218-219
Cuisenaire rods, 362

Day care, 383-384, 388, 390
Depth perception:
  discussion of, 292
  objectives of, 292
  movement experiences, 292-294
    hoops, 294
    jumping, 294
    balance beam, 294
    boxes, 294
Development, 22-23
Developmental differences, 63
Differences, individual, 54
Differentiation, 52
Direct teaching methods, 130
Directional awareness:
  definition of, 96-97
  activity ideas, 97-98
  discussion of, 278
  objectives of, 278
  movement experiences, 278-284
    clock games, 278
    swinging ball, 279
    commands, 279
    over, under and around, 280
    walking-board, 280
    unilateral, bilateral and cross-lateral, 281
    directional throwing, 281
    chalkboard activities, 282
    ladder activities, 282
    twist-board, 283

creeping and walking, 284
  ball activities, 284
Disturbed, emotionally, 355-357
Dodging, 135
Drama, creative, 355

Economic conditions, 380
Education of the young, 379-400
Encouragement, 124
Endurance:
  muscular, 72
  circulatory respiratory, 72-73
Evaluation:
  physical fitness, 68-69
  motor fitness, 75-76
  perceptual-motor, 103-105
Experience, 24, 55-57
Expectations, 123

Failure, 113-115
Flexibility, 73
Figure ground perception:
  discussion of, 246-297
  objectives of, 297
  movement experiences, 297-299
    discrimination, 297
    sorting, 297
    attention, 297
    ladder maze, 297
    target toss, 298
    egg-shell walk, 298
    rope walk, 298
    paddle balance, 298
    rope maze, 298
    candyland, 298
    tetherball, 298
    find hidden objects, 298
    finger fixation, 298
    pencil-wall fixation, 298
    paper-punch picture, 299
Finger plays:
  discussion of, 229
  objectives of, 229-230
  movement experiences, 230-234
    here is the beehive, 230
    this little clown, 230
    I'm a little teapot, 230
    over the hills, 230
    row, row, row, 231
    dig a little hole, 231
    ten fingers, 231

little fish, 232
bunny, 232
birds, 232
if I were a bird, 232
two little, 233
the flowers, 233
left and right, 233
miscellaneous, 269-270
Fixation, 85
Form perception:
  discussion of, 294
  objectives of, 295
  movement experiences, 295-296
    shape walking, 295
    tracing, 295
    making things, 295
    body shapes, 296
    shape tag, 296
    stepping shapes, 296
    matching shapes, 296
    beanbag toss, 296
    shadow pantomine, 296
Formal operation, 36
Fundamental movement abilities:
  definition of, 5
  discussion of, 61-68, 261
  locomotion in childhood, 65
  manipulation, 66
  sequence of emergence, 65-68
  stability, 68

Galloping, 65, 155
Games:
  discussion of, 178-179
  objectives of, 180, 199
  locomotor games, 180-199
    brownies and fairies, 180
    crows and cranes, 181
    squirrels in the trees, 182
    frozen tag, 183
    red light, 183
    colors, 184
    magic carpet, 184
    flowers and the wind, 185
    midnight, 186
    stop and go, 187
    red rover, 187
    automobiles, 188
    back-to-back, 189
    huntsman, 190
    space ship, 191

touch and follow, 191
walk, walk, run, 192
where's my partner?, 193
whistle stop, 194
frog in the sea, 195
crossing the brook, 196
jump the shot, 196
jack be nimble, 197
come along, 197
skip for your supper, 198
manipulation games, 199-213
poison ball, 199
hot potato, 201
teacher ball, 202
guess who, 202
moon shot, 203
call ball, 204
spud, 204
circle dodgeball, 204
keep away, 206
tunnel ball, 205
roll and catch, 207
roll it out, 208
I'll roll it to..., 208
kick-away, 209
free ball, 209
cross the line, 210
balloon volleying, 211
bounce and catch, 211
teacher's choice, 212
General movement abilities, 5-6
Grasping, 66
Growth, 22
Growth rate, 51-52
Guidelines, program, 391-396
Gustatory perception, 88

Head-start, 368, 385-386, 390
Heart myth, 69
Home day care, 388, 390
Hoops, 161-162, 173
Hopping, 65
Horizontal ladder, 147-149

Indirect teaching methods, 129-130
Individual differences, 54
Individualized instruction, 118-119
Infant perception, 82-87
auditory perception, 84, 87
gustatory perception, 84, 87
visual perception, 84, 85-86

Initiative, 30, 38-39
Immature, children, 355
Inner tubes, 142-143
Instruction, individualized, 118-119
Integration, 52
Intensity, 218
Interest centers, 371-372
Intuitive thought, 35-36

Jump and crawl standards, 163-164
Jumping, 65, 155

Kicking, 66, 168-170
Kindergarten, 388-390

Ladders, horizontal, 147-149
Landing, 135-136
Language arts:
discussion of, 327
specific objectives, 328
movement experiences, 328-337
following directions, 328
describing objects, 329
verbal direction discrimination, 330
letter shapes, 330
big letters, small letters, 331
colors and color words, 32
do what I say, 333
acting out words, 333
story relay, 334
same or opposite, 35
relay spelling, 335
read and follow directions, 336
Leaping, 156-157
Learning disabilities, 266
Light sensitivity, 85
Listening skills:
discussion of, 299
objectives of, 299
movement experiences, 300-302
traditional games, 300
hot and cold, 300
clap clap, 300
poems, 300
music, 300
bounce bounce, 301
active animals, 301
hands, 301
echo, 301
movement clapping, 301
listening walk, 301

it is I, 301
tape-recorder sounds, 302
voice recording, 302
freeze and melt, 302
marching, 302
Locomotion:
  definition of, 4
  in infants, 59-60
Locomotor activities:
  discussion of, 150-151
  objectives of, 151
  movement experiences, 151-164
    walking, 151-154
    running, 154-155
    jumping, 155
    galloping, 155
    skipping, 156
    leaping, 156-157
    with small equipment, 157-164
      ropes, 159-160
      stretch ropes, 160-161
      hoops, 161-162
      jump and crawl standards, 163-164
      boxes and stairs, 163-164
Locomotor games, *see* Games

Manipulation, 4
Manipulation games, *see* Games
Manipulative activities:
  discussion of, 164-165
  objectives of, 165-166
  movement experiences, 166-175
    rolling, 166-167
    throwing, 167-168
    catching, 167-168
    kicking, 168-170
    trapping, 168-170
    stroking, 170-171
    with small equipment, 172-175
      beanbags, 172-173
      hoops, 173
      balloons, 174
      scoops, 175
Mathematic abilities, 337-345
  discussion of, 337
  specific objectives, 337-338
  movement experiences, 338-345
    measuring volume, 338
    measuring lengths, 339
    shape, size and color discrimination, 339
    money twister, 340

number sequence, 341
    jump and measure, 341
    beanbag addition and subtraction, 342
    addition relay, 343
    odd and even, 343
    math hopscotch, 344
    skip count, 345
Maturation, 23, 55-57
Mental health, 355
Methods, teaching:
  direct, 130
  indirect, 129-130
Models of child development, 28-36
Mothering, 397
Motor development:
  phase of, 4-7
    reflexes, 4-5
    rudimentary movement abilities, 5
    fundamental movement abilities, 5
    general movement abilities, 5-6
    specific movement abilities, 6
    specialized movement abilities, 6-7
    responsibilities, 381-382
Motor fitness, 8-9
Movement:
  abilities, 2-7
  centers, 372-373, 375-376
  exploration, 129-130
Movement experiences:
  stability activities, 131-150
  locomotor activities, 150-164
  manipulative activities, 164-175
Music, 216, 300-301

Nonachievers, 113-114
Nursery schools, 386-387, 390
Nursery Rhymes:
  discussion of, 234
  objectives of, 234
  movement experiences, 234-240
    my hands, 234
    the noble Duke of York, 235
    Choo-Choo, 235
    windy weather, 235
    funny clown, 236
    my little puppy, 236
    how creatures move, 236
    jack-in-the-box, 236
    stormy days, 237
    follow the leader rhymes, 237-238
    drawing numerals in space, 238

head, shoulders baby, 239
Miss Mary Mack, 239
miscellaneous, 267-269

Obesity, 116
Olfactory perception, 88
Ontogenetic, 54
Outward Bound, 116

Parent helpers, 398-399
Peer relations, 17-18
Perception:
    olfactory, 88
    infant, 82-87
    gustatory, 88
    form, 86
    depth, 292-297
    visual, 291-299
Perceptual-motor, 11-12, 116, 259-288, 316
Perceptual-motor development:
    in infancy, 81-84
    visual, 84, 85-86
    auditory, 84, 87
    olfactory, 84, 87
    gustatory, 84, 87
    in childhood, 87-100
    training programs, 100-101
    readiness and remediation, 101-103
    evaluation, 103-105
Perceptual-motor training programs, 100-101
Phylogenetic, 54-55
Physical abilities, 7-9, 68-78
    physical fitness, 8, 71-73
    motor fitness, 8-9, 73-78
Physical fitness, 8
Piers-Harris, 117
Play, 17-18, 354-360
    developmental aspects, 357-370
    egocentric, 359
    infant, 359
    preschoolers, 360
    primary grades, 360
    sedentary, 357
    toddler, 359-360
    why?, 355-357
Play spaces, 369-376, 393
    indoors, 371-372
    indoor movement center, 372-373
    outdoors, 373-375
    outdoor movement center, 375-376
Poems, 300. *See also* Nursery rhymes

Power, 76
Preoperational, 34-35, 37
Preschool programs, 382-390
    day care centers, 383-384
    head-start, 385-386
    nursery schools, 386-387
    parent cooperatives, 387
    home day care, 388
    kindergarten, 388-389
Preschoolers, number of, 382-383
Principles of development, 51-56
Problem solving, 119
    stability activities, 132-150
    locomotor activities, 150-164
    manipulation activities, 164-175
Program guidelines, 391-396
Proximodistal, 51
Psychomotor development, 2-9, 49, 79
    principles of, 51-57

Qualities of movement, 130

Readiness, 12-14, 52-54, 57, 101-103, 260
Reading, 101-103
Reflexes, 4-5, 58
Rhymes, 234-269
Rhythm, 216, 218
    objectives of, 216
    elements of, 217-218
    creative, 218-227
Rhythmic abilities, 216
Rhythmic pattern, 218
Rhythms:
    auditory:
        finger plays, 229-234
        nursery rhymes and poems, 234-240
        singing rhythms, 240-256
    interpretative:
        discussion of, 224
        objectives of, 224
        movement experiences, 225-227
            interpreting feelings and moods, 225
            interpreting art through movement, 225
            interpreting action sequences, 226
            interpreting pendular movements, 226
            interpreting special holidays, 226
    imitative:
        discussion of, 219-220
        objectives of, 220
        movement experiences, 220-223
            imitating living creatures, 220

imitating things in nature, 220
imitating objects, 221-223
imitating events, 223
singing:
discussion of, 240
objectives of, 240
movement experiences, 240-256
bingo, 240
did you feed my cow?, 241
hey Betty Martin, 242
little red caboose, 243
mulberry bush, 241
ten little jingle bells, 245
lobby loo, 246
blue bird, 248
ten little Indians, 249
farmer in the dell, 250
how do you do my partner, 251
round and round the village, 252
I see you, 253
a hunting we will go, 254
did you ever see a lassie?, 254
jolly is the miller, 255
Reinforcement, 124
Rolling, 166-167
Ropes, 157-160
Rudimentary movement abilities, 5, 58-60
Running, 65, 154-155

Science abilities:
discussion of, 317
specific objectives, 318
movement experiences, 318-327
leverage, 318
machines, 319
leaf study, 320
seasons, 321
similarities and differences, 322
animals with horns, 323
shadows, 324
parts of a plant, 325
inertia, 325
absorption of force, 325
rotary motion, 327
Scoops, 175
Self-concept, 14-17, 39
definition of, 108-111
social status, 111-112
poor self-concept, 113-115
influences of movement, 115-124
Sensori-motor, 33-34, 82

Sequencing tasks, 121
Singing rhythms, *see* Rhythms, singing
Skipping, 65, 156
Social studies abilities:
discussion of, 345
specific objectives, 345-346
movement experiences, 346-351
it is I, 346
it eats, plays and works, 347
shopping basket, 348
community helpers, 348
map of the community, 349
mulberry bush, 349
traffic signs, 350
equator, 351
Space for play, 369
Space world, 91
Spatial awareness:
definition, 94-95
activity ideas, 95-96
objectives of, 271-272
movement experiences, 273-277
big and small, 273
maze walk, 273
rope walking, 274
back space, 274
obstacle course, 275
body space, 275
other space, 276
near and far, 276
twister, 276
maps, 276
miscellaneous, 277
Specialized movement abilities, 6-7
Specific movement abilities, 6
Speed, 76
Stability:
definition of, 3-4
in infants, 59-60
Stability activities:
discussion of, 131-132
objectives of, 132
movement experiences, 132-150
bending, 132-134
stretching, 134
twisting, 134
turning, 134-135
swinging, 135
dodging, 135
landing, 135-136
stopping, 135

rolling, 135
upright supports, 136-137
inverted supports, 137
with small equipment, 137-143
  balance boards, 137-139
  balance blocks, 139
  coffee can stilts, 139-140
  barrels, 140
  wands, 140-141
  balance ropes, 141
  inner tubes, 142-143
  beanbags, 143
with large equipment, 143-150
  balance beam, 144-146
  benches, 146-147
  horizontal ladder, 147-149
  bounding board, 149
  trampoline, 149-150
Stairs, 163-164
Stilts, 139-140
Stopping, 136
Strength muscular, 71-72
Stretch ropes, 160-161
Stretching, 134
Striking, 66, 170-171
Success, 117-119, 124
Supports, 136-137
  inverted, 137
  upright, 136
Swinging, 135

Tactile discrimination:
  discussion of, 309
  objectives of, 309
  movement experiences, 309-311
    collections, 309
    textural paintings, 310
    collages, 310
    creative movement, 310
    mystery bag, 310
    tag an object, 310
    geometric shapes, 311
    shape trace, 311
    heavy and light, 311
    sand paper sort, 311
    tough tag, 311
    search, 311
Tactile matching, *see* Tactile discrimination
Tactile memory:
  discussion of, 311
  objectives of, 312

movement experiences, 303-312
  where is it?, 312
  guess who?, 312
  put in order, 312
  memory ball, 312
  sandpaper numbers-letters, 313
Tactile perception:
  discussion of, 307-309
  tactile discrimination, 309-311
  tactile memory, 311-313
Teacher, qualifications, 396-398
Teaching methods:
  direct, 130
  indirect, 129-130
Tempo, 218
Temporal awareness:
  definition of, 98-99
  activity ideas, 98-100
  discussion of, 285
  objectives of, 285
  movement experiences, 285-288
    ball activities, 285
    rhythmic activities, 286
    my beat, 286
    free flow, 286
    moving-target toss, 286
    balloon-volleying, 287
    miscellaneous, 287
Temporal world, 91
Theorists, developmental, 28, 29
Throwing, 66, 167-168
  games, *see* Manipulation
    games
Toys:
  affective value, 361-363
  appropriate, 364
  choosing of, 367-368
  cognitive values, 362-363
  educational, 361-363
  libraries, 368-369
  safety, 365-367
  therapeutic value, 362
  war, 363-365
Trial and error, 355
Tracking, 85
Traditional approach, 130
Trampoline, 149-150
Trapping, 168-170
Trust, 29-30, 110
Turning, 135
Twisting, 134

Visual acuity, 86
Visual perception:
   discussion of, 291-292
   depth perception, 292-294
   form perception, 294-296
   figure-ground perception, 296-299

Walking, 65, 151-154
Wands, 140-141
White House Conference on Children,
   381
Women's liberation, 380